FIRST EDITION

READINGS IN AFRICAN AMERICAN CULTURE

RESISTANCE, LIBERATION, AND IDENTITY FROM THE 1600S TO THE 21ST CENTURY

by Angela Schwendiman

EASTERN WASHINGTON UNIVERSITY

Bassim Hamadeh, CEO and Publisher
Michael Simpson, Vice President of Acquisitions and Sales
Jamie Giganti, Senior Managing Editor
Miguel Macias, Senior Graphic Designer
Michelle Piehl, Project Editor
Kristina Stolte, Senior Field Acquisitions Editor
Alexa Lucido, Licensing Coordinator
Rachel Singer, Associate Editor

Cover images: United States Senate, "BarackObamaportrait," https://commons.wikimedia.org/wiki/
        File:BarackObamaportrait.jpg. Copyright in the Public Domain.
        Copyright © Dave Brinkman (ANEFO) (CC BY-SA 3.0) at https://commons.wikimedia.org/
        wiki/File:JohnColtrane1961orig.jpg.
        Copyright © Herbert Behrens / Anefo (CC BY-SA 3.0) at https://commons.wikimedia.org/
        wiki/File:Louis_Armstrong_(1955).jpg.
        "Frederick Douglass," https://commons.wikimedia.org/wiki/File:Motto_frederick_doug-
        lass_2.jpg. Copyright in the Public Domain.
        United States Information Agency, "Ralph Ellison photo portrait seated," https://commons.
        wikimedia.org/wiki/File:Ralph_Ellison_photo_portrait_seated.jpg. Copyright in the Public
        Domain.
        "Family of slaves in Georgia, circa 1850," https://commons.wikimedia.org/wiki/
        File:Family_of_slaves_in_Georgia,_circa_1850.jpg. Copyright in the Public Domain.
        Copyright © Depositphotos/kozzi2.

Printed in the United States of America

ISBN: 978-1-63487-314-7 (pbk) / 978-1-63487-315-4 (br)

CONTENTS

Introduction

*T*he emergence of African Americans as a distinct cultural identity would occur over the span of several centuries and undergo the influence of specific historical and social phenomena. The Trans-Atlantic slave trade facilitated the largest forced migration known to human history. Also known as the African diaspora, the dispersal of people from the west coast and central regions of Africa brought millions of enslaved to the shores of North and South America and to the West Indies from the 17th through the 19th centuries. While only a relatively small portion, roughly 500,000–600,000 Africans, would reach North America, out of this population developed a unique ethnicity based not only on the genetic origins of their ancestry, but on the culture of a people who were primarily raised in slavery, but who had not altogether forgotten their West African traditions and had incorporated the colonial American ideals of egalitarianism and European culture.

Slave owners controlled their properties' bodies, but they could not dictate what was in their hearts and minds. Secret societies for worship emerged, and the slaves combined African rituals and rhythms to Christian hymns, forming the soulful spirituals and "sorrow songs," as W. E. B. Du Bois would call them, that would validate their existence as human beings. A caste system, informally known as the "color line," precluded even free blacks from realizing the benefits of American citizenship, but the end of slavery promised a future of equality for all Americans. In the North, free black Americans organized their own churches and created social organizations for the express purpose of meeting the needs of the newly freed former slaves still adjusting to society, as well as assisting the millions still enslaved to realize freedom. In the South, industrial forms of slavery dispensing the assignment of tasks and work groups allowed the African descendants to incorporate the call-and-response song style brought from West Africa into their everyday work songs. African folklore and storytelling such as the tale of the tortoise and the hare allowed the slaves to teach values to their children and preserve their history in an oral tradition practiced in African homes. The relative isolation, as well as the numbers of slaves from West Africa, enabled them to preserve cultural traditions found in the preparation of food and in the types of food, particularly rice, which the slaves brought with them from Africa and then were later forced to produce and harvest along the coastal regions of Georgia and South Carolina. The Africans taught their enslaved descendants a very physically demanding form of dancing, including spinning and leaping in the air and in time to the complex rhythms, multiple harmonies, and improvised melodies played on the drums, flutes, and banjos fashioned after the instruments played in West Africa. Thus, the sounds of West Africa permeated the air surrounding the slave cabins. The tonal style of speaking, including the West African diction of uh-huh and uh-uh would replace the English spoken words of yay and nay for yes and no and influence the creation of the southern drawl.

By the 19th century, civil war tore the nation asunder; in 1863, President Lincoln issued the Emancipation Proclamation and declared the conflict a war to end slavery. The announcement inspired millions of blacks, and 200,000 slaves would join the ranks of the Union to fight for freedom. After four years of war, the nation began the slow and arduous process of rebuilding. More than 4 million blacks—descendants of Africans who had preserved remnants of their former identities and African culture through the isolation of slavery, the vast majority largely uneducated (for this had been prohibited by law)—entered the American economy with nothing more than the skills they had acquired through years of forced drudgery along with the scars of inhumanity.

During Reconstruction, Congress would pass the nation's first civil rights legislation embodied in the 13th, 14th, and 15th Amendments to the Constitution, articulating the end of slavery and acknowledging birthright citizenship for the first time, regardless of race, equal protection under the law, and guaranteeing, for men, at least, the right to vote. In 1896, *Plessy v. Ferguson* made the doctrine of "separate but equal" the law of the land, and the dark period of Jim Crow began. Institutionalized racism, epitomized by legal segregation, sowed the seeds for the ongoing struggle for equality and identity that would dictate the lives and characterize the culture, as well as the social philosophy, of African American people. Some scholars theorize it was the failure of Reconstruction to integrate blacks into the fabric of American society, as well as their long sojourn on American soil as slaves, that provided the basis for the emergence of a distinct African American identity. This trait unified a people not only by race, but by a shared collective memory of slavery, which helped to construct the identity of a people. The trauma of slavery, experienced in retrospect by their descendants through their missing family histories, identities, and exclusion from American culture, society, and history, would unite African Americans in the United States.

The readings included in this book attempt to explore not only how African Americans and their culture and identity were expressed and formed, but features articles that analyze the role of collective memory in providing a people with a collective identity, as well as a means for developing narratives and coping strategies to deal with the trauma of slavery in retrospect and as an ongoing entity of exclusion from mainstream American history, culture, and society. Examining white privilege in American society today allows students to explore and discuss the many ways in which "race-neutral" policies and social practices perpetuate racial disparities embedded within the nation's institutions and thereby continue to favor and unconsciously validate white identity.

Scholarship and readings that challenge the tales of slave traders who encountered 16th-century Africans and perceived them as inferior reject established, preconceived notions that blacks had no culture or any written histories. Modern translations of written manuscripts once buried beneath the sand dunes of former West African empires and universities reveal the glory of Africa's past and refute the previously accepted worldview of blacks as perceived through the racialized lens of 19th-century historians during the height of Eurocentric thinking. Theories and scholarship included in this book provide groundwork for students to discuss why Victorian scholars removed documentation from history that supported the existence of advanced black African civilizations that predated European intervention in West Africa prior to the Trans-Atlantic slave trade. Such readings also lay the foundation for examining the early work of Pan-Africanists, who sought to unify people of African descent on the diaspora in attempts to address the effects of colonialism and the color line, as well as provide a historical context from which to analyze the role of Afrocentrists, who not only sought to reclaim Africa's history, but sensed the unique desire to recognize an essential black identity, vindicate her people, and restore them and the continent to their former glory.

Research enclosed in the book reveals the different ways in which the former slaves constructed new identities for themselves, as well as identifies the major historical events that contributed to a knowledge and understanding of an emergent, postbellum African American cultural group and identity that would at once embrace its roots in slavery while anticipating their assimilation into the larger culture and fabric of American society. The shattered dreams of this delay would fracture the black community into multiple variations and expressions of black culture and identity, from rejecting any connection with slave culture and identity and embracing a separatist black nationalism, to espousing cultural pluralism, where the black community could recognize its ancestral culture and ethnicity while embracing its American identity through pluralism, to rejecting both identities, classifying themselves as neither being "essentially African nor essentially American," but defined within a broader, universal context of being "human," to rejecting all previous racial categories and identifying solely as American.

Lastly, the text allows students to explore the creation and expression of black power and the Black Panther Party, as well as to understand the logic and reasoning behind the rise of its associated visual culture which overtook radicals in the 1960s after the demise of Dr. King's Student Nonviolent Coordinating Committee when it became evident to young black activists that their nonviolent efforts to politically organize blacks in the South were not enough. The Black Panther political ideology was subsequently embraced and expressed, as well as defined by black artists during the emergent black cultural arts movement through the development of a black aesthetic that would spawn revolutionary ways of expressing and perceiving black thought and politics in literature, poetry, films, and music. The goal of the artist was liberation—i.e., to decolonize minds and transform individuals through raising a consciousness of the conditions that contributed to the oppression of the black community, and to find and develop a new language by which to express those thoughts. The appeal to reinvent identity through restructuring the formal context of art would later characterize a new and emerging art form in the ghetto known as rap, and the hip-hop culture that would follow.

PART
ONE

DEFINING AFRICAN AMERICAN CULTURE AND IDENTITY: THE TRAUMA OF SLAVERY

*R*econstructing a cultural identity from a past that was erased through slavery, as well as redefining a collective identity apart from the dominant culture, has been the task of African Americans who did not experience the "normal" process of assimilation into American society (Eyerman). African Americans, therefore, are left to "discover" their blackness and what that means in terms of its significance and the prospects for healing and reconciliation for approximately 40 million people who are descendants of slaves today.

SELECTED READING:

Cultural Trauma: Slavery and the Formation of African American Identity
   BY RON EYERMAN

Cultural Trauma

Slavery and the Formation of African American Identity

Ron Eyerman

*I*n this chapter I explore the notion of cultural trauma in the formation of African American identity from the end of the Civil War to the Civil Rights movement. The trauma in question is slavery, not as institution or even experience, but as collective memory, a form of remembrance that grounded the identity-formation of a people. As has been discussed elsewhere in this volume and as will be further developed here, there is a difference between trauma as it affects individuals and as a cultural process. As cultural process, trauma is linked to the formation of collective identity and the construction of collective memory. The notion of a unique African American identity emerged in the post–Civil War period, after slavery had been abolished. The trauma of forced servitude and of nearly complete subordination to the will and whims of another was thus not necessarily something directly experienced by many of the subjects of this study, but came to be central to their attempts to forge a collective identity out of its remembrance. In this sense, slavery was traumatic in retrospect, and formed a "primal scene" that could, potentially, unite all "African Americans" in the United States, whether or not they had themselves been slaves or had any knowledge of or feeling for Africa. Slavery formed the root of an emergent collective identity through an equally emergent collective memory, one that signified and distinguished a "race," a people, or a community, depending on the level of abstraction and point of view being put forward. It is this discourse on the collective and its representation that is my focus.

That slavery was traumatic can be thought to be obvious, and for those who experienced it directly, it must certainly have been. In a recent attempt to trace the effects of slavery on contemporary African American behavior patterns, Orlando Patterson (1998, 40) writes, "Another feature of slave childhood was the added psychological trauma of witnessing the daily degradation of their parents at the hands of slaveholders ... to the trauma of observing their parents' humiliation was later added that of being sexually exploited by Euro-Americans on and off the estate, as the children grew older." While this may be an appropriate use of the concept of trauma, it is not what I have in mind here. The notion of an African American identity, however, was articulated in the latter decades of the nineteenth century by a generation of blacks for whom slavery was a thing of the past, not the present. It was the memory of slavery and its representation through speech and art works that grounded African American identity and permitted its institutionalization in organizations such as the National Association for the Advancement of Colored People (NAACP), founded in 1909–10. If slavery was traumatic for this generation, it was so in retrospect, mediated through recollection and reflection, and, for some black leaders and intellectuals, tinged with a bit of strategic, practical and political, interest.

While exploring the meaning of cultural trauma is part of the aim of this and other chapters, some notion of the parameters of its usage should be stated here. As opposed to psychological or physical trauma, which involves a wound and the experience of great emotional anguish by an individual, cultural trauma refers to a dramatic loss of identity and meaning, a tear in the social fabric, affecting a group of people that has achieved some degree of cohesion. In this sense, the trauma need not necessarily be felt by everyone in a community or experienced directly by any or all. While some event may be necessary to establish as the significant cause, its meaning as traumatic must be established and accepted, and this requires time to occur, as well as mediation and representation. Arthur Neal (1998) defines a "national trauma" according to its "enduring effects," and as relating to events "which cannot be easily dismissed, which will be played over again and again in individual consciousness" and which then become "ingrained in collective memory." In this account, a national trauma must be understood, explained, and made coherent through public reflection and discourse. Here mass media and their representations play a decisive role. This is also the case in what we have called cultural trauma. In his chapter, Neil Smelser offers a formal definition of cultural trauma that is worth repeating: "a memory accepted and publicly given credence by a relevant membership group and evoking an event or situation that is a) laden with negative affect, b) represented as indelible, and c) regarded as threatening a society's existence or violating one or more of its fundamental cultural presuppositions." In the current case, the phrase "or group's identity" could be added to the sentence. It is the collective memory of slavery that defines an individual as a "race member," as Maya Angelou (1976) puts it.

In Cathy Caruth's (1995, 17, and Caruth 1996) psychoanalytic theory of trauma, it is not the experience itself that produces traumatic effect, but rather the remembrance of it. In her account there is always a time lapse, a period of latency, in which forgetting is characteristic, between an event and the experience of trauma. As reflective process, trauma links past to present through representations and imagination. In such psychological accounts, this can lead to a distorted identity-formation, in which "certain subject-positions may become especially prominent or even overwhelming, for example, those of victim or perpetrator ... wherein one is possessed by the past and tends to repeat it compulsively as if it were fully present" (LaCapra 1994, 12).

Allowing for the centrality of mediation and imaginative reconstruction, one should perhaps not speak of traumatic events, but rather of traumatic effects (Sztompka in this volume). While trauma necessarily refers to something experienced in psychological accounts, calling this experience *traumatic* requires interpretation. National or cultural trauma (the difference is minimal at the theoretical level) is also rooted in an event or series of events, but not necessarily their direct experience. Such experience is mediated, through newspapers, radio, or television, for example, which involve a spatial as well as temporal distance between the event and its experience. Mass-mediated experience always involves selective construction and representation, since what is visualized is the result of the actions and decisions of professionals as to what is significant and how it should be presented. Thus, national or cultural trauma always engages a "meaning struggle," a grappling with an event that involves identifying the "nature of the pain and the nature of the victim and the attribution of responsibility" (Alexander in this volume). Alexander calls this the *trauma process* when the collective experience of massive disruption, a social crisis, becomes a crisis of meaning and identity. In this trauma process "carrier groups" are central in articulating claims, representing the interests and desires of the affected to a wider public. Here intellectuals, in the term's widest meaning (Eyerman and Jamison 1994), play a significant role. *Intellectual,* as used here, refers to a socially constructed, historically conditioned role rather than to a structurally determined position or a personality type. Although bound up with particular individuals, the concept refers more to what individuals do than who they are. Generally speaking, intellectuals mediate between the cultural and political spheres that characterize modern society, representing and giving voice not so much to their own ideas and interests, but rather articulating ideas to and for others. Intellectuals are mediators and translators, between spheres of activity and differently situated groups, including the situatedness of time and space. In this sense, intellectuals can be film directors, singers of song, as well as college professors. In addition, social movements produce "movement intellectuals" who may lack the formal education usually attributed to intellectuals, but whose role in articulating the aims and values of a movement allow one to call them by that name.

As with physical or psychic trauma, the articulating discourse surrounding cultural trauma is a process of mediation involving alternative strategies and alternative voices. It is a process that aims to reconstitute or reconfigure a collective identity, as in repairing a tear in the social fabric. A traumatic tear evokes the need to "narrate new foundations" (Hale 1998, 6), which includes reinterpreting the past as a means toward reconciling present/future needs. There may be several or many possible responses to cultural trauma that emerge in a specific historical context, but all of them in some way or another involve identity and memory. To anticipate, the appellation "African American," which may seem more or less obvious and natural today, was one of several paths or reactions to the failure of reconstruction to integrate former slaves and their offspring as Americans, and to the new consensus concerning the past in the dominant culture in which slavery was depicted as benign and civilizing. Among the alternatives, the idea of returning to Africa had been a constant theme among blacks almost from the first landing of slaves on the American continent. Another alternative, later in its development, also involved emigration, but to the north to Canada or the free states and territories like Oklahoma, rather than to Africa. Such a move, which was discussed and realized in the later decades of the 1800s did not necessarily exclude a new identity as an African American, but did not necessarily include it either. This alternative, however, did involve an openness to new forms of identification and the attempt to leave others behind.

Developing what W. E. B. Du Bois would describe as a "double consciousness," African *and* American, offered another possibility, one that implied loyalty to a nation but not necessarily to its dominant culture or way of life. In 1897 Du Bois posed the question, "What, after all, am I? Am I an American or a Negro? Can I be both? Or is it my duty to cease to be a Negro as soon as possible and be an American?" (Du Bois 1999, 16–17). However this dilemma, as an aspect of the process of cultural trauma, is resolved, the interpretation and representation of the past and the constitution of collective memory is central. The meaning of slavery was a focal point of reference. A similar process, under way among whites and black attempts to negotiate cultural trauma, was intimately intertwined with this national project. By the mid-1880s the Civil War had become the "civilized war" and "a space both for sectional reconciliation and for the creation of modern southern whiteness" (Hale 1998, 67). As the nation was re-membered through a new narration of the war, blacks were at once made invisible and punished. Reconstruction and blacks in general were made the objects of hate, an Other against which the two sides in the war could reunite. The memory of slavery was recast as benign and civilizing, a white man's project around which North and South could reconcile.

COLLECTIVE MEMORY

> *The history of the study of memory is a tale of the*
> *search for a faculty, a quest for the way in which the*
> *mind-brain codes, stores and retrieves information.*
> *Only with the recent interest in language and in cultural*
> *aspects of thinking has there emerged the wider view*
> *of remembering as something that people do together,*
> *reminding themselves of and commemorating*
> *experiences which they have jointly undertaken.*
>
> *Alan Radley (1990)*

Memory is usually conceived as individually based, something that goes on "inside the heads" of individual human beings. "Memory has three meanings: the mental *capacity* to retrieve stored information and to perform learned mental operations, such as long division; the semantic, imagistic, or sensory *content* of recollections; and the *location* where these recollections are stored" (Young 1995). Theories of identity formation or socialization tend to conceptualize memory as part of the development of the self or personality and to locate that process within an individual, with the aim of understanding human actions and their emotional basis. In such accounts, the past becomes present through the embodied reactions of individuals as they carry out their daily lives. In this way, memory helps account for human behavior. Notions of collective identity built on this model, such as those within the collective behavior school, theorize a "loss of self" and the formation of new, collectively based, identities as the outcome of participation in forms of collective behavior like social movements. Here memory, as far as it relates to the individual participant's biography, tends to be downplayed, because it is thought to act as a barrier to forms of collective behavior that transcend the normal routines of daily life. The barrier of memory once crossed, the new collective identity is created sui generis, with the collective, rather than the individual, as its basis. The question of whether this collective may develop a memory has, as far as we know, rarely been addressed by this school.

Alongside these individually focused accounts of memory have existed a concern with collective identity and with "how societies remember," with roots in Durkheim's notion of collective consciousness (Connerton 1989). Here collective memory is defined as recollections of a shared past "that are retained by members of a group, large or small, that experienced it" (Schuman and Scott 1989, 361–62). Such memories are retained and passed on either as part of an ongoing process of what might be called public commemoration, in which officially sanctioned rituals are engaged to establish a shared past, or through discourses more specific to a particular group or collective. This socially constructed, historically rooted collective memory functions to create social solidarity in the present. As developed by followers of Durkheim such as Maurice Halbwachs (1992), memory is collective in that it is supra-individual, and individual memory is always conceived in relation to a group, be this geographical, positional, ideological, political, or generationally based. In Halbwachs' classical account, memory is always group memory, both because the individual is derivative of some collectivity, family, and community, and also because a group is solidified and becomes aware of itself through continuous reflection upon and re-creation of a distinctive, shared memory. Individual identity is said to be negotiated within this collectively shared past. Thus while there is always a unique, biographical memory to draw upon, it is described as being rooted in a collective history. Here collective memory provides the individual with a cognitive map within which to orient present behavior. In this sense, collective memory is a social necessity; neither an individual nor a society can do without it. As Bernhard Giesen (in this volume) points out, collective memory provides both individual and society with a temporal map, unifying a nation or community through time as well as space. Collective memory specifies the temporal parameters of past and future, where we came from and where we are going, and also why we are here now. Within the narrative provided by this collective memory, individual identities are shaped as experiential frameworks formed out of, as they are embedded within, narratives of past, present, and future.

The shift in emphasis in the social sciences and humanities toward language-based, text-oriented analysis and to the effects of "visual culture" on identity formation has brought new developments to the study of memory. In the field of comparative literature, for example, more attention is being paid to the importance of collective memory in the formation of ethnic identity and the role of literary works in this reflective process. With the cultural turn to focus on the centrality of cognitive framing and the emphasis on language and intertextuality, memory is located not inside the heads of individual actors, but rather "within the discourse of people talking together about the past" (Radley 1990, 46). This is a development that has its roots in forms of analysis often called "poststructuralism" and in feminist theory and practice. In the 1970s feminists developed techniques of "consciousness raising" that attempted to make the personal political, to theorize the development of the self within a politically as well as symbolically structured social context. Armed with theories of socialization that combined Marx and Freud (and sometimes G. H. Mead), feminists developed techniques for liberating individuals from the distorted identity formation of male-dominated society. Like the collective behavior school mentioned above, with whom they shared many theoretical assumptions, some feminists viewed individual memory as a barrier to collective political action. "Memory work" was one technique developed by feminists after the women's movement moved into the academy, as a way of recalling faded or repressed images of domination.

A more recent development concerns the idea of collective memory itself. The editors of a volume concerning developments in literary theory (Singh, Skerrett, and Hogan 1994) define collective memory as "the combined discourses of self: sexual, racial, historical, regional, ethnic, cultural, national, familial, which intersect in an individual." These form a net of language, a metanarrative, which a community shares and within which individual biographies are oriented. Here Foucault and poststructuralism unite with the Durkheimian tradition referred to above. Collective memory is conceived as the outcome of interaction, a conversational process within which individuals locate themselves, where identities are described as the different ways individuals and collectives are positioned by, and position themselves, within narratives. This dialogic process is one of negotiation for both individuals and for the collective itself. It is never arbitrary.

From this perspective, the past is a collectively articulated, if not collectively experienced, temporal reference point that shapes the individual more than it is reshaped to fit generational or individual needs. This is a necessary addendum, especially where political motivation is concerned. In response to what he calls the "interest theory" of memory construction, where the past is thought to be entirely malleable to present needs, Michael Schudson (1989) suggests several ways in which the past is resistant to total manipulation, not least of which is that some parts of the past have been recorded and thus obtain at least a degree of objectivity. Supporting this, Barry Schwartz (1982, 398) writes that "given the constraints of a recorded history, the past cannot be literally constructed; it can only be selectively exploited." In this context a distinction between collective memory and recorded and transcribed history is useful. If, as Halbwachs suggests, collective memory is always group memory, always the negotiated and selective recollections of a specific group, then collective memory is similar to myth. This, in fact, is how Arthur Neal (1998) conceives of it in his work on national trauma. From Halbwachs's "presentist" perspective, collective memory is essential to a group's notion of itself and thus must continually be made over to fit historical circumstance. While this collective memory makes reference to historical events, that is, events that are recorded and known to others, the meaning of such events is interpreted from the perspective of the group's needs and interests, within limits of course. History, especially as a profession and academic discipline, aims at something wider, more objective, and more universal than group memory. Of course, history is always written from some point of view and can be more or less ethnocentric, but as an academic discipline, even within the constraints of nationally based institutions, its aims and, especially, its rules of evidence, are of a different sort from the collective memory of a group. At the very least, professional historical accounts can be criticized for their ethnocentricism.

An overheard conversation between a historian and a Holocaust victim can perhaps illustrate what I mean. In this conversation the victim was recalling his memories of an infamous Jewish guard in a Polish ghetto. He vividly recalled his personal experience of this man. The historian pointed out that this could not have occurred, as this guard was in another camp at that particular time and could document that claim. The victim remained skeptical, but, perhaps because he was also a scientist, was willing to consider the claim. Later, the historian, who specializes in atrocities such as the Holocaust, recounted that he often faces this problem of the difference between memory and documented history.

While the focus on language and ways of speaking has had many liberating effects on the study of collective memory and identity, there are limitations as well. According to Alan Radley, "This movement ... still falls short of addressing questions related to remembering in a world of things—both natural and products of cultural endeavor—where it concentrates upon memory as a product of discourse. The emphasis upon language tends to hide interesting questions which arise once we acknowledge that the sphere of material objects is ordered in ways upon which we rely for a sense of continuity and as markers of temporal change" (Radley 1990). Viewing memory as symbolic discourse, in other words, tends to downplay or ignore the impact of material culture on memory and identity formation. From the point of view of discourse analysis, objects gain meaning only when they are talked about. Radley's point is that the way things are organized, whether the objects of routine, everyday experience, like the furniture in a room or the more consciously organized objects in a museum, evokes memory and a "sense of the past," whether this is articulated through language or not. Food and household items can evoke memory, such as suggested by the examples found in the African American cookbook *Spoonbread and Strawberry Wine.*

The authors (Darden and Darden 1994, xi) write, "Aunt Norma's biscuit cutter, Aunt Maude's crocheted afghan, our father's old medicine bottles (representing a medical practice of over sixty years) all evoke powerful and loving memories." The same can be said of other cultural artifacts, like music and art objects. Listening to a particular piece of music or gazing at a painting can evoke strong emotional responses connected to the past and can be formative of individual and collective memory. Memory can also be embedded in physical geography, as illustrated by Maya Angelou's vivid descriptions of her youth in a small Southern hamlet (Angelou 1974), and as discussed in Barton (2001).

There is a point to the poststructuralism argument, however, that the actual significance of this response, what it "really" means, is fashioned through language and dialogue and may change depending on the context. Thus, while the arrangement of material artifacts may evoke a sense of the past or of something else, what exactly this 'sense' is requires articulation through language.

This points further to the issue of representation. How is the past to be represented in the present, to individuals, and, more important in this context, to a collective? If we take the preceding arguments into account, the past is not only recollected, and thus represented through language, but it is also recalled through association with artifacts, some of which have been arranged and designated for that purpose. If narrative, the "power of telling," is intimately intertwined with language, with the capacity and the possibility to speak, representation can be called "the power of looking" (Hale 1998, 8) and can be associated with the capacity to see and the possibility to make visible. The questions of who can speak and to whom, as well as the issue of who can make visible, are thus central.

These are matters of great interest in the present study. How was slavery represented, in whose interests, and for what purposes? What role if any did former slaves have in this process of collective remembering through public representation? How slavery was represented in literature, music, the plastic arts, and, later, film is crucial to the formation and reworking of collective memory by the generations that followed emancipation. What social movements provide is a context in which individual biographies and thus memories can be connected with others, fashioned into a unified collective biography and thereby transformed into a political force. Social movements reconnect individuals by and through collective representations; they present the collective and represent the individual in a double sense, forging individual into collective memory and representing the individual as part of a collective.

THE PLACE OF GENERATION IN COLLECTIVE MEMORY

If collective memory is always group based and subject to adjustment according to historically rooted needs, what are the spatial and temporal parameters that mark this process of reinterpretation? As social groups are mobile, so too are the borders of their memory and collective identity formation. The spatial parameters marking these borders vary and have attained more fluidity with the exponential development of mass media. Their basis may be political, rooted in relatively specified geographic boundaries, but still they span much space to cover exiles and expatriates. They may also be ethnic and religious, which equally can be fixed locally or widespread. While Halbwachs and Durkheim before him rooted memory in real communities, that is, those that have face-to-face contact, recent approaches expand this notion to include the "imagined" communities (Anderson 1991). This possibility and its recognition in academic literature has to do in part with the rise to significance of electronic mass media and the migration of populations, both of which fall under the umbrella term *globalization*. As Igartua and Paez (1997, 81) put it after studying the symbolic reconstruction of the Spanish civil war, "Collective memory does not only exist in the individuals, but that in fact it is located in cultural artifacts. Analyzing the contents of cultural creations, as for example films, one may see how a social group symbolically reconstructs the past in order to confront traumatic events for which it is responsible." This means that the collective memory that forms the basis for collective identity can transcend many spatial limitations when it is recorded or represented by other means. The Armenian-Canadian filmmaker Atom Egoyan records in his films traces of remembrance of the slaughter of Armenians by Turks in 1915, an event that has shaped the collective identity of Armenians ever since. This group is now spread over the globe, but its identity-forming collective memory remains apparently intact, partly due to media such as film as well as the stories passed within the community itself. Temporally the parameters of collective memory appear a bit more fixed. Research on memory has brought forth the generational basis of remembrance and forgetting as key to adjusting interpretations of the past. Survey-based research such as that carried out by Howard Schuman and Jacqueline Scott (1989) investigated whether or not there are particular events that distinguish generations and shape the actions of individuals through memory. Their study focused on Americans in the post–World War II era and found that those who came of age during the Vietnam war shared a distinctive collective memory of that period, something that distinguished this cohort from others. Other studies of "traumatic events," such as the Spanish civil war (Igartua and Paez (1997), have made similar findings. Taking their starting point in Karl Mannheim's theory of generation, these studies tend to show that "attributions of importance to national and world events of the past half century tend to be a function of having experienced an event during adolescence or early adulthood" (Schuman, Belli, and Bischoping 1997, 47).

Mannheim's original formulation proposed that those events experienced during adolescence are the ones most likely to "stick" in later life and to influence behavior. Also those passing through the life cycle at the same point in time are likely to recall the same events; thus one can speak of generational memory.

In what would generational memory consist? How would it be produced and maintained? Mannheim had a very optimistic and positive account of generational memory, at least concerning its general function, before it is filled with the historically determined specifics. The function of generational memory for Mannheim consists in offering "fresh-contact" with "the social and cultural heritage" of a social order, which "facilitates re-evaluation of our inventory and teaches us both to forget that which is no longer useful and to covet that which has yet to be won"(Mannheim 1952, 360). Here collective forgetting is as important as collective remembering for a society's self-reflection; it is in fact the role of youth or the new generation: to provide society with a fresh look at itself. Aside from this general, and generally positive, role, generational memory consists of a record of and a reaction to those "significant" events that an age cohort directly experiences. These events are those that the cohort encounters between the ages of seventeen and twenty-five, in Mannheim's calculation, that shape their worldview and set the framework that will guide their actions and responses for their entire existence. As noted, for Mannheim this means having direct experience. Later investigators have also added mediated experiences, both as formative of a generation and also in terms of retention or reproduction of that generation and others. Thus, not all those who lived through the 1960s participated in social movements, but many experienced them via television. Probably those who participated directly would have a stronger sense of belonging to "the sixties' generation," but those who experienced the events via television and are of the same age might also feel a strong sense of belonging. The question is, would those of a different age who saw the events of the 1960s on TV have any sense of belongingness, and where would the age-related boundaries fall? In any case, the role of mass media in producing and reinforcing generational identity is a much more central question in the current age than in Mannheim's.

THE CYCLE OF (GENERATIONAL) MEMORY

The notion of cultural trauma implies that direct experience is not a necessary condition for the appearance of trauma. It is in time-delayed and negotiated recollection that cultural trauma is experienced, a process that places representation in a key role. How an event is remembered is intimately entwined with how it is recollected. Here the means and media of representation are crucial, for they bridge the gaps between individuals and between occurrence and its recollection. Social psychological studies provide grounds for a theory of generational cycles in the reconstruction of collective memory and the role of media in that process.

After analyzing various examples, Pennebaker and Banasik (1997) found that approximately every twenty to thirty years individuals look back and reconstruct a "traumatic" past. In applying this theory to their study of the remembrance of the Spanish civil war, Igartua and Paez list four factors that underlie and help explain this generational cycle:

1. The existence of the necessary psychological distance that remembering a collective or individual traumatic event requires. Time may soothe and lessen the pain that remembering a traumatic event produces.

2. The necessary accumulation of social resources in order to undergo the commemoration activities. These resources can usually

be obtained during one's middle age. The events are commemorated when the generation which suffered them has the money and
power to commemorate them.

3. The most important events in one's life take place when one is
12–25 years old. When these people grow older they may remember the events that happened during this period.

4. The sociopolitical repression will cease to act after 20–30 years
because those directly responsible for the repression, war, and so
on, have either socially or physically disappeared. (1997, 83–84)

If we leave aside the assumption that an event can be traumatic in
itself, this framework is useful in the analysis of collective memory and
cultural trauma. Igartua and Paez emphasize the difference between a
generation shaped by the direct experience of an event and those that
follow, for whom memory is mediated in a different way. They also point
to the issues of power and access to the means of representation, which
are essential for public commemoration and thus collective memory.
They also place special emphasis on the role of art and of representation
generally in this process.

A discussion of representation seems appropriate here, as this is
an issue that will arise throughout this chapter. Representation can
be analyzed along several dimensions, as re-presenting, that is, as the
presentation through words or visual images of something else where
considerations of form are at least as important as content; this can
be considered an aesthetic dimension. That the form may itself have a
content has been pointed out by White (1987). Representation can refer
to a political process concerning how a group of people can and should
be represented in a political body, such as a parliament or other public
arena, from the mass media to a museum. Representation has a moral
dimension, which can involve both aesthetic and political aspects, when
questions like "How should a people be represented?" are raised. There
is a cognitive dimension, wherein representation becomes the preroga-
tive of science and of professionals (museum curators, historians, and
so on), who develop procedures and criteria of and for representation,
claiming special privileges regarding the materials presented. As in
representativeness, representation can refer to types and exemplars, as
in Emerson's *Representative Men* (1851) or Du Bois' "talented tenth,"
in which individuals are said to be types that express the "best" of a race
or civilization.

The complex and problematic issues of representation have been of central concern to black Americans from the earliest periods of the slave trade to the present. In what can be properly called "the struggle for representation" (Klotman and Cutler 1999), black Americans have fought for the right to be seen and heard as equals in social conditions that sought to deny it. This struggle for representation occurred in literary, visual, and more traditional political forms. It encompassed a fight to be seen as well as heard and involved who would define what was seen and heard. The first written accounts from inside the culture were the slave narratives from Briton Hammon's *Narrative* (1760) to Harriet Jacobs's *Incidents in the Life of a Slave Girl* (1861) (Klotman and Cutler 1999, xiv). The abolitionist movement and the associated free black press were important mediators and facilitators of this representation, something that affected the mode of presentation, as we will see in the following chapters.

Painting and other forms of visual representation from the inside were later to emerge. What have now come to be called the historically black colleges and universities, inaugurated during the southern "reconstruction" after the Civil War, were important in the production, conservation, and display of artifacts by black artists. These schools and their collections were central to the education of future artists, as well as other black scholars and intellectuals. Music, especially as related to work and religion, was one of the few means of cultural expression publicly available to blacks, and its importance as a means of representation as well as expression has been duly acknowledged, not least by black intellectuals such as W. E. B. Du Bois, in their attempts to find grounds for the narration of black collective identity in the trauma following the end of reconstruction. What Du Bois would call the "sorrow songs" of the slaves embodied and passed along across generations and geographical space the memories of slavery and hopes of liberation. The first film documentary by a black American appeared in 1910. Bearing the title *A Day at Tuskegee,* it offered a representation of the "new Negro" and was commissioned by Booker T. Washington. Commercial black filmmakers and music producers began to play an increasingly important role from the 1920s on, as the urban migrations and better living conditions created a sophisticated audience for "race" movies and recorded music.

Even if these representations were made from the inside, by blacks themselves, the issues of whose voice and whose image were represented was not thereby resolved. The black "community" was always diverse, even as it was unified by enforced subordination and oppression. Internal discussions concerning proper representation, as well as the means and paths of liberation, were many and divergent. This was especially so in the urban public sphere that emerged with the "great migration" in the first quarter of the twentieth century. After emancipation and the urban migrations, the possibility that a single issue could define and unite the black community and focus representation was undercut. Thus, "since there is no single, unchanging black community, the 'burden of representation' involves varying viewpoints, differing degrees of objectivity and subjectivity, and competing facts and fictions" (Klotman and Cutler 1999, xxv). Here different voices and visions clamored to be seen and heard, even as representation was still intimately entwined with subordination and the desire for liberation. This created a situation in which representation was a responsibility and burden; it could not easily or merely be a form of personal expression, as a black artist was always black in the eyes of the dominant culture.

Resolving cultural trauma can involve the articulation of collective identity and collective memory, as individual stories meld into collective history through forms and processes of collective representation. Collective identity refers to a process of "we" formation, a process both historically rooted and rooted in history. While this common history may have its origins in direct experience, its memory is mediated through narratives that are modified with the passage of time and filtered through cultural artifacts and other materializations that represent the past in the present. Whether or not they directly experienced slavery or even had ancestors who did, blacks in the United States were identified with and came to identify themselves with slavery. The historical memory of the Civil War was reconstructed in the decades that followed, and blackness came to be associated with slavery and subordination. A common history was thus ascribed and inscribed as memory, as well as indigenously passed on. In this sense, slavery is traumatic for those who share a common fate and not necessarily a common experience. Here trauma refers to an event or an experience, a primal scene, that defines one's identity because it has left scars and thus must be dealt with by later generations who have had no experience of the original event. Yet each generation, because of its distance from the event and because its social circumstances have altered with time, reinterprets and represents the collective memory around that event according to its needs and means. This process of reconstruction is limited, however, by the resources available and the constraints history places on memory.

The generational shifts noted by Pennebaker and others can be said to temporally structure the formation of collective memory, providing a link between collective (group) memory and public (collective) memory. Groups, of course, are public, but a particular group's memory may not necessary be publicly, that is officially, acknowledged or commemorated. If a collective memory is rooted in a potentially traumatic event, which by definition is both painful and also open to varying sorts of evaluation, it may take a generation to move from group memory to public memory. Sometimes it may take even longer; sometimes it may never happen at all. The case of American slavery is an example. As Ira Berlin notes in his introduction to *Remembering Slavery* (1998), slavery is remembered differently in the United States depending upon which time period and which racial group and regional location one starts from. He writes:

> Northerners who fought and won the (civil) war at great cost incorporated the abolitionists' perspective into their understanding of American nationality: slavery was evil, a great blot that had to be excised to realize the full promise of the Declaration of Independence. At first, even some white Southerners—former slave-holders among them—accepted this view, conceding that slavery had burdened the South as it had burdened the nation and declaring themselves glad to be rid of it. But during the late nineteenth century, after attempts to reconstruct the nation on the basis of equality collapsed and demands for sectional reconciliation mounted, the portrayal of slavery changed. White Northerners and white Southerners began to depict slavery as a benign and even benevolent institution, echoing themes from the planters' defense of the antebellum order ... Such views, popularized in the stories of Joel Chandler Harris and the songs of Stephen Foster, became pervasive during the first third of the twentieth century. (Berlin 1998, xiii–xiv)

There was a long history of visual representation to draw upon as well. In his account of the "visual encoding of hierarchy and exclusion," Albert Boime (1990, 15–16), shows how "a sign system had been put into place," which supplemented written and oral justifications for slavery. Especially in the nineteenth century, white artists produced paintings that reinforced beliefs about the "happy slave," contented in his/her servitude. This was filtered through popular culture, especially through minstrelsy, wherein black-faced white actors parodied black dialect and behavior in staged performances. American culture was permeated with words, sounds, and images that took for granted that slavery was both justified and necessary, beneficial to all concerned. At the same time, there existed a countercurrent that "remembered" the opposite.

Against the attempt to reconstruct slavery to fit particular interests stood the recollections of former slaves, those passed down orally, in story and song, as well as in the written slave narratives being hailed today by many as the origins of a distinctive African American aesthetic. These voices, though significant and strong after emancipation were secondary to the optimistic hope for integration. It was this future orientation, not a reflected upon common past, that unified blacks after the Civil War. As former slaves died out, the voice of direct experience began to disappear. Already in 1867 a group of musically interested collectors could write about the songs they were about to publish, "The public had well-nigh forgotten these genuine slave songs, and with them the creative power from which they sprung" (Allen, Ware, and Garrison 1867) In the 1880s, as the dreams of full citizenship and cultural integration were quashed, the meaning of slavery would emerge as the issue of an identity conflict, articulated most clearly by the newly expanded and resourceful ranks of highly educated blacks. Through various media and forms of representation these black intellectuals reconstituted slavery as the primal scene of black identity. In this emergent identity, slavery, not as institution or experience but as a point of origin in a common past, would ground the formation of the black "community." This was not the only source of revived memories of slavery, however. In face of repressive, often violent, reactions from whites, many blacks fled the South as reconstruction ended. One of their prime motivations for migrating was the fear that slavery would be reinstated (Painter 1976). In the trauma of rejection, slavery was remembered as its memory re-membered a group. Slavery defined, in other words, group membership and a membership group (Smelser, in this volume). It was in this context that slavery was articulated as cultural trauma.

As stated previously, the idea of an African American was one result of this identity struggle. It is important to keep in mind that the notion "African American" is not itself a natural category, but rather a historically formed collective identity that first of all required articulation and then acceptance on the part of those it was meant to incorporate. It was here, in this identity formation, that the memory of slavery would be central, not so much as individual experience, but as collective memory. It was slavery, whether or not one had experienced it, that defined one's identity as an African American; it was why you, an African, were here, in America. It was within this identity that direct experience, the identification "former slave" or "daughter of slaves" became functionalized and made generally available as a collective and common memory to unite all blacks in the United States. "African American" was a self-imposed categorization, as opposed to and as meant to counter those imposed by the dominant white society. In this sense, the memory of slavery by African Americans was what Foucault would call a "counter-memory." This clearly marks a difference between black and white in social and historical understanding. While whites might have condemned slavery as an evil institution and bemoaned its effects on the body politic of American society, blacks viewed slavery as a social condition, a lived experience, producing a distinctive way of life, a culture, a community, and finally, an identity. This collective identification affected not only the past and the present, but also future possibilities, recognizing the effects of racial distinction that would reinforce the tendencies of the dominant culture to ascribe common destiny. Thus a distinct gap formed between the collective memory of a minority group and the dominant group in the society, the one that controlled the resources and had the power to fashion public memory. Even here, however, differences between regions, North and South, winners and losers of what some have called the first modern war, created conflicting modes of public commemoration and thus public memories. While both sides avoided slavery as mode of experience, except of course for the North's celebration of its role as liberator and the South's as paternalistic romanticists, to focus on the Civil War itself as a traumatic event in the nation's history, each side offered a different interpretation and developed different ceremonies and rituals to officially and publicly commemorate that event.

There were some dissenting voices, especially among liberals and radicals in the North. Kirk Savage (1994, 127), cites one very influential Northern point of view, that of William Dean Howells, America's foremost literary critic writing in the *Atlantic Monthly* in 1866, who believed that commemoration following the war should focus not on soldiers and battles, but on the ideals and ideas that the war was fought over. Howells, in what must have been a minority view, thought "ideas of warfare itself—organized violence and destruction—unfit for representation" (Savage 1994, 127). As an alternative he pointed to "The Freedman," a sculpture of a freed black slave done in 1863, as "the full expression of one idea that should be commemorated" (cited in Savage 1994, 128). Needless to say, this suggestion went unfulfilled. Instead, each side, North and South, built monuments to its soldiers and their battlefields. In his analysis of these monuments, Savage writes that "issues such as slavery were at best subsidiary in the program of local commemoration, lumped in with stories of Christian bravery and other deed of heroism"(131). With slavery out of the picture, there could be reconciliation between the opposing sides, each being allowed to mark its own heroes, thus sweeping aside one of the main contentions of the war: "Commemoration and reconciliation, two social processes that were diametrically opposed in the aftermath of the Civil War, eventually converged upon a shared, if disguised, racial politics" (132).

Without the means to influence public memory, blacks were left to form and maintain their own collective memory, with slavery as an ever shifting and reconstructed reference point. Slavery has meant different things for different generations of black Americans, but it was always there as a referent. In the 1920s, after the first wave of what has come to be called the "great migration" in the context of a newly forming black public sphere, two distinct frameworks for narrating and giving meaning to the past took form, one progressive and the other tragic. These narrative frameworks were articulated by activists in two social movements, the Harlem renaissance and Garveyism, both of which were directed primarily inward, toward the transformation of racially based collective identity. It was not until the 1950s, even the 1960s, that slavery moved outside group memory to challenge the borders, the rituals and sites, of public memory. Again it was a social movement, the civil rights movement that reopened the sore and helped transform the cultural trauma of a group into a national trauma. Since then and only since then has slavery become part of America's collective memory, not merely that of one of its constituent member's. At the end of the current century the meaning, commemoration, and representation of slavery continues to evoke emotionally charged responses.

RE-MEMBERING AND FORGETTING

*Memories of slavery disgrace the race, and race
perpetuates memories of slavery.*

Tocqueville

Four million slaves were liberated at the end of the Civil War. In the first comprehensive historical account written by an American black, George Washington Williams (1882) offered this description: "Here were four million human beings without clothing, shelter, homes, and alas! most of them without names. The galling harness of slavery had been cut off of their weary bodies, and like a worn out beast of burden they stood in their tracks scarcely able to go anywhere" (1882, 378).

This was written nearly twenty years after the event and is an act of remembrance as much as historical writing. The author was part of a literary mobilization within the black middle class that emerged in the decades after the Civil War. The collective aim of this semicoordinated movement was to counter the image of blacks being put forward by whites. As the "full and complete" integration promised by radical reconstruction gave way to new forms of racial segregation in the South and elsewhere, such mobilizations were of utmost importance. It was within the context of such efforts that a new form of racial consciousness began to take form. In addition to this monumental work, which also appeared in a condensed "popular" version, Williams produced an equally monumental history of black soldiers during the Civil War. Along with these historical works were a few biographies, such as Sarah Bradford's *Harriet, the Moses of Her People* (1886) a dramatization of the life of Harriet Tubman, leading black Abolitionist.

While constantly growing in number, the black reading public was not the prime audience of these and other literary efforts by the few black authors of the time. The contemporary audience was more likely the sympathetic white reader, in need of bolstering in this reactionary period, and, one can assume, later generations of blacks who would require alternative histories to those offered by mainstream white society. Thus, these writers walked a narrow and rocky path between countering white stereotypes and pleasing the tastes and desires of their predominantly white reading public. Williams's historical accounts, for example, moved between portraying blacks as victims and depicting them as heroes in the struggle for racial dignity and recognition. The quotation cited above begins with the victim, in part as preparation for the heroic message of racial uplift to follow. It was just as plausible to argue, as sympathetic white historians later would and contemporary black novelists (who will be discussed below) were about to, that slavery produced hidden social networks that permitted blacks not only to survive, but also to maintain their dignity and traditions. These networks, which some would identify as a distinct cultural form, were an important resource after emancipation and reconstruction. As Linda McMurry (1998, 20–21) writes, "On many plantations and farms, the slave community functioned as an extended family. In freedom those informal support networks became structurally organized as church groups or benevolent organizations provided aid to families in crisis." Williams painted the former slaves as victims, survivors who would triumph over their condition, proving their worthiness, only to be rejected by a white society busy painting pictures of its own.

Here lie the roots and routes of cultural trauma. For blacks this rejection after the raised hopes engendered by emancipation and reconstruction forced a rethinking of their relation to American society. This was traumatic not only because of the crushed expectations, but also because it necessitated a reevaluation of the past and its meaning regarding individual and collective identity. Many blacks and a few whites had hoped that reconstruction would, if not entirely eliminate race as the basis for identity, at least diminish its significance, as former slaves became citizens, like other Americans, and the caste system associated with servitude disappeared. This was now clearly not the case, making it necessary to reevaluate the meaning of the past and the options available in the future. Once again it would be necessary to attempt to transform tragedy into triumph with the uncovering of new strategies in the struggle for collective recognition, in the face of the threat of marginalization.

Some significant changes had occurred during reconstruction, even if the period later would be viewed as a failure. One of these concerned education and literacy. Along with presenting a military presence, the federal government organized Freedmen's Bureaus in the defeated South designed to aid former slaves, a program that included providing the grounds, if not the sufficient funds, for their formal education as well as that of their offspring. Such funding was aimed at individuals but had a collective effect in that a system of segregated schools sprung up in the South, creating the grounds for a dramatic rise in literacy rates among blacks as well as solidifying a sense of togetherness in seperatness. According to a report published by the commissioner of the bureau, Major General O. O. Howard, in 1870, five years after work had begun "there were 4,239 schools established, 9, 307 teachers employed, and 247,333 pupils instructed" (cited in Williams 1882, 385). Such figures reflected only an aspect of this education revolution, as "the emancipated people sustained 1,324 schools themselves, and owned 592 school buildings" (ibid.). The federal program was thus supplemented by self-help, some of which was sponsored by organizations such as the African Methodist Episcopal (A.M.E.) and other black churches. As a result of these efforts, by 1870, "black illiteracy in the South had been reduced to 79.9%" (Christian 1995, 231).

Reconstruction had an ambiguous effect on the black church and its leaders. On the one hand, as blacks were permitted a more active role in public life, the authority of the church and its ministers, long centers of the shadow black community, was eroded. However, as ministers were among the only literate and educated blacks, the role of the black minister, if not the church, was enhanced. As will be discussed, the earliest black newspapers in the South were dominated by ministers. In addition, black churches were central in the organizing and distributing of resources during and after reconstruction. In this the church expanded its role as the center of black social as well as religious life. The two, like the sacred and the secular generally, were intimately entwined.

Along with growing literacy, an improved means of communication helped reinforce a sense of collective identity, as well as common destiny, within this first generation. Benedict Anderson (1991) has argued that it is with the assistance of mass media that "imagined" as well as "real" communities are constituted and sustained. For this generation, newspapers were the most important form of mass media. The growth in literacy, permitted by the education revolution following the end of the war, went hand in hand with the growth of black-owned and -read newspapers. The first black-owned newspaper, *Freedom's Journal,* appeared in New York City in 1827. By the 1850s most northern cities contained at least one black-owned paper, whose prime editorial concern was the abolition of slavery. Between 1865 and the end of reconstruction, 115

Southern-based, black-owned newspapers were started. According to one study (Simmons 1998, 14) the publication of black-owned newspapers in the South "signaled the first change in editorial philosophy—one from freeing slaves to one of reestablishing the racial identity of Afro-Americans and educating them so that they could survive in society." It was through this medium that self-identity could be debated and a new postslavery collective identity articulated.

The success of the failure of reconstruction was an expanding institutional base for sustaining a black community, as segregated schools and newspapers were added to the churches and other counterinstitutions like the conferences and the semisecret societies and fellowships, the Masons and Elks. Two streams existed side by side, one, the drift toward a separate black community within a dominate white society, and the other, the continuing hope that (black) community and (white) society would eventually converge. This consolidating and expanding "Negro World," as Drake and Cayton would later write in their classic study *Black Metropolis* (1945, 116), had existed since the eighteenth century.

"Through the years it had been developing into an intricate web of families, cliques, churches, and voluntary associations." It was, as they write, "the direct result of social rejection by the white society." It was just this rejection that was articulated as cultural trauma in the late nineteenth century and consolidated in the notion of the African American as a distinct "race."

POPULAR MEMORY, POPULAR CULTURE, AND IDENTITY POLITICS

With the end of the Civil War, slavery was something that was thought by many, black as well as white, best forgotten rather than commemorated. History was not a centerpiece of the new system of education. Former slaves were, as said, more concerned with the future than with remembering slavery as anything more than a means of orienting collective agency. Alexander Crummell, an early supporter of emigration to Africa, who had lived for many years there, liked to distinguish memory from recollection in regard to slavery. On Memorial Day 1885 at Harper's Ferry, where blacks gathered to commemorate John Brown's raid, Crummell told his audience, "What I would fain have you guard against is not the memory of slavery, but the constant recollection of it" (cited in Blight 1997, 161). Popular commemoration by blacks supported this view. Since emancipation, blacks had developed their own political calendar, and where they used that of the dominant culture, as in the example above, they transformed its meaning. Thus, New Year's Day and July 4 commemorated black emancipation, rather than American independence. Slavery, or rather the emancipation from it, was taken as the symbolic starting point for hope of a new relation with American society. At the same time, the grounds of a distinct, and separate, collective consciousness was being formed through such rituals.

Other forms of popular culture carried memories of slavery into future generations. Earlier, the abolitionist movement had provided the context for the publication and spread of the so-called slave narratives, texts written by former slaves about their experiences. The aim of these texts was decidedly political, their primary purpose being to recruit supporters to the antislavery cause. Still, these narratives were the first representations of slavery from the point of view of the victim and had become central to the construction of a counter, collective memory, both in the articulation and resolution of cultural trauma. As representations, the images called forth in these narratives are framed by the circumstances of their production—they are what can be called movement texts—and their reception has varied according to time and place. Even when read as firsthand accounts of slavery, these are moral tales, which identify heroes and villains, giving voice to the pain of subordination as well as faces to the perpetrators. They help in the process of turning victims into agents and tragedy into triumph. For later generations, these narratives have functioned as exemplary texts, examples of a "black literature" and as sources of collective identity, as they recall a common heritage. Their direct political meaning thus has diminished. An exemplary slave narrative that gave voice to the aspirations of the first generation after emancipation was Booker T. Washington's *Up from Slavery* (1901), a book that moves between slave narrative and autobiography in its focus on subjectivity and agency. This tale of willful triumph over adversity is one full of hope for the future, even though it was published at a reactionary age. It would become one of the exemplary texts of what can be described as the progressive narrative, one of two competing frameworks through which black experience in the United States is remembered.

The slave narratives developed into autobiography and adventurous novels at a time when literacy rates were improving for blacks in the United States, and they played a part in the struggle over the memory of slavery. A new generation of black writers emerged out of the small black middle class, giving voice to its aspirations, as well as providing a counter-memory to that which dominated American popular culture. Examples are Paul Dunbar (1872–1906), James Weldon Johnson (1871–1938), Charles Chesnutt (1858–1932), and Frances Harper (1825–1911). What makes such writers constitute a "generation" is not their year of birth so much as their collective articulation of the aspirations of those who had experienced the raised hopes of emancipation and the crushing effects of the failure of reconstruction. Their poetry and fiction objectified, as it represented, the memory of slavery, at the same time as it articulated a generational consciousness formed in the cultural trauma that accompanied the end of reconstruction and the reestablishment of "racially" based otherness.

For this generation of black intellectuals, writers, teachers, journalists, lawyers, and others who thought of themselves as representing the collective by means of the intellect and imagination, questions of representation were intimately bound up with moral and political, as well as aesthetic, concerns. As "race" and the slave past became the prime means through which the collective was identified and more or less forced to identify itself, the issue of how the collective should be represented before and to the dominant white society became increasing central as blacks slowly attained the possibility to represent themselves through cultural means.

To understand this process as traumatic one must recall the racial stereotyping and the shifting grounds of popular memory recurrent in the dominant culture. The ending of reconstruction brought with it a resurgence of nostalgia for the "good old days" of the antebellum South. Popular culture was flooded with images of genteel whites and contented slaves, as minstrel shows and other forms of popular and serious entertainment created the so-called plantation school of literature as well as the roots of what has been called the "cult of the Confederacy" (Foster 1987). It was this conservative and reactionary cultural offensive that the black authors sought to counter with their own representations. Since for the most part whites controlled the means of representation and also made up the overwhelming majority of the reading public, this was indeed a process of delicate negotiation—one that often involved a developed sense of tongue in cheek and double entendre.

TRAUMA'S DIALECTIC: TRANSFORMING NEGATIVE INTO POSITIVE

The term "New Negro," which in the 1920s would become the title of a groundbreaking collection of literary and artistic works, first appeared in an 1895 newspaper editorial, where it was applied to a "new class of blacks with education, class, and money" that had appeared in the thirty years since the end of the Civil War (Wintz 1988, 31). What the phrase implied was that blacks in increasing numbers had achieved social position of influence in at least some corners of American society and could more freely express feelings of racial pride in public, that is, for white eyes. If one was going to be ascribed racial status, one need not necessarily accept the ranking system of the dominant society—not, that is, if one had some means to counter it. This emerging black middle class was coming of age in a context shaped not by slavery or the hopes and expectations of emancipation, but by the failure of reconstruction and by white backlash. It was gaining a sense of itself, a generational consciousness as well as a racial one, and some cultural capital of its own. This would correspond with the schema of generational memory presented earlier, where it was noted that cultural trauma and the search for resolution would take at least a generation before the most affected groups were in a position to express their feelings publicly.

The late nineteenth century was a period of nation-building, and the notion of the grounds of collective identity for such "imagined" communities was a matter of great interest and debate. Race, by which one meant cultural heritage more than physical characteristics, was often argued as a most useful ground for collective identification. The various immigrant groups streaming into the United States were often referred to as "races." In 1896, speaking in favor of imposing limitations on immigration, U.S. senator Henry Cabot Lodge asked rhetorically what "the matter of race (was) which separates the Englishman from the Hindoo and the American from the Indian." He answered,

It is something deeper and more fundamental than anything which concerns the intellect. We all know it instinctively, although it is so impalpable we can scarcely define it, and yet it is so deeply marked that even the physiological differences between the Negro, the Mongol, and the Caucasian are not more president or more obvious. When we speak of a race then ... we mean the moral and intellectual characters, which in their association make the soul of a race, and which represent the product of all its past, the inheritance of all its ancestors, and the motives of all its conduct. The men of each race possess an indestructible stock of ideas, traditions, sentiments, modes of thought, an unconscious inheritance from their ancestors, upon which argument has no effect. What makes a race are their mental and, above all, their moral characteristics, the slow growth and accumulation of centuries of toil and conflict. (quoted in Stocking 1993, 4–16)

The point here is that from the end of reconstruction to the turn of the century, "race," in this very particular sense, was perhaps the most common reference point for collective identity. When the United States vigorously restated its intentions to exclude blacks from full and acknowledged participation in the construction of American society little more than a decade before Lodge was explaining the meaning of race to his colleagues in the Senate, it is not surprising that some black intellectuals seized upon the notion of race to ground the countercollective identity of this once again marginalized group. A leading spokesman for the notion of an African American race was W. E. B. Du Bois (1868–1963), a Harvard-educated sociologist, whose essay collection *The Souls of Black Folk* (1903) became the manifesto of the new Negro movement. While race may have been a pliable concept at the turn of the century, blackness was now firmly associated with subordination and difference in the minds of most white Americans. Popular and "serious" culture had been brought to bear; minstrelsy, literature, and the visual arts had cultivated the association of color with passivity, laziness, naive good humor, child-like behavior, and "primitive" sexuality. To counter these images, intellectuals like Du Bois called upon a section of the educated black middle class, a cultural avant garde he called the "talented tenth," to mount a more concerted counterattack with the means at their disposal. Toward this end, he helped form a core group of intellectuals who became known as the Niagara Movement (1905) and then the National Association for the Advancement of Colored People (NAACP) in 1909–10. Du Bois was appointed editor of the association's periodical, *Crisis,* in which he published short stories by Chesnutt and poems by Johnson alongside more directly political pieces.

As "New Negroes," black intellectuals began an earnest search for some common grounding upon which to secure a new collective identity for American blacks once again degraded by the dominant society. In the process, a long tradition of black separatism, which called for a return to Africa, was transformed into something less radical, a racially based identity that combined African and American elements into something unique, an African American (see Moses 1978). From an African American perspective, blacks in the United States were "Americans by citizenship, political ideals, language, and religion" (Rampersad 1976)— and African in terms of heritage, something that made them members of a "vast historic race" of separate origin from the rest of America. The distinctiveness of American blacks stemmed not from slavery, but rather from an African past, one filled with greatness. It was this and not the circumstances of their coming to America or the "culture" they scratched out of those circumstances that was at the heart of their racial distinctiveness.

Race functions here not only as a unifying concept, but also as one that endows purpose. Being a "sort of seventh son, born with a veil, and gifted with a second-sight in this American world" (Du Bois 1903, 3), the African American had the task to reveal to this still young and unfinished American nation a true picture of itself. Another task was to offer "civilization the full spiritual message they are capable of giving," to become a "co-worker in the kingdom of culture" (ibid.). Race involved the duty of speaking truth to power and of producing greatness. The aim here was to find the positive in the negative, the distinctiveness in the distinction. The trauma of rejection produced the need for positive identification and a plan of action, a cultural praxis as well as political and economic practice. After the hopes of full political participation faded, leaving "the half-free serf weary, wondering, but still inspired" (ibid., 5) another ideal emerged "to guide the unguided" on the path of self-knowledge. Though this, too, proved futile, "the journey at least gave leisure for reflection and self-examination; it changed the child of Emancipation to the youth with dawning self-consciousness, self-realization, self-respect." The race saw itself for the first time, "darkly as through a veil," yet "some faint revelation of [its] power, of [its] mission" emerged (ibid., 6). Du Bois'

Hegelian perspective, the coming to be of racial consciousness, was one of the first steps in articulating what I will call the "progressive narrative," wherein slavery would be viewed as a stage, even a necessary one, in a path toward civilization, self-fulfillment, if not acceptance.

Elsewhere in the world, the nation-state was being held up as the ultimate measure and expression of the distinctiveness of a people, and nationalist movements were especially active in Europe. Unlike their European counterparts (the Irish, for example), American blacks "lacked an immediately accessible native language in which to center their cause" (Mishkin 1998, 48). Black speech or dialect was being parodied in popular culture and although Africa was being rediscovered as a cultural and spiritual heritage, there existed no common African language to draw upon. While writers and poets like Dunbar, Chesnutt, and Harper drew upon black dialect and character types, stories, and jokes in their attempts to locate a distinctive folk culture developed through slavery, Du Bois pointed to another sort of language, what he called "sorrow songs" and the underlying humble, good-natured character that slavery had produced and which these songs expressed. While these sorrow songs had African roots, their development was the result of a unique mixture of Africa and America. It was this that grounded the "soul" of a new race, the African American. It was this identity, born of slavery, which united all blacks in the United States, whether they lived in the North or South, in the city or the countryside, whether they were highly educated or had no schooling at all. The Massachusetts-born Du Bois wrote of his experience upon hearing the sorrow songs that expressed this commonality, "Ever since I was a child these songs have stirred me strangely. They came out of a South unknown to me, one by one, and yet at once I knew them as of me and of mine" (Du Bois 1903, 177). Here, as elsewhere in *Souls,* Du Bois spoke through his own experience to that of the "race." Like the slaves themselves, fragmented and dispersed across the continent, a new generation of blacks in America was articulating the trauma of the dashed hopes of reconstruction in a struggle to combat the solidifying national consensus concerning blacks' "otherness." They could consolidate and unify as African Americans, Du Bois reasoned, as they found solace and their common soul in the sorrow songs, as he had.

As he moved the field of struggle to cultural politics, Du Bois could contrast a soulless American culture with a soulful slave culture: "Will America be poorer if she replace her brutal dyspeptic blundering with light-hearted but determined Negro humility? Or her coarse and cruel wit with loving jovial good-humor? Or her vulgar music with the soul of the Sorrow Songs?" (ibid.). His answer was a gently put "no." While Du Bois tended to restrict the positive outcome of slave culture to sorrow songs and a distinctive character type, the next generation would expand it to include an entire way of life. This was a way of turning tragedy into triumph, uncovering a progressive route out of cultural trauma. This cognitive transformation would be articulated in the mid-1920s as a renaissance, by new "New" Negroes.

A USABLE PAST: THE PROGRESSIVE AND TRAGIC NARRATIVES

The First World War brought unforeseen changes in the material and spiritual conditions of blacks in the United States. For one, even though the American military maintained strictly segregated conditions, black soldiers volunteered for service and went into combat with equal enthusiasm as whites. Black Americans were as patriotic as their white counterparts, something that is astonishing given their treatment. Although many of those who volunteered for military service were turned away due to the racial ideas and discriminatory practices of admission boards (this was before the national draft) "more than 400,000 African Americans served in the United States armed forces during World War I, and about half of those saw duty in France" (Stovall 1996, 5). These veterans, filled with an increased sense of national and racial pride, would return to the same segregated America and all the frustrations felt by those left behind.

A year after the war's end the country suffered some of the worst race riots in its history, something that can at least in part be attributed to the perceived threats of a new, urban Negro. At the same time as the triumphant returning black veterans marched up New York's Fifth Avenue, all the way into Harlem, to the strains of an all-black orchestra directed by James Reese Europe, other, equally symbolic, events were taking place. In 1919, twenty-five race riots occurred in northern cities involving direct clashes between whites and blacks, something that would distinguish the riots from later occurrences, which were largely internal to black neighborhoods. In Chicago alone, thirty-eight persons, black and white, were killed, and five hundred were injured. In the South, there was a distinct rise in the number of lynchings, which could be attributed to the threat posed by returning veterans. Eighty-five blacks were lynched in 1919 in what was called the "Red Summer of Hate," as the KKK organized "over 200 meetings throughout the country" (Christian 1995, 316). Writing in the *Crisis,* Walter White listed the following as causes to the rioting: "racial prejudice, economic competition, political corruption and exploitation of the Negro voter, police inefficiency, newspaper lies about Negro crime, unpunished crimes against Negroes, housing, and reaction of whites and Negroes from war" (quoted in Christian 1995, 317).

In addition to the return of veterans and the raised expectations for integration and acceptance, other changes were occurring in the black population. Stimulated by the war, developments in farm production were changing the rural workforce, creating a significant decrease in the need for unskilled manual labor. The production of cotton, the mainstay of black labor, was particularly affected. These and other factors, such as the need for unskilled industrial labor in northern cities, precipitated what has come to be called the "great migration," a population shift of such magnitude that it would change the conditions of African Americans forever. In a period of sixty years (1910–70) more than six and a half million black Americans would move northward, shifting from farm to industrial work and from rural to urban living. During World War I alone, "the black population of the North increased by almost 80 percent, from 900,000 to 1.6 million. Another 350,000 African Americans joined the armed forces, and many of these soldiers resettled in the North after the war" (Barlow 1999, 16). In Chicago the black population increased 148 percent between 1910 and 1920; Columbus, Ohio, increased 74 percent; and Philadelphia, St. Louis, Kansas City, and Indianapolis all expanded their black populations by about 50 percent in the same period (Christian 1995: 319). This population shift wrought major changes in the social conditions of African Americans. For black authors, artists, and intellectuals, the shift helped produce a new audience and a new self-confidence. In 1920, New York's Harlem "contained approximately 73,000 blacks (66.9 percent of the total number of blacks in the borough of Manhattan); by 1930 black Harlem had expanded ... and housed approximately 164,000 blacks (73.0 percent) of Manhattan's blacks" (Wintz 1988, 20).

What could be called a black public sphere emerged as urban areas expanded to accommodate the waves of migrants arriving from the southern regions of the country and soldiers home from war. Within the neighborhoods that were created or transformed, small clubs and meeting halls, restaurants, movie houses, theaters, and dance halls sprung up in the teeming black sections of Chicago, Detroit, Cleveland, and Philadelphia. Forms of popular entertainment were created as the newly arrived refitted their ways of life to fit the urban environment. In a sense, one could say that this new urban public sphere expanded upon and competed with the much smaller ones created and maintained by the educated black middle class of the previous generation. While the book clubs, lyceums, concerts, and theater that helped constitute the previous generation had been limited to a small elite with intimate knowledge of each other and maintained through networks that built on face-to-face contact, this new black public was more anonymous and open. Further, what previously had been carried and motivated by small groups and exemplary individuals was now borne by collective movements of a different type. There existed a tension between these social formations, one exclusionary and personal and the other open and anonymous, that would express itself in part as a generational struggle between an aging new Negro and a younger offspring in the 1920s.

The development of concentrated and literate black populations facilitated the emergence of social and cultural movements that would articulate as well as signal a new social awareness and a revisioning of the collective past. The urban environment opened blacks to intellectual and political impulses, such as the cultural radicalism of Greenwich Village and the political radicalism associated with it: socialism and communism, as well as nationalism. These processes were interconnected through a range of magazines, journals, and newspapers that served to link the wide-ranging and socially diverse racial community, and through which "race leaders" sought to influence the formation of the collective identity. Periodicals included Marcus Garvey's *Negro World*, A. Philip Randolph and Charles Owen's socialist *Messenger*, both of which began publication in 1917. Randolph, who would found the all-black Brotherhood of Sleeping Car Porters Union in 1925, was the son of slaves, while Garvey was a Jamaican immigrant.

Besides the *Crisis*, which remained under Du Bois' editorship, another journal central to the development of the Harlem renaissance was

Opportunity: Journal of Negro Life, founded in 1923 as the organ of the National Urban League. Its editor was Charles S. Johnson, a University of Chicago–trained sociologist born in 1893 and coauthor of *The Negro in Chicago* (1922), which followed the path opened by Du Bois' *The Philadelphia Negro* in providing a professional, sociological, and social work perspective on urban blacks. *Opportunity* was the organizer of literary prizes for promising young blacks. It was at the first awards dinner in 1925 that the poet Langston Hughes met the anthropologist Zora Neale Hurston for the first time, as they were each awarded prizes, as was Countee Cullen, whose poems are discussed below. There emerged, simultaneously, a developing interest in black history, literature, and art, especially within the smaller circles of the growing urban African American middle class, and a market for a race-oriented consumer culture. Additionally, the new, urban environment opened blacks to aesthetic movements like cultural radicalism; the bohemian lifestyle and modernist ideology of Greenwich Village, with its interest in "primitivism"; and to a new mass consumer culture. More directly, political movements and ideologies such as socialism and communism also found their way into these urban black communities. Along with new forms of black nationalism, they would compete for the attention of a black population in a period of great fluctuation.

TWO VOICES

Out of this exciting cacophony, two guiding frameworks emerged that would prove resilient in providing a cognitive map for mediating the past, present, and future orientation of the new, urban Negro. The cultural-political movement that has become known as the Harlem renaissance articulated a modernist, progressive narrative framework in which the past was interpreted as a stepping-stone toward a brighter future. And a social movement identified through the name of its leader, Marcus Garvey, gave voice to a traditionalist-romantic, tragic narrative framework, in which the past was something to be redeemed through the future. These narrative frames structured alternative ways of regarding the African and the American, as well as the meaning of slavery. These frames were articulated in a context wherein generational experience and social class were significant factors in understanding both their emergence and their acceptance.

Someone is always at my elbow reminding me that I am a grand-daughter of slaves. It fails to register depression with me. Slavery is sixty years in the past. The operation was successful and the patient is doing well, thank you. The terrible struggle that made an American out of a potential slave said "On the line!" The Reconstruction said "Get set!"; and the generation before me said "Go!" I am off to a flying start and I must not halt in the stretch to look behind and weep. Slavery is the price I paid for civilization, and the choice was not with me. It is a bully adventure and worth all that I paid through my ancestors for it. (Zora Neale Hurston, 1928, quoted in Watson 1995)

A core figure in the Harlem renaissance, Hurston (1891–1960) voices a modernist approach to the past, filtered through a narrative that is evolutionary and progressive. This is a past that points to the future. Slavery is not here forgotten, but is regarded as a usable past, an experience that can be appropriated. As heritage and tradition, the slave past can and should be collected, written down, and written about, as Hurston and others went on to do. Conceived as folk culture and compiled as source material, the past can be mined and used, a form of cultural capital to which blacks could be argued to have privileged access. From such a perspective, re-collecting the past could also be considered valuable activity, not only from the standpoint of racial pride. From an evolutionary perspective, preserving artifacts from an earlier way of life, one possibly threatened with extinction, could be viewed as socially, politically, and professionally useful. A progressive and evolutionary perspective views the past with the attitude of the outsider, though in Hurston's case, the outsider is also an insider. Raised in the small, black town of Eatonville, Florida, Hurston studied anthropology with Franz Boas at Barnard College in New York and under his direction would return to her birthplace and other areas of the South to collect this now exotic material. Together with the poet Langston Hughes (1902–1967), Hurston would return south in search of material for a play under the auspices of a wealthy white New York patron, as she would do later with the help of the W.P.A.

Here the collective past is usable in at least two senses: it is central to the maintenance of group identity, part of a collective memory, and it is source material, a cultural resource for a distinct aesthetic, explored and exploited not only by members of the group itself but by others as well. This applied equally to the visual arts. In the cultural politics of the renaissance, culture was a weapon in the struggle for racial recognition and acceptance. Many hours and pages had been spent discussing the relation between art and propaganda and "how should the Negro be represented" in aesthetic terms. Through the active intervention of Charles Johnson and Alain Locke, critic and central mediator in the representation of the Harlem renaissance, Aaron Douglas, a young, college-educated high school art teacher from Kansas, was recruited to visualize the New Negro and his/her historical coming-to-be. Following a path laid out by his mentor W. Reiss, a white, European modernist portrait artist, Douglas set out to transform internalized American ideals that identified beauty with European features and whiteness. European modernism had recently discovered Africa, and Reiss encouraged Douglas to do the same. Douglas's Africa centered on the Nile and Egyptian painting, with its flat, elongated bodies and faces drawn in profile. As one of the few black artists, Douglas not only painted but also was called upon to illustrate the novels and poetry of his fellow renaissance authors. His art deco illustrations are probably the most well known, with their lush primitive themes and flatly drawn figures.

Douglas was primarily a mural painter, and it is here that the progressive narrative behind his work is most apparent. In the murals he painted at Fisk University, black history is presented as progressive and evolutionary. While the African scenes are depicted as idyllic, they are also primitive, though in the positive sense of the term; figure and surroundings meld together in a natural, organic totality. These scenes are imagined and painted through a modernist prism, exotic and colorful, although in Douglas's work these colors tend to be muted, more like Modigliani than Gauguin. His contemporary images carried traces of this rhythmical, exotic primitivism, but he often introduced a political comment, such as the threatening noose that hangs down in the center of a cabaret in *Charleston,* an illustration that appeared in Paul Morand's *Black Magic* in 1929. Douglas's depictions of slavery, particularly in the murals *An Idyll of the Deep South* and *Slavery Through Reconstruction,* both from 1934, are done in the same style, idyllic in its depiction of the slave community, where oppression is amended by collective solidarity, expressed through work, music, and struggle. In all of these, the past is an essential link to the present/future but nothing to redeem or return to.

As it was for Douglas, Africa provided an important resource in this generation's search for identity. In the progressive narrative, Africa appears not so much as a geographical place, somewhere to actually escape to, but as metaphor for a long lost and forgotten past. This can be seen in the following poem by Countee Cullen, which appeared in the Urban League's *Survey Graphic* and then in *The New Negro,* both edited and introduced by Alain Locke in 1925.

> *What is Africa to me:*
> *Copper sun and scarlet sea,*
> *Jungle star or jungle track,*
> *Strong bronzed men, or regal black*
> *Women from whose loins I sprang*
> *When the birds of Eden sang?*
> *One three centuries removed*
> *From the scenes his father loved,*
> *Spicy grove, cinnamon tree,*
> *What is Africa to me?*

"Heritage," the title of Cullen's poem, is revealing in itself. As part of a generational reconstitution of collective memory, the concept of heritage adds a new dimension to reinterpreting the slave past by looking beyond it to something more glorious. It places emphasis on the African in re-configuring the relationship between the African and the American. As heritage, this past is still meant to be useful in the present, something of which one sings and re-visions in order to look forward toward the future, but it is something more than a stepping-stone. The "strong bronzed men" and "regal black women" are "three centuries removed" but can be called upon to orient and solidify a community facing quite another world. It is the African, rather than the slave, culture that is the heritage of African American. It is a different Africa that is called upon in the tragic recon-struction of historical memory. The tragic and redemptive narrative that guided Garveyism and other forms of black nationalism viewed Africa as the homeland and would drop the American altogether.

TRAGIC NARRATIVE

The same urban public sphere in which this progressive narrative was articulated produced an alternative, tragic and redemptive, narrative frame. This narrative took form in conjunction with the development of an internationally based movement for Pan Africanism, a form of black nationalism with roots in the previous generation of American blacks, including W. E. B. Du Bois. This international movement was articulated locally through a broad-based social movement associated with the Jamaican-born Marcus Garvey and his United Negro Improvement Association (UNIA). The international basis of the movement was reflected in the figure of Marcus Garvey himself, in the role of West Indians in the reconstruction of black collective identity in this period. Like some groups of European immigrants, some West Indians brought with them an anticolonialist perspective, as well as an openness to ideologies like marxism and socialism. Garvey had come to the United States looking for support in the racial self-help philosophy of Booker T. Washington but ended up in Harlem as the leader of what has been called the largest black-based social movement in the history of the United States.

The grounding aim of the UNIA was "to promote the spirit of race pride and love; to reclaim the fallen of the race; to administer to and assist the needy; to assist in civilizing the backward tribes of Africa; to strengthen the imperialism of independent African States; to establish Commissionaires or Agencies in the principal countries of the world for the protection of all Negroes, irrespective of nationality" (quoted in Moses 1978, 19).

Speaking on Emancipation Day in 1922, Garvey began:

> Fifty-nine years ago Abraham Lincoln signed the Emancipation Proclamation declaring four million Negroes in this country free. Several years prior to that Queen Victoria of England signed the Emancipation Proclamation that set at liberty hundreds of thousands of West Indian Negro slaves. West Indian Negroes celebrate their emancipation on the first day of August of every year. The American Negroes celebrate their emancipation on the first of January of every year ... We are the descendants of the men and women who suffered in this country for two hundred and fifty years under the barbarous, the brutal institution known as slavery. You who have not lost trace of your history will recall the fact that over three hundred years ago your fore-bearers were taken from the great Continent of Africa and brought here for the purpose of using them as slaves. Without mercy, without any sympathy they worked our fore-bearers. They suffered, they bled, they died. But with their sufferings, with their blood, which they shed in their death, they

had a hope that one day their posterity would be free, and we are assembled here tonight as the children of their hope. ... each and everyone of you have a duty which is incumbent upon you; a duty that you must perform, because our fore-bearers who suffered, who bled, who died had hopes that are not yet completely realized ... No better gift can I give in honor of the memory of the love of my fore-parents for me, and in gratitude of the sufferings they endured that I might be free; no grander gift can I bear to the sacred memory of the generation past than a free and redeemed Africa—a monument for all eternity—for all times. (Garvey in Lewis 1994, 26–27)

This is a different view of the slave past than the one offered by Zora Neal Hurston and others associated with the Harlem renaissance. In Hurston's account slavery was a stepping-off point for evolutionary development. Framed through a progressive narrative, the past was a stepping-stone to the present/future and opened up for scientific excavation, for ethnological and archeological expeditions looking for traces and remnants, which could be collected and perhaps even used by those at a new stage of development. Garveyism was neither progressive nor scientific in the sense meant here, although it did contain elements of a civilizing mission. The future will look more like the past in his account; the aim of present action is to restore and renew lost glory. Rather than catalog and trace the steps out of the past, Garvey holds the past up as a model, a vision that will regenerate the present and the future. This is not a progressive vision but one of tragedy and redemption, of loss and retrieval. While Hurston's ethnological perspective required that the past be treated with respect, as evidence and as resource, Garvey's past demanded retribution. Slavery, which now would also include colonialism, was more than theft and the loss of freedom in forced labor; it denied a people their dreams and stripped them of their civilization. This lost generation now had to be redeemed by their progeny. Slavery in other words created a duty to redeem the memory of enslaved.

These two narratives formed two opposing and often opposed ways of relating the past to the present and future. United by the primal scene of slavery and the previous generation's attempts to deal with the trauma of rejection, each in its own way served as the basis for collective identity, by linking the individual to the collective through the concept of racial pride and the role of culture in that process. With their respective interpretations of the past they offered different paths to the future, however. The progressive evolutionary view articulated by Hurston pointed toward eventual integration into American society, on the basis of racial regeneration made possible through sifting the past for present use. The tragic-redemptive narrative pointed to a racial nation in a revitalized Africa.

These perspectives on the slave past were fashioned by small groups of intellectuals, in what Karl Mannheim would call "generational units," which were largely restricted to urban environments. In some sense, they, especially the Harlem renaissance, could be called an avant garde of a new generation. This was, however, a different sort of avant garde than the "talented tenth" envisioned by Du Bois and others of the previous generation for whom "culture" reflected and re-presented the best and the brightest of the race. This view of black culture was rejected by younger members of the Harlem renaissance in favor of a modernism that was at once "primitive" and realistic, creating an idyllic past as it represented the present, warts and all. Through incorporating folk traditions, such as jokes, folktales ("Hell: Ginny Gall way off in Ginny Gall/ where you have to eat cow cunt, skin and all," Hurston, cited in Watson 1995), and blues music into high cultural forms, such as poetry and painting, and including sexuality, desire, and everyday life as significant content, this avant garde younger generation blurred the borders drawn by their elders, as they reached out to and drew inspiration from, the surrounding mass black public. Its leadership was not exemplary in the same way, manner, or form as the moralistic, religious, and Euro-centered talented tenth. There were exceptions, of course—Countee Cullen being one—and overlaps, but there were, as I discuss below, great tensions between these two conceptions of racial representation and their respective views and uses of the past. Africa and the slave past were present as reference points for both, as that from which we came, but were interpreted in different ways by the different generations. The older generation found such language as Hurston's (recorded above) embarrassing and demeaning, just as they did blues lyrics and performance. For Du Bois and the generation formed by reconstruction and its failed promise of integration, the cultural trauma generated by the failures of reconstruction and the marginalization it engendered created a standpoint and a filter through which to judge present practice, which constituted a distinct generational habitus. For the new generation, the past, as Hurston expressed it, was a jumping-off point, a starting block in the race toward the future, which, because it looked black, was an open door.

Although offering another way of viewing the past, Garveyism was also optimistic about the future, but with another outcome in mind. Here Africa was a place to return to, a home in more than the spiritual sense. Rather than viewing Africa through the lens of modernism, Garveyism was traditionalist and mystical. Ethiopia was both a real place and the site of spiritual redemption: "We as a people, have a great future before us; Ethiopia shall once more see her day of glory" (cited in Moses 1978, 267). The uniforms and rituals of the Garvey movement reflected this nineteenth-century traditionalist view, as much as they did the fantasies of Garvey's predominantly working-class followers. They were part of a backward-looking movement into the future. As opposed to the progressive narrative for whom the slave past was negated by a future that transcended it, in Garvey's tragic narrative, the future realized rather than negated the past.

CIVIL RIGHTS AND MODERNIZED BLACK NATIONALISM: THE POSTWAR GENERATION

These narrative frames developed out of the cultural trauma initiated by the failure of emancipation and then renewed in a continuous cycle of raised and crushed expectations. Transmitted as collective memory, they organized experience, providing cognitive maps that guided present actions. As such they could be transmitted from one generation to the next and, in the process, reworked and revived to fit new situations and needs. It perhaps should be repeated that "cultural trauma" is a process, one that in this case was kept in motion through the continual degradation and marginalization of American blacks. The specific content of the trauma varied, as it is articulated, given voice and image in different historical circumstances. In the 1960s two social movements, civil rights and a modernized black nationalism, provided a context for their revitalization. These two movements, here exemplified through two who most visibly represented them, Martin Luther King Jr. and Malcolm X, at once reflected the changes that American society and its black minority had undergone since the end of the Second World War and the continued reworking of the trauma of rejection as the basis of collective memory. These movements were shaped in part by a new social and historical context in which the United States assumed the role of political, economic, and, most important, moral world leader. The image of the United States was one of a democratic nation, in which the notion of individual freedom and the right to participate in the pursuit of happiness were central pillars in the legitimization of this role. The new role and self-image affected domestic relations, increasing pressures to include blacks both culturally and politically, adding leverage to the claims by blacks as marginalized second-class citizens. It was such claims, and their remedy, that the two social movements articulated, and in this sense they expressed a continuity with the past.

The development of electronic mass media, especially color television, added a new factor in the representation of the present and remembrance of the past. Television, which seemed to offer an authentic representation of events as they occurred, would play a central role in the development of these social movements, including the lives of their most visible representatives/representors. Television also helped in changing the perception of Africa by bringing images of waves of anticolonial movements that swept the continent in the 1960s into American homes. These movements would have a dramatic impact on American race relations. Through this medium and the more traditional means of communication, such as the press and the public meeting, national and international movements contributed significantly in the struggle to articulate and define "blackness" and the African American, the preferred names and collective identities that would constitute the postwar generation. In this struggle, the meaning and memory of slavery and the failure of emancipation to fully integrate American blacks would remain the point of departure of collective memory and identity formation, as the primal scene of cultural trauma.

The great northward migration and the urbanization of blacks in both the North and the South continued after the Second World War, leading to an ever-greater concentration of America's black population. This encouraged a modernization of Garveyism and other forms of black nationalism developed by previous generations, a process that Malcolm X both expressed and represented, but which came to fruition after his death in 1965 in the black power community control movements in the urban ghettos. A key factor in this modernization was the birth of a "new" Africa, as anticolonial movements spread across the continent in the 1960s and inspired a new generation of American blacks. As previously, these forms of black nationalism centered in the continually expanding northern urban ghettos and were internally oriented to articulating and organizing this "community." As social movements, they developed their own institutions and cultures, from religious temples and self-defense to ways of dress, talk, marriage, and child rearing. Here "blackness" came to be associated with liberating oneself from the ways imposed by the "white devil," especially through religious teaching and education. These movements more and more came to represent themselves through un-compromising images of moral, mental, and physical toughness, which many, if not most, whites considered aggressive and threatening. For Malcolm X these representations offered a role model for oppressed and "brainwashed" urban blacks: "We Muslims regarded ourselves as moral and mental and spiritual examples for other black Americans" (Haley 1965, 396), making imagery and representation a form of exemplary action. For the developing feminist consciousness, these movements were considered to represent and be dominated by male values and by educated, middle-class blacks as ghetto or street culture, one that was at the same time attractive and repelling, a continued sign of social malad-justment as well as an outcome of marginalization and racist exclusion perpetrated by the dominant society. These images, no matter how they were interpreted, were projected and magnified through television and other mass media, in which the phrase "black power" and the image of the leather-clad, bereted man with a rifle complemented the pursed lips and tough words of Malcolm X and Amiri Baraka. This image of blackness contrasted sharply with that promoted by the civil rights movement, whose "good Negro" was represented either in suit or bib overalls and cotton dress, armed with a Bible and espousing nonviolent, Christian love.

What became known as the civil rights movement was by tradition and intention rooted in interaction with whites and white society. Its audience and its activists were multiracial and inclusionary. The black leaders it produced could mediate between black and white worlds. The movement exemplified Du Bois' "double consciousness," as well as the desire for integration, a concept that nationalists like Malcolm X ridiculed. Drawing on a tradition of protest reaching back to abolition-ism, the civil rights movement was rooted in the black church as much as in organizations like the NAACP and the Urban League. While the latter included whites as members, the black church developed its own religious traditions largely separate from white institutions, especially concerning day-to-day activities. The civil rights movement also developed its own internal media and means of communication, but it was from the beginning directly engaged with whites. The landmark decision by the Supreme Court in 1954, which questioned the constitutionality of segregated schools, created a new sense of possibility. Martin Luther King Jr. explained its importance this way: "Along with the emergence of a 'New Negro,' with a new sense of dignity and destiny, came that memorable decision of May 17, 1954 ... This decision came as a legal and sociological death blow to an evil that had occupied the throne of American life for several decades" (King 2003, 137–38). The movement began with protest concerning public transportation, reaching back to Ida Wells and others in the nineteenth century, and with boycotts of white stores and other services. Its demands concerned the inclusion of blacks, and its vision of America was decidedly along the lines specified in the Constitution and the Bill of Rights: "one nation, indivisible, with freedom and justice for all."

The black church, as mentioned earlier, originated in response to the segregationist policies of white religious denominations and developed parallel to them. As perhaps no other institution in American society, the southern black church embodied the cultural legacy of slavery and the hope of its transcendence. Through the ritualized performance of sermon and song, the southern black church recalled the slave past as it remembered the black community. The largest denomination and the most central in the civil rights movement was the Baptist Church, which particularly retained a southern basis, as well as rural flavor. Baptist minister Martin Luther King Jr. exemplified the role of the prophet in the church's Old Testament theology, as he set out to redeem the soul of America. What became the movement's representation of "the good Negro" was southern and rural, the hard-working, former slave who now wanted the full citizenship promised with emancipation. This was an image congenial to many whites, especially in the North. Even northern blacks who traveled south to participate in the movement found this image appealing and took it on; Harvard-educated Bob Moses even changed his name to fit the biblical references and worldview that guided the movement.

King rose to national prominence with the Montgomery bus boycott, an event that served to catalyze what is now called the civil rights movement. In many ways this movement and Martin Luther King Jr. himself exemplified the progressive narrative. As the movement developed, its aim was to include blacks as first-class American citizens. King often expressed this demand in his sermons and speeches. King opened his first public address, a speech given at the Holt Street Baptist Church directly after Rosa Parks's arrest in December 1955, with "You are American citizens." He later continued, "This is the glory of our democracy. ... If we are wrong, the Constitution of the United States is wrong. If we are wrong, God almighty is wrong!" In his sympathetic and incisive analysis of King's sermons and preaching techniques, Richard Lischer (1995, 148) reveals that King's sermonic material "reflects the same world-view and ethos to which white Baptists, Methodists, and Presbyterians had long been accustomed, the Brotherhood of Man and the Fatherhood of God." This view he received from his mentors within the black church and he revitalized and re-voiced to fit the needs of mobilization in the struggle to include blacks into this brotherhood on the secular plane of American society. One of the tasks King was to perform was to transform the traditions of the black church to fit the framework of the progressive narrative and to convince his fellow blacks to act according to its aims. He mobilized and motivated within the framework set by this narrative. "His goal", according to Lischer, "was the merger of black aspirations into the American dream" (142). To achieve this, King at times criticized the black church and some of his fellow ministers for passivity regarding the struggle for inclusion and civil rights; one must remember that the majority of ministers, especially in the South, were conservative and even opposed to King and *his* movement. Such publicly expressed criticism was made only before black audiences, however. Further, King had to convince those blacks who accepted the goals of inclusion and were willing to actively participate in the movement that nonviolence was the best way to achieve this end. Here it was not so much motivation that was necessary, but more a brake on the choice and use of more aggressive means.

The point is that what I've called the progressive narrative provided a framework for making action meaningful in a different way from the traditional messages of black religion, yet still within bounds set by them. As exemplified in the sermons of Martin Luther King Jr., the narrative frame enabled the mixing of the sacred and secular in ways that black religion had done since the slave era, with a message that combined sustenance here and now with hope for a better, more just future. This future was usually understood to be on earth as in heaven, that is, there was no sharp gap between the world of man and the world of God. Black preachers can be divided between the "sustainers" and the "reformers." The former was a tradition begun with the slave preachers, slave converts to Christianity and (later) free Black preachers, who "stimulate(d) hope while deferring reward" as they "projected a heavenly vision against the dark, low ceilings of slavery and segregation" (ibid., 29). This preaching strategy does not necessarily have to be cased as "otherworldly," "pie in the sky," or as the "opiate of the people." It can be seen as a strategy for sustaining human dignity for a people "not yet able to act and thereby avert(ing) the disaster of premature revolution" (Gayraud Wilmore in Lischer 1995, 29). Because of the constant threat of violence and the subordinate position of blacks generally, "sustaining" always contained a political dimension, in that the maintenance of hope in such a situation is always subversive. What the civil rights movement did was to take this hope beyond the walls of the church in a more collectively active way. This was a strategy that identified the reformer, a role that King learned from his own minister-father, Martin Luther King Sr., who, like many black ministers, combined sustaining with a more active engagement with the wider condition of blacks in American society.

The progressive narrative frame was flexible enough to contain the sustaining and reforming aspects of the black church in the move toward collective action. The movement itself took over the role that the individual minister had earlier played. Christian doctrine and nonviolence provided the sustaining, proving the moral worthiness of the movement activist. Nonviolence and a Christian worldview provided a moral high ground from which to reveal the immorality, the evilness, of segregation and the goodness of integration. Movement activists were thus doing God's work in bringing justice to the world. This strategy of inclusion thus included whites, not only as activists on the side of justice, but also those whites who currently opposed the movement, for in the end, they would inhabit a better world. This inclusion involved an underlying belief in conversion at the base of King's strategy. As opposed to the views of Malcolm X, who saw whites as "devils," enemies incapable of seeing the potential goodness in a new world that included blacks as equals, King's Christian beliefs were based on the hope not only of inclusion but also upon the conversion of enemies into brothers.

It was in this context that the new, modernizing Africa became important not so much as a root of culture and certainly not as the site of redemption, but as a symbol for freedom. This changed view of Africa, sparked by the anticolonialist movements of the early 1960s, marks a clear difference between this and the previous generation. What King found in Africa was "a throbbing desire; there seems to be an internal desire for freedom within the soul of every man" (King 2003), a universalistic notion that he found expressed in Montgomery and in the civil rights movement as a whole. This is a form of freedom based in the individual and in self-determination at the individual, rather than collective, level. The collective, the community, was a means to this end, not the end itself.

The community is one born and borne of necessity, out of segregation, and it is a source of strength and an agent of liberation, if not yet freedom. The basis of the community is the congregation, but its roots are wider, reaching back to slavery and to an ascribed racial identity, that is, to the historically reflective process of collective memory and to cultural trauma. History had created the black community, just as segregation had created the black church. It is this historical memory, accumulated over years of struggle and humiliation, that King recalls and calls upon to gather this community to collective action:

> We have ... seen the old order in our own nation, in the form of segregation and discrimination. We know something of the long history of this old order in America. It had its beginning in the year 1619 when the first Negro slaves landed on the shores of this nation. ... The great tragedy of physical slavery was that it led to mental slavery. So long as the Negro maintained this subservient attitude and accepted this "place" assigned to him, a sort of racial piece existed. ... Then something happened to the Negro. Circumstances made it necessary for him to travel more. His rural plantation background was gradually being supplanted by migration to urban and industrial communities. His economic life was gradually rising to decisive proportions. His cultural life was gradually rising through the steady decline of crippling illiteracy. All of these factors conjoined to cause the Negro to take a new look at himself. Negro masses began to reevaluate themselves. The Negro came to feel he was somebody. (King 2003, 136–37)

Just as Du Bois recognized himself in the sorrow songs of slave, which gave voice to the hope of redemption as well as weariness with the present condition, King uncovers the collective in a shared history of humiliation and the desire for freedom that began with slavery. The dream that was by this time shattered was one King articulated earlier in his famous "I have a dream" speech. This too was part of a heritage rooted in the black church and colored by the memory and image of slavery.

Through his sermons and speeches, King linked the individual to the collective, just as he reinvented a black religious tradition through their performance. Through drawing upon set formulas and phrases, common points of reference and association, and couching them in familiar musical speech patterns, King linked the individual and collective, the past and the present, as he "transformed the prosaic discouragement of his audiences into the poetry of a Movement" (Lischer 1995, 104). Whether he quoted from Paul Dunbar or James Weldon Johnson or lifted phrases from the Bible or Shakespeare, King used a formulaic speech that turned the I into the We and the mundane into the historically significant. "His audiences would cheer when he *began* one of his set pieces the way fans respond to the first bars of their favorite song at a rock concert. The formulas not only verified the identity of the speaker; they also guaranteed a collaborative role for the hearer in an important moment of history" (ibid., 104).

Slavery was the first point of reference and inclusion into the American dream, the end point around which all revolved. As the dream faded, the references became more "black": "Too many Negroes are ashamed of themselves, ashamed of being black. A Negro gotta rise up and say from the bottom of his soul, 'I am somebody. I have a rich, noble, and proud heritage. However exploited and however pained my history has been, I'm black, but *I'm black and beautiful*' " (ibid., 101). Yet his narrative frame and that of the civil rights movement as a whole remained progressive and inclusionary. Toward the end of his life, as the frustrations stemming from the failures of white society and increasing violent resistance and corresponding calls for black power by a younger generation of activists, King may have more and more played the role of prophet, venting his and others' rage against American society, emphasizing its shortcomings rather than its promise, but this was done within the narrative of universal deliverance and a philosophy of Christian love. As Lischer puts it, "deliverance and love were needed by everyone in America" (217). Here he was more like Marx, who believed that the liberation of the oppressed proletariat would also entail the liberation of their oppressors.

MALCOLM X AND MODERNIZATION OF AMERICAN BLACK NATIONALISM

The story of Malcolm X is well known, having been reconstructed for and by Alex Haley (1965) in a posthumously published best-selling autobiography and represented on film by Spike Lee. The white world first heard of the Nation of Islam's minister Malcolm X through the local New York broadcast of a television news program called "The Hate That Hate Produced" in 1959. Born in Omaha, Nebraska, in 1925, with the family name Little, Malcolm X was assassinated in Harlem in 1965. Like others of his generation, his life was shaped not only by skin color and gender, which conditioned his participation in the migration to the northeast, but also by the Great Depression and the Second World War. Malcolm inherited his late developing nationalism from his father, a Baptist minister and Garvey supporter, whose apparent murder at the hands of white racists represented an individual trauma for the six-year-old Malcolm. Malcolm recounts,

> I remember seeing the big, shiny photographs of Marcus Garvey that were passed from hand to hand. My father had a big envelope of them that he always took to these meetings. The pictures showed what seemed to me millions of Negroes thronged in parade behind Garvey riding in a fine car, a big black man dressed in a dazzling uniform with gold braid on it, and he was wearing a thrilling hat with tall plumes. I remember hearing that he had followers not only in the United States but all around the world, and I remember how the meetings always closed with my father saying, several times, and the people chanting after him, "Up, you mighty race, you can accomplish what you will!" (Haley 1965, 85)

As a teenager, Malcolm migrated to Boston to live with an older half-sister. Here, despite his sister's efforts to push him in the direction of middle-class inclusion, Malcolm discovered the excitement of urban ghetto life. He became a small-time hustler, for whom regular work was called a "slave" and considered something only fools or status conscious blacks would pursue. He worked as a shoe shine boy, a railroad porter, and a dish washer, only to better allow him to negotiate his hustle and "hip" lifestyle. Eventually this led him to New York and to Harlem, the center not of black art and culture, but of the hustle and the game. Imprisoned along with a friend and their two white women for robbery, Malcolm avoided direct participation in the war. In prison, he discovered Islam and the teachings of Elijah Muhammad. According to his own account this occurred through the efforts of his younger brothers and sisters, who, now living in Detroit, had become Muslim activists. He began corresponding with Elijah Muhammad, and by the time of his release had himself become a convert.

His years of correspondence with Elijah Muhammad created a bond between them and an entry into the inner circle of the religious movement. Putting his street knowledge and hustling skills to work in the movement's service, Malcolm X was soon rewarded with the title of "minister" and the role of chief organizer. He moved from city to city laying the groundwork for new temples through his recruiting talents. In part due to his efforts, the organization grew from a sect to a movement, as temples were established in most major cities with a large black population. The prime sources of recruits were the poorest sections of the ghettoes and the prisons, where blacks greatly outnumbered whites. Favorite targets were the recent migrants who peopled the storefront Christian churches. "We went 'fishing' fast and furiously when those little evangelical storefront churches let out their thirty to fifty people on the sidewalk. ... These congregations were usually Southern migrant people, usually older, who would go anywhere to hear what they called 'good preaching'" (Haley, 318–19).

What Malcolm X offered potential recruits was "good preaching"— about how the "white devil" used Christianity to keep blacks enslaved— and an alternative religion created for and by blacks. At the core of these sermons, at least in this stage of recruitment, was what Malcolm called "the dramatization of slavery" (ibid., 312):

> I know you don't realize the enormity, the horrors, of the so-called *Christian* white man's crime. ... Not even in the *Bible* is there such a crime! God in His wrath struck down with *fire* the perpetrators

of *lesser* crimes! *One hundred million* of us black people! Your grandparents! Mine! *Murdered* by this white man. To get fifteen million of us here to make us his slaves, on the way he murdered one hundred million! I wish it was possible for me to show you the sea bottom in those days—the black bodies, the blood, the bones broken by boots and clubs! The pregnant black women who where thrown overboard if they got too sick! Thrown overboard to the sharks that had learned that following these slave ships was the way to grow fat! (ibid., 311)

Dramatic images of slavery acted as a magnet to draw new recruits to a new religion, "a special religion for the black man" (ibid., 320). "Well, there *is* such a religion. It's called Islam. Let me spell it for you, I-s-l-a-m! *Islam!*" What the new religion offered was a strict moral code, an ethos, that would circumscribe a new collective identity and an entire way of life. This identity connected the urban black to a global community of black people and to a new understanding of themselves and their place in the world. Africa, the black continent, was a source of inspiration as well as a common point of origin. This new identity was necessary, Elijah Muhammad had preached, because "You are the planet Earth's only group of people ignorant of yourself, ignorant of your own kind, ignorant of your true history, ignorant of your enemy! ... You are members of the Asiatic nation, from the tribe of Shabazz!" (ibid., 357).

Important here is to reveal how Malcolm X modified the redemptive narrative he inherited from Marcus Garvey and Elijah Muhammad, with special reference to the meaning and recollection of slavery. Equally well known as the details of his life is the fact of Malcolm X's break with the Nation of Islam and his attempts to redirect black nationalism in a more secular direction. Just prior to his assassination in February 1965, Malcolm X completed a "Basic Unity Program" that would ground this new nationalism. It was addressed to "Afro-Americans, people who originated in Africa and now reside in America," advising them to "speak out against the slavery and oppression inflicted upon us by this racist power structure." The stated aim of the organization, which sought to unify and represent all black Americans, was to "launch a cultural revolution which will provide the means for restoring our identity that we might rejoin our brothers and sisters on the African continent, culturally, psychologically, economically, and share with them the sweet fruits of freedom from oppression and independence of racist governments" (Van Deberg 1997, 108).

One major factor influencing this revised and revitalized reference to Africa was the wave of national liberation movements that swept that continent in the 1960s, movements that inspired not only African Americans, but the political left generally. The emergence of postcolonial Africa also revitalized Pan-African ideas and moved the African continent into the political and ideological forefront. The marxist political theory motivating many of the leaders of these movements also was important in changing the modes of interpreting reality among black Americans. The marxism and socialism of the 1930s had been severely hindered by the Cold War and McCarthyism. This began to change in the 1960s as a new generation rediscovered marxist theory. The largely white "new" left developed its theoretical politics with the help of the same "Third World" national liberation movements that affected developments in black nationalism in the United States. Theories of "colonialism," "imperialism," and "underdevelopment" turned on issues of class and race, as well as self-determination. This new positive picture of Africa in Europe and America stimulated the transformation of black nationalism, from being religiously based to politically based.

Malcolm X was one of the first to articulate this transformation. One of the cornerstones of this new phase of Africanism was the idea of self-determination as a form of redemption, with the locus now moved from the individual and the group to the nation. In the Program, Malcolm X put it this way, "We assert that we Afro-Americans have the right to direct and control our lives, our history and our future rather than have our destinies determined by American racists" (ibid., 109). Central to self-determination was the control over history and its representation: "We are determined to rediscover our true African culture which was crushed and hidden for over four hundred years in order to enslave us and keep us enslaved up to today ... We, Afro-Americans, enslaved, oppressed and denied by a society that proclaims itself the citadel of democracy, are determined to rediscover our history, promote the talents that are suppressed by our racist enslavers, renew the culture that was crushed by a slave government and thereby to again become a free people" (ibid., 109).

Here slavery is not something relegated to the past; it is forever present. This slavery is economic, involving the exploitation of black labor, but it is primarily cultural, a form of slavery of the mind, which denies to the enslaved the possibility to develop their own talents. Here it would be impossible to view slavery as a past stage of development, which may have either hindered that development or promoted it. It would also be difficult to see slavery as a resource, itself the basis of a form of culture, no matter how distorted and misformed. Rather, this slavery is something lived and living; it forms a habitus that determines current behavior and thus requires a radical spiritual transformation in order to be rooted out. The rediscovery of one's true past is central to this transformation.

As developed in the Program, a central part of this rediscovery was the opening of communication channels between the new Africa and black America. This was meant in a more than symbolic sense and involved developing mass media, "independent national and international newspapers, publishing ventures, personal contacts and other available communications media" (ibid., 110). The new Africa could teach black Americans not only about their past but also their possible future. Concerning the past, Africa could teach black Americans "the truths about American slavery and the terrible effects it has on our people. We must study the modern system of slavery in order to free ourselves from it. We must search out all the bare and ugly facts without shame, for we are all victims, still slaves—still oppressed" (ibid., 111).

In this narrative, redemption will come through rejecting the legacy of slavery and, most important, the psychological burden it continues to impose on African Americans and through being reborn as blacks, no longer Negroes, hyphenated Americans or anything else than original and authentic black people. Black self-determination, whether in Africa or in separate communities or city-states on the American continent is the goal. Blacks are sojourners in the United States, a diasporic condition, an existence that can be redeemed only through rejecting the cultural heritage imposed by the white enemy. Thus the significance of renaming, either with an African-sounding name or with the even more symbolic and provocative "X." Elijah Muhammad put it this way, "Your slavemaster, he brought you over here, and your past, everything was destroyed. Today, you do not know your true language. What tribe are you from? You would not recognize your tribe's name if you heard it. You don't know nothing about your true culture. You don't even know your family's real name. You are wearing a *white man's* name! The white slavemaster, who *hates* you!" (quoted in Haley 1965, 357).

Elijah Muhammad had also preached slavery as part of a divine plan, a test of strength and thus a necessary step toward redemption. "Our slavery at the hands of John Hawkins and his fellow-slavetraders and suffered here in the Western Hemisphere for four hundred years was actually all for a Divine purpose: that Almighty Allah … might make himself known through us to our enemies, and let the world know the Truth that He alone is God" (quoted in Essien-Udom 1962, 132–33). Following a tradition reaching back at least to Du Bois, but with much older religious roots, this view endows not only a collective identity through creating a common past, but also a sense of purpose, a mission to tell or reveal the truth. This, combined with a strict program for changing individual behavior, a program of reform aimed at changing habits seen as stemming from slavery, provided a powerful link between individual and collective behavior and identity. Even as it could be interpreted as part of a divine plan, the memory of slavery was part and parcel of a continuing cultural trauma, one that was still very much alive. It was alive because the contemporary society and its culture were understood as an all-encompassing and oppressing Other, a totality from which one was alienated as well as excluded and against which one must struggle, so as not to be its victim or dupe. The movement and its regimen were thus a means of dealing with and resolving trauma, offering support and strength in the struggle to resist temptation and provide a path and a vehicle for redemption.

Each of the two narratives described here offers a framework for interpreting and resolving the cultural trauma that emerged at the failure of reconstruction to fully integrate blacks into American society. I have ended in the 1960s for reasons of space, but the trauma continues to this day and can be recognized in the work of Toni Morrison, Alice Walker, Charles Johnson, and other writers, as well as in other areas of popular culture such as music and film. It also can be seen in the field of sociology in the continuing debate about the success or failure of integration, in the writings of Orlando Patterson and William Julius Wilson, for example. For this generation, which came of age in a context dominated by the struggles for civil rights, feminism, and the rise of modern black nationalism, reflections and recollections upon an imagined slave past catalyzed a burst of creative energy as well as debate. This can perhaps be understood as part of a search for collective roots by an educated, professional middle class searching for ways to link itself with other black Americans who live under entirely different conditions. The rise of black studies programs at many if not most universities was a major contributing factor here. An important outcome of the civil rights movement, and part of that movement's institutionalization, these programs provided employment opportunities and a ready audience, both face to face and mediated through books and other expressive forms. The interest in "black culture," including the history and experience of slavery, expanded greatly, encouraged and magnified by mediated events, such as the television dramatization of Alex Haley's collective biography *Roots*. These, and other factors, including legislation, made possible increasing access to the means of cultural production, providing this generation with unprecedented opportunity to articulate and represent a countermemory. That this countermemory, while collective, is not univocal, can be seen in the various interpretations of the meaning of the slave past, not only for blacks, but for American society, that abound among black intellectuals, broadly defined, today.

As proscribed by melting-pot theories and supported by empirical research, the "normal" process of assimilation, wherein "each succeeding generation becomes more 'American,'" a process in which, as Philip Roth (1999) so dramatically expresses, "immigrants flowed into America and America flowed into them," appears to have been reversed for blacks because of the cultural trauma described here. Although with apparently less cultural baggage to hinder their acculturation, succeeding generations of American blacks have rediscovered their slave past and their blackness with increasing intensity. What is specific and contextual in the contemporary reworking of cultural trauma is the rejection of the separatism and marxism that characterized the 1960s' nationalism and thus an implicit convergence through the idea of the African American as black American. This reveals the possibility of accepting the collective identification "African American" without necessarily accepting the linear form of the progressive narrative. Progress can mean something other than shedding or overcoming the past. It also gives new meaning to the idea of integration by drawing on the later Du Bois and a modernized nationalism, where a reworking of the past leads through cultural autonomy rather than assimilation. In the context of postcolonialism and the resurgence of ethnic politics generally, this permits a reconciliation not only of an internal conflict, but also of cultural trauma. This is accomplished through the coexistence of a distinctive and relatively autonomous collective history and the progressive political and economic integration into an American society that is also altered in the process.

DISCUSSION QUESTIONS

1. Discuss the role of trauma in the formation of a collective memory and identity.

2. What is cultural trauma? Do people need to experience trauma directly to form unity or cohesion? Why?

3. How does trauma link the past to the present? What is its negative impact at the psychological level?

4. How did the failure of Reconstruction to integrate the former slaves help to formulate an African American identity?

5. Why can professional historical accounts be criticized for their ethnocentrism? How does history play a role in collective memory, even when it is inaccurate? How does collective memory, then, become more similar to myth?

6. Discuss and explain why the struggle for representation for black Americans has been both complex and problematic.

7. How did the meaning of slavery change according to different time periods, regions, and racial groups? What does this reveal about the power of collective memory and identity, as well as history, historical events, and their reconstruction and representation?

8. Why did slavery become the "primal scene of black identity?" Why is this significant in terms of history, collective memory, identity, and representation?

9. How did the civil rights movement transform the cultural trauma of a group into a national trauma? How did that movement place slavery into America's collective memory?

10. How did blacks and whites view slavery differently, and why is this significant in the development of a "counter memory?"

11. Discuss the impact of national and regional commemorations of the Civil War without any physical reminders—i.e., statues, memorials—in reference to slaves as a part of the construction of that event or its historical memory.

THE PRIVILEGE OF WHITENESS

A different picture of racism emerges when racism is understood as a sense of group position and as the organized accumulation of racial advantage, a system best understood by observing actual behavior (Brown et al.). While overt racism is considered a thing of the past, racial grouping and the ability to exclude people of color from social institutions reflects a benefit as well as a "cardinal principle of white identity" that perpetuates racial disparities (Brown et al.). How do we effectively address racism in society when the privileged status of the dominant group goes unnoticed by them and is as natural to its members as water is to fish?

SELECTED READING:

Of Fish and Water: Perspectives on Racism and Privilege
   *BY MICHAEL K. BROWN, MARTIN CAMOY, AND
   ELLIOT CURRIE*

Of Fish and Water

Perspectives on Racism and Privilege

By Michael K. Brown, Martin Carnoy and Elliot Currie

> There ain't no white man in this room that will change places with me—and I'm rich. That's how good it is to be white. There's a one-legged busboy in here right now that's going:
> "I don't want to change. I'm gonna ride this white thing out and see where it takes me."
> Chris Rock

*A*ccording to a well-known philosophical maxim, the last thing a fish notices is the water. Things that are unproblematic seem natural and tend to go unnoticed. Fish take the water they swim in for granted, just as European Americans take their race as a given, as normal. White Americans may face difficulties in life—problems having to do with money, religion, or family—but race is not one of them. White Americans can be sanguine about racial matters because their race has not been (until recently) visible to the society in which they live. They cannot see how this society produces advantages for them because these benefits seem so natural that they are taken for granted, experienced as wholly legitimate.[1] They literally do not see how race permeates America's institutions—the very rules of the game—and its distribution of opportunities and wealth.

Blacks, Latinos, and other people of color in the United States are racially visible, and everyone seems to notice their race. For them, the same culture, law, economy, institutions, and rules of the game are not so automatically comfortable and legitimate. In a white-dominated society, color brings problems.[2] And if people of color cry foul, if they call attention to the way they are treated or to racial inequality, if they try to change the distribution of advantage, if they try to adjust the rules of the game, white Americans (whose race and racial advantage are invisible) see them as asking for special privileges. They are seen as troublemakers.

What this means is that there is no such thing as a "view from nowhere"—to use Thomas Nagel's apt phrase.[3] People's perspectives on race reflect their

Michael K. Brown, Martin Carnoy and Elliot Currie, "Of Fish and Water: Perspectives on Racism and Privilege," *Whitewashing Race: The Myth of a Color-Blind Society*, pp. 34-65, 259-269. Copyright © 2005 by University of California Press. Reprinted with permission.

experience on one side of the color line or the other. Whites routinely misperceive the reality of black lives. For example, even though blacks are about twice as likely as whites to hold low-paying jobs and are more than twice as likely to be unemployed, 50 percent of whites say the average black is about as well off as the average white person. (Blacks, on the other hand, tend to be more realistic and accurate in their perceptions of their economic status relative to whites.[4]) If white Americans make no effort to hear the viewpoints and see the experiences of others, their awareness of their own privileged racial status will disappear. They can convince themselves that life as they experience it on their side of the color line is simply the objective truth about race. But while this allows them to take their privileged status for granted, it also distorts their understanding. This error poses serious problems for conservatives' analysis of racial inequality.

Of course, individual views within racial groups vary. Not everyone who shares the same subjective perspective will draw the same conclusions about policy. But any perspective that is unreflectively locked inside its own experience is limited, and this is particularly so when that perspective reflects the dominant culture. Failure to understand that they take whites' racial location for granted leads racial realists to ignore the ways in which race loads the dice in favor of European Americans while simultaneously restricting African Americans' access to the gaming table. White privilege, like the water that sustains fish, is invisible in their analysis.

This chapter is about perspective, and how definition—the power to name—determines perception, and ultimately, prescription. It traces the difference it makes if one group's perspective pervades almost everything, from culture to law. Apostles of the new perspective on race insist that racism is primarily a thing of the past. They come to this conclusion because they filter their evidence and their judgment through an outdated, discredited understanding of racism as intentional, obvious, and individual. These misconceptions are not unique to any particular writer or writers. Many white Americans and American institutions, including the current Supreme Court majority, hold parallel views. Because racial conservatives ignore the variability of racial reality in America, they do not recognize that racism is lodged in the structure of society, that it permeates the workings of the economic, political, educational, and legal institutions of the United States. Without that recognition, however, we will be unable to resolve the pernicious problems of race that confront us as Americans.

CONCEPTIONS OF RACE AND RACISM AFTER THE CIVIL RIGHTS REVOLUTION

In the new conventional wisdom about race, white racism is regarded as a remnant from the past because most whites no longer express bigoted attitudes or racial hatred. The Thernstroms note that despite black riots and crime in the streets in 1968, "nowhere in the voluminous polling evidence available for these years is there any sign that whites were drifting in the direction of the virulent anti-black sentiments so prevalent in the 1940s and 1950s."[5] Indeed, the real story for most whites is that racism has almost disappeared. Marianne Means flatly asserts, "We all agree that slavery was evil. But the blood of slavery does not stain modern mainstream America."[6] The Thernstroms concur. "White racial attitudes have truly altered," they write. "Whites with a pathological hatred of African Americans can still be found, of course. But the haters have become a tiny remnant with no influence in any important sphere of American life."[7]

Racial realists conclude that racism has ended because of the massive change in white attitudes toward blacks over the past sixty years. For example, more than half of all whites once believed that blacks were intellectually inferior. In 1994, however, only 13 percent of whites believed that blacks had "less in-born ability to learn" than whites. Whites also used to favor school segregation by overwhelming majorities, but now 90 percent favor school integration. In the 1940s whites believed they should be favored in competition for jobs. Today, on the other hand, whites unanimously agree that "blacks and whites should have an equal chance to compete for jobs."[8] The Thernstroms go so far as to assert that white attitudes had already changed for the better before the civil rights movement erupted in the 1960s.[9]

To racial realists, this evidence means that the color line has been radically altered. Although many whites still accept one or more negative stereotypes about African Americans, a recent study by Paul Sniderman and Thomas Piazza asserts that only 2 percent of the population could be considered old-fashioned bigots who subscribe to a large number of racist stereotypes.[10] Consequently, it is rare today to find cases of discrimination such as the ones involving Texaco's executives calling African Americans "black jelly beans," a member of the Dallas school board referring to African Americans as "niggers," and the "raw racism" experienced by black secret service agents in a Baltimore Denny's restaurant.

The evidence cited by racial realists indicates that they, like many whites, use a particular understanding of racism.[11] This notion assumes that racism is motivated, crude, explicitly supremacist, and typically expressed as individual bias. Racism, in short, is a form of "prejudice." Paul Sniderman and Thomas Piazza define it as "a consistent readiness to respond negatively to a member of a group by virtue of his or her membership in the group, with the proof of prejudice being thus the repetitiveness with which a person endorses negative characterization after negative characterization."[12]

Given this concept of racism and the use of opinion surveys to measure it, one should hardly be surprised that many people believe racism is a thing of the past. After all, virulent anti-black sentiments have diminished, formal barriers based on malicious intent have in large part been dismantled, and few Americans would accept publicly sanctioned racial barriers today. Were these its undisputed characteristics, one might be tempted to agree that racism is obsolete.

The law institutionalizes the American ideal of equality, and it provides remedies for those hurt by bias. Current law embraces the concept of racism as intentional individual prejudice, and also its corollary—that whites today are often unfairly accused of being racist. Evolving doctrine in racial discrimination cases reflects what Angela Harris has called an "essentially moralistic" view.[13] In several reverse discrimination lawsuits, for example, the Supreme Court has explicitly worried that affirmative action plans impose unacceptable burdens on "innocent" third parties (read whites).[14] In equal protection cases, the Court has increasingly emphasized invidious intention as a necessary element for finding actionable discrimination.

But this perspective has its critics. Twenty-five years ago, Alan Freeman documented how, after a brief period of attention to what he called a "victim perspective" in the jurisprudence of equality, the Court moved decisively to adopt a "perpetrator perspective" on issues of race.[15] Adopting the perpetrator perspective means looking at contested race issues from the vantage point of whites. The "perpetrator perspective" in law, like the conservatives' understanding of racism, is preoccupied with white guilt or innocence. It largely ignores whether people of color have suffered injury or loss of opportunity because of their race. Other critics have raised analogous arguments, paying attention to group subordination or disadvantage.[16] Ignoring these analyses, the courts have extended and deepened their attachment to the perpetrator perspective as the racial law of the land.

The Supreme Court's standard for white innocence is very low. Before the modern civil rights era, the Supreme Court often insisted that analysis of motive was inappropriate in constitutional adjudication.[17] During the past several decades, however, the Court has increasingly required that plaintiffs in equal protection discrimination cases not only may, but must, probe defendants' motives. To be successful, plaintiffs must prove specific and conscious bad intentions, the equivalent of the concept of racism as personal prejudice. Under the equal protection clause of the Fourteenth Amendment, the Court holds it is not enough to show that people would reasonably know the discriminatory consequences of their actions. Nor is it enough that actors foresaw the predictable effects of their actions and still proceeded in spite of them. To gain or sustain a remedy for racial injustice, litigants must meet a very high standard: they must show specific discriminatory purpose or malice. Reva Siegel argues on the basis of credible evidence that the Court knew this was a level of responsibility plaintiffs would "rarely be able to prove."[18]

Under congressional statutes, the role of intent is somewhat reduced. The Court has sometimes said that proof of employment discrimination may be based on a demonstration that policies have a disparate impact rather than on a showing of intent—proving, for example, that African Americans or other racial groups are more likely to be disadvantaged by an employment practice than whites.[19] Although the courts give lip service to unintentional bias in cases involving claims of discriminatory treatment, particularly in employment, most of the governing precedents require that plaintiffs prove intentional bias.[20] In 2001 the Supreme Court further extended that requirement. It held that under Title VI of the Civil Rights Act, which prohibits the discriminatory use of federal money, proving disparate impact would no longer be sufficient to win discrimination suits by private parties against federally funded contractors or institutions.[21]

The Court now requires proof of invidious intention in most cases of racial discrimination. But it does not apply this standard of intent in age discrimination cases where the relevant statutory language is identical to that in Title VII. In these cases, the courts have accepted a distinction between motive (a factor in causing action) and intent (a specifically proven state of mind) that is more favorable to plaintiffs alleging discrimination.[22] In other settings that address harms caused by others, such as personal injury law, courts assess liability and compensate victims not simply for intentional harms but also for injuries caused accidentally, that is, negligently. Plaintiffs do not have to prove malice or purpose unless they seek punitive damages.[23]

Choosing to make the specific intentions of identifiable individuals the criterion of racism is neither neutral nor appropriate. It is self-aggrandizing and misguided to judge others by their actions but ourselves only by our intentions.[24] In Supreme Court decisions and in the minds of many whites, the relevant "ourselves" are predominantly white or, in Freeman's phrase, potential "perpetrators." Many whites want to determine whether racism exists by exploring their explicit personal intentions. If we are deciding whether to put someone in jail, then assessing his intentions may be appropriate.[25] However, where disputes do not involve criminal charges but rather decisions about social, educational, welfare, or employment policy, questions of guilt, innocence, and punishment are not the issue. No one goes to jail for discrimination.[26] In discrimination litigation, the focus is on the legitimacy and fairness of the distribution of scarce opportunities and resources. To ameliorate injustice and achieve a more desirable state of civil affairs, it is more important to examine the problems of discrimination, injuries, and unfairness than to evaluate the culpability and motives of particular perpetrators.

The Court's narrow definition of discrimination, like the realists' equation of racism with prejudice, severely restricts what counts as bias or as evidence of bias. This definition tends to exonerate whites, blame blacks (by default), and naturalize (render unobjectionable) the broad realities of race-based subordination in the United States. This definition of racism, as we have already noted, is also empirically and conceptually flawed. It depends almost exclusively on attitudinal evidence uncovered by opinion polling. This poses two problems. First, even on its own terms, this interpretation of racism ignores significant research that shows how racist attitudes have persisted. In his recent book *The Ordeal of Integration*, Orlando Patterson examined a variety of evidence and concluded that "all things considered, it is reasonable to estimate that about a quarter of the Euro-American population harbors at least mildly racist feelings toward Afro-Americans and that one in five is a hard-core racist."[27] This is not a small number. If Patterson is correct, the Thernstroms' "miscreants of the night" are hardly a fringe.

Second, by relying on survey questions written in the 1950s, this research ignores possible changes in the character of racism and is, therefore, incorrectly measuring modern expressions of it. Donald Kinder and Lynn Sanders write that "a new form of prejudice has come to prominence, one that is preoccupied with matters of moral character, informed by the virtues associated with the traditions of individualism. Today, we say, prejudice is expressed in the language of American individualism."[28] Statements about individual failure, in other words, may be racially coded expressions of a derogatory stereotype.

There are also abundant survey data documenting the persistence of widespread racial prejudice forty years after the civil rights revolution. Many writers who use polling data to show the decline of racism cherry pick among these surveys and omit this evidence. Some of the most compelling evidence of tenacious prejudice comes from studies of residential discrimination. In 1992, the Detroit Area Survey found that 16 percent of whites said they would feel uncomfortable in a neighborhood where 8 percent of the residents were black, and nearly the same percentage said they were unwilling to move to such an area. If the black percentage rose to 20 percent, 40 percent of all whites indicated they would not move there, 30 percent said they would be uncomfortable, and 15 percent would try to leave the area. Were a neighborhood to be 53 percent black, 71 percent of whites would not wish to move there, 53 percent would try to leave, and 65 percent would be uncomfortable.[29] A more recent study of four cities (Atlanta, Boston, Detroit, and Los Angeles) yielded similar results. Camille Zubrinsky Charles found that more than half of whites in these four cities expressed a preference for same-race neighborhoods, while blacks expressed a strong preference for integrated neighborhoods.[30]

Contrary to the optimism of racial realists, one finds precious little evidence, even in the polling data they use, that many white Americans believe in integrated neighborhoods, especially if that means a neighborhood with more than a very few black families. Pejorative racial stereotypes are not restricted to one's choice of residence. They continue to be fundamental to (white) American culture. When the University of

Chicago's National Opinion Research Center asked people to compare blacks and other ethnic groups on a number of personal traits in 1990, they discovered that 62 percent of nonblack respondents believed that blacks were lazier than other groups, 56 percent stated that they were more prone to violence, and 53 percent thought they were less intelligent.[31] Another report suggests that white Americans are still substantially opposed to intimate contact with African Americans. In one national survey conducted in 1978, 70 percent of whites rejected interracial marriage on principle.[32] This hardly represents the significant change in whites' attitudes trumpeted by the proponents of racial realism.

Both the meaning of survey data and the way they are used by these cheerleaders for racial progress are also problematic. Because the typical questions used to measure changes in racial attitudes essentially gauge how closely attitudes conform to the American creed enshrined in the Declaration of Independence, it is not surprising to find that most (white) Americans sound tolerant. This is because when prejudice and tolerance are evaluated by these criteria, the questions assess only whether people subscribe to American ideals. It is hardly a major discovery to find that racism has declined when individuals are asked whether they believe in equal job treatment and integrated schools. Because the ideals of equality and formal tolerance are central to American identity, most Americans know the "correct" answers to such questions. Thus, rather than representing a decline in racism, these polling data actually measure adherence to the principles of American society.

Because most surveys tap only surface commitment or verbal adherence to ideals, polling data may reveal more about the correlation between self-presentation and socioeconomic class than about the persistence of racism. When tolerance means verbalizing principles acquired through exposure to liberal middle-class institutions, lower- and working-class whites will appear to be more racist than middle-class whites. Surveys that find prejudice and intolerance declining among America's white middle class also link racist sentiments disproportionately to poor and working-class white Americans, or to the "lunatic fringe." This finding is not new. As long ago as 1966, Paul Sheatsley found that the highest scorers on his "pro-integration scale" shared three features in common: they attended college, their earnings were high, and they were professionals.[33] But the narrow catch of this racism net reflects only its limited definition of racism. The behavior between classes may not differ much, but, unlike well-educated middle- and upper-class whites, poorly educated working-class white people are nearly precluded from this conception of "tolerance" because they have not learned the "proper" ways to present their racial views to pollsters.

Some writers promoting the new orthodoxy on racial inequality also seem unaware that evidence based on broad changes in opinion is insufficient to assess a complex, multifaceted problem like the persistence of racism. The gap between what people tell survey researchers and what they actually do or believe is wide, and a very different picture emerges when one moves from political abstractions to routine behavior.

Discrepancies between racial attitudes and behavior are large and pervasive. White Americans overwhelmingly endorse civil rights principles. When asked, 88 percent of whites in 1978 agreed that blacks have a right to live wherever they want to, up from 76 percent in 1970. By 1980, in fact, just 5 percent of whites were willing to tell a pollster they preferred strict segregation.[34] Yet only 40 percent said they would vote for a law stating "a homeowner cannot refuse to sell to someone because of their race or skin color."[35] White Americans may support the principle of fair housing, but less than half say they are willing to act on this principle. In fact, when actual patterns of racial isolation are examined, it is clear that very few whites prefer integrated to segregated neighborhoods.

American Apartheid, an award-winning study of housing segregation by Douglas Massey and Nancy Denton, reveals just how wide the gap is between attitudes and behavior. Using demographic data about where African Americans and whites actually reside, Massey and Denton demonstrated that levels of residential segregation have hardly changed since the 1960s. Applying a sophisticated index of segregation to thirty metropolitan areas with the largest black populations between 1970 and 1980, they discovered that in northern cities, "this (segregation) index averaged over 80 percent in both 1970 and 1980."[36] The index declined a mere 4 points over the decade of the 1970s and only 2 percent during the 1980s, and most of the decline occurred in small cities with small black populations. Massey and Denton conclude that "blacks living in the heart of the ghetto are among the most isolated people on earth."[37]

The Thernstroms challenge this conclusion, arguing that Massey and Denton exaggerate the persistence of residential segregation. But they provide no counterevidence, nor do they generate demographically grounded indices of integration. Rather, they attempt to refute Massey and Denton with an analysis that is laughable. "The strongest proof that residential segregation has been declining for a generation," they write, "comes from national surveys [that] have intermittently asked blacks and whites whether members of the other race live in the same neighborhood as they do." They find the patterns "striking" and report "fully two-thirds of all African Americans at the time (1964) said that they had white neighbors." The fact, they write, "that the figure was as high as five out of six in 1994" is evidence that residential apartheid has declined.[38] The Thernstroms apparently imagine that people's beliefs about who lives in their neighborhood are a more accurate indication of residential segregation than measures of where and how people actually live.

Similar gaps between attitudes and behavior are found in most contexts where race is an issue. These gaps become especially obvious when the reality of one's everyday life is directly affected. Support for desegregation of schools was relatively free of cost so long as no busing was involved or one's own children attended private schools. On-the-job equality also had an all-American sound to it, especially when there were very few blacks in one's occupation. Upgrading blacks from unskilled to skilled work was a fine goal if one's own work was white-collar or professional. But as black enrollments in prestigious universities and professional schools increased, constitutional amendments eliminating affirmative action became the order of the day.[39] When the demands of people of color hit closer to home and directly affect middle- and upper-class whites, these traditionally color-blind Americans begin to sound distinctly less tolerant and become seriously concerned with the color of people's skin.

These empirical flaws in studies purportedly demonstrating that racism has declined are compounded by fundamental conceptual problems. By now, the prejudice approach to the study of racism has been discredited and has become almost completely obsolete. The challenge to the prejudice paradigm began as early as 1958 when sociologist Herbert Blumer first argued that racism was better understood as a sense of group position than as a collection of bigoted individual attitudes. Since Blumer's groundbreaking article, a long line of sociologists, social psychologists, and legal theorists have moved beyond the outdated notion of racism employed by most advocates of color-blind ideology.[40] Instead of locating racism in intentions, attitudes, and obviously crude supremacist expressions or in pathological individual psyches, these scholars use a more complicated conception. Their analysis assumes that racism is often unintentional, implicit, polite, and sometimes quite normal. They look for racism in behavior as well as in attitudes and find it in culturally and economically produced systems of advantage and exclusion that generate privilege for one racially defined group at the expense of another.

Using this more realistic conception of racism, it becomes apparent that those who argue racism has declined ignore critical evidence that contradicts their assumptions. Their understanding of race paints a one-sided, terribly inaccurate portrait of racism in modern America. A very different picture emerges when racism is understood as a sense of group position and as the organized accumulation of racial advantage, a system best understood by observing actual behavior.

RACIAL PRIVILEGE AND GROUP POSITION

Because it extends far beyond individual attitudes, permeating the very structure and organization of American society, race strongly determines the ways in which Americans are treated and how they fare. White Americans, whether they know it or not, benefit as individuals and as a group from the present social pecking order. The social, political, and economic benefits of being white encourage white Americans, argues George Lipsitz, to invest in whiteness as if it were a form of venture capital and to work at increasing its value. When it comes to race, white Americans' social choices are very often molded by the relationship between whiteness and accumulated racial advantages.[41]

The possessive investment in whiteness is like property. And as a kind of property, the value of whiteness, as Cheryl Harris points out, lies in "the unconstrained right to exclude" or to deny communities of color opportunity or the chance to accumulate assets.[42] Exclusion, as is evident in the case of residential segregation, is a cardinal principle of white identity. To paraphrase Harris, those who possess whiteness have, until recently, been granted the legal right to exclude others from the advantages inherent in whiteness; they have accumulated wealth, power, and opportunity at the expense of the people who have been designated as *not* white. In this sense, the experiences of white and non-white Americans are intimately connected. The benefits of being white are related to the costs of being nonwhite. This is why it makes more sense to analyze racism in terms of group position rather than in terms of the bigoted attitudes of individuals.

White privilege is pervasive. Most discussions of racial inequality focus on labor markets, the criminal justice system, residential segregation, and education. But race also counts in ways that are less obvious, indeed typically invisible, to white Americans. While often unrecognized, these patterns of racial disadvantage point to the insidiously pervasive power of racism in American life. Because most Americans use such a narrow conception of racism, it is not surprising that they fail to recognize these subtle expressions of racial inequality that are woven into the fabric of society.[43]

To see the pervasiveness of white privilege, consider first something as ordinary as consumer trade. As we noted in the introduction, blacks and other minorities are denied mortgages far more frequently than whites with comparable incomes.[44] But even in other situations, including those where market forces would be expected to eclipse racial factors, race plays a powerful role. Researchers studying automobile dealerships in the Chicago area found, for example, that salespeople offer significantly lower sales prices to white men than to women or blacks, even when economic factors and bargaining strategies are held constant.[45] A more recent study shows that in the 1990s blacks paid significantly more for car loans arranged through dealers than whites did, despite having comparable credit histories.[46] Similarly, clerks in retail stores are frequently more concerned with the color of shoppers' skin than with their ability to pay. Cignal Clothing, a subsidiary of Merry-Go-Round Enterprises, for example, stamped an information form on the back of personal checks. The form included a section marked "race," and shoppers were classified "W" for white, "H" for Hispanic, and "07" for black.[47] Sociologist Joe Feagin, drawing on thirty-seven in-depth interviews with middle-class blacks in several American cities, found widespread evidence that black shoppers were treated less respectfully than their middle-class white counterparts. "No matter how affluent and influential," he reports, "a black person cannot escape the stigma of being black even while relaxing or shopping."[48]

Health care is another realm where significant disparities exist between blacks and whites—disparities that often mean life itself. We have already noted the wide gaps in mortality rates and access to primary care between blacks and whites. Similar disparities cut across every aspect of health and health care, and few of these differences can be fully attributed to social class or genetics. For example, the National Cancer Institute (NCI) recently reported that cancer death rates are increasing much faster for blacks than whites, sometimes by as much as twenty to one hundred times as fast. Black women are more likely than white women to die of breast cancer, even though the incidence of the disease is lower among blacks.[49] According to the NCI report, "Black men have a cancer-death rate about 44 percent higher than that for white men."[50] In fact, African American men between the ages of fifty and seventy are nearly three times as likely to die from prostate cancer as white men, and their prostate cancer rate is more than double that of whites.[51]

Higher death rates for blacks diagnosed with cancer are a recent development. In the 1930s, blacks were only half as likely as whites to die of lung cancer. Since 1950, however, the rate of lung cancer deaths among black men has increased at three times the rate for white men, and age-adjusted figures reveal that the rate was actually 40 percent higher among black men by the 1970s.[52] An increase in smoking rates is not the likely culprit behind the change. Exposure to environmental toxins and carcinogens, which are disproportionately located in poor and minority communities, is one important reason for the racial disparities in cancer mortality rates. Differential access to screening, prevention, and treatment is another reason for the disparities. One of the chief reasons black women are more likely to die of breast cancer is that they are not diagnosed until the disease has reached an advanced and more lethal stage.[53] A study of operable non–small cell lung cancer found that the rate of surgery for black patients was 12.7 percent lower than that for whites with the same diagnosis. The authors of this study concluded that "the lower survival rate among black patients ... is largely explained by the lower rate of surgical treatment among blacks."[54] Racial differences in mortality rates for cervical cancer remain significant even after adjusting for age and poverty, and are likely attributable to disparities in screening and diagnosis.[55]

Racial disparities in mortality rates for stroke and coronary heart disease are also significant. The black mortality rate for strokes is 80 percent higher than the white rate and the black mortality rate for coronary heart disease is 40 percent higher.[56] Racial differences in hypertension are well documented and are particularly pronounced among low-income African Americans. One study rejected the common assumption that hypertension among blacks is genetic, concluding that socioenvironmental factors like the stresses of low job status and income are responsible for the different rates of hypertension.[57]

Access to sophisticated diagnostic and treatment procedures for coronary heart disease and related ailments also accounts for significant health differences between blacks and whites. Once differences in age, sex, health care payer, income, and diagnoses for all admissions for circulatory disease or chest pains to Massachusetts hospitals had been accounted for, a 1985 study found that whites underwent significantly more angiography and coronary artery bypass grafting than blacks.[58] More recent studies confirm the results. One study, for example, found that after controlling for differences in age, gender, disease severity, comorbidity, geography, and availability of cardiac facilities, blacks were 60 percent less likely to have had coronary angioplasty or coronary bypass surgery and 50 percent less likely to have had thrombolytic therapy.[59] Similarly, researchers who investigated stroke treatments found that "white patients were approximately 50 percent more likely to receive imaging than were black patients"; they also found that of patients deemed appropriate for carotid endarterectomy, two-thirds of white patients but only half of blacks underwent the surgery.[60]

Ironically, amputation of a lower limb is the one advanced procedure that blacks receive far more often than whites.[61] African Americans are more likely to have such last-resort procedures because of inadequate treatment of hypertension and diabetes—illnesses that reflect inadequate care and treatment.[62] This is a perfect illustration of how disaccumulation works: small deficits in health care add up over time, leading to the disaccumulation of health and a perverse outcome.

Neither income nor social class adequately explains these differences in mortality rates and treatment. Rather, the burden of evidence contained in these studies indicates that race is a crucial variable. A recent National Bureau of Economic Research study, for example, found that income inequality between racial groups—not income inequality within racial groups—explains the differences in mortality rates.[63]

Race has a powerful and widespread impact on health treatment and thus health outcomes. Blacks and Latinos are less likely than whites to have access to basic health insurance.[64] Another serious obstacle to quality care for black and Latino patients is that minority doctors, who typically treat disproportionate numbers of minority patients, have greater difficulty than white physicians securing authorization for care. Nationwide, about one-third of black and Latino doctors report difficulty obtaining necessary hospital admissions, compared to one-quarter of white physicians.[65] Racial differences in infant mortality and prenatal care are also linked to a perverse version of racial profiling. Hospitals and clinics with high proportions of minority patients often conduct more systematic and intrusive screening for drug abuse and sexually transmitted disease than do those that treat white women, even though that pattern is not justified by prevailing rates of substance abuse.[66] This in turn discourages many black women from seeking needed prenatal care. Another study found that low-income African American mothers in Chicago who reported being the victims of racial discrimination were twice as likely to give birth to very low-weight babies compared to mothers reporting no discrimination.[67]

Racial bias is another important source of the differences in the ways life-threatening diseases are treated. Recent evidence suggests that racial stereotyping, and even discrimination, influence doctors' treatment recommendations for patients. K. Schulman and his colleagues asked doctors to respond to videotaped interviews with "patients" who were actually actors with identical medical histories and symptoms. Only the race and gender of the actors were different.[68] Doctors turned out to be significantly less likely to refer black women for aggressive treatment of cardiac symptoms than other categories of patients with the same symptoms. Doctors were also asked about their perceptions of patients' personal characteristics. Black male actor-patients, whose symptoms and comments were identical to white male actor-patients, were perceived to be less intelligent, less likely to participate in treatment decisions, and more likely to miss appointments. Doctors in the study thought that both black men and women would be less likely to benefit from invasive procedures than their white counterparts, less likely to comply with doctors' instructions, and more likely to come from low socioeconomic backgrounds.[69] In other words, where actor-patients were identical except for race, black patients were usually seen as low-income members of an inferior group.

Although few doctors may be intentionally racist, not very many are immune to America's racial history and the resulting cognitive bias.[70] In his pathbreaking article on unconscious racism, Charles Lawrence III has observed that "[racism] is part of our common historical experience and ... culture. It arises from the assumptions we have learned to make about the world, ourselves, and others as well as from the patterns of our fundamental social activities."[71] Because doctors, health insurance officials who authorize treatment procedures, and grievance hearing officers exercise considerable discretion, there is ample room for cognitive bias and stereotypes to influence their decisions. Discretion arises because only a small proportion of medical treatments are scientifically validated, because experts have differences of opinion about appropriate treatment, and because approaches must be individualized for the specific characteristics of each patient.[72] Discretion is inescapable in medicine. But combined with other sources of racial bias, it accentuates differences in treatment and health care. This pattern of racially biased discretion is similar to patterns in the criminal justice system, another institution whose practitioners wield wide powers of discretion.

Sports, a third arena in which race matters, is perceived by many as one of the most meritocratic, color-blind institutions in American life. If there is any realm in which the color line should have disappeared by now, it is professional sports, where measures of achievement are supposedly obvious, numerical, and uncontested. Yet even though 79 percent of National Basketball Association (NBA) players in the 1996–97 season were black, 76 percent of the head coaches were white. By 2001, the proportion of white coaches had dropped to 66 percent, as ten NBA head coaches were black. And although 66 percent of the National Football League (NFL) players in the 1996–97 season were black, 90 percent of the head coaches were white.[73] By the 2000–2001 season, the numbers had not changed; there were still only three African American head coaches, accounting for 10 percent of NFL coaches.[74]

The situation is not much different in college sports. Sixty-one percent of Division I-A male basketball players were black in the 1996–97 season, but 81.5 percent of the head coaches were white. The numbers barely changed at the end of the 2001 season, as the proportion of white head basketball coaches decreased to 78 percent. And although 52 percent of the Division I-A football players were black during the 1999–2000 season, 92.8 percent of the coaches were white. By 2001, nearly 97 percent of the head coaching positions had gone to whites.[75]

These discrepancies are unlikely to even out anytime soon. After the 1996–97 college football season, there were twenty-five openings for head coach of Division I-A teams. Only one of those schools—New Mexico State University—even interviewed a black candidate. During the 1997 and 1998 seasons, thirteen head coaches were named in the NFL, a turnover of almost 50 percent in the thirty-team league. Not one of the replacements was black. The situation did not change much in the next three years. Although the NFL turnover rate was 75 percent between 1998 and 2001, only one African American was hired as a head coach.[76]

Can these racial discrepancies be explained by the concept of merit? Some may think these head coaches got their jobs because they had the best records. The evidence, however, does not support this explanation. There have been only four black head coaches in the history of the NFL. Each of them has either played for or coached on a Super Bowl championship team, or was a college conference coach of the year. By contrast, as of 2001 only thirteen of the twenty-seven white NFL head coaches held this distinction. An analysis of the turnover among NFL coaches at the end of the 1997–98 season makes it obvious that merit is not the sole criterion for being a head coach. The potential pool of blacks has included (to name just a very visible few) Johnny Roland, all-American running back and Pro-Bowler who has been an NFL assistant coach for twenty-two years; Art Shell, former NFL Pro-Bowler with a 56-41 record as head coach of the Raiders and currently an NFL assistant coach; and Sherman Lewis, ten-year offensive coordinator (next in line to head coach) for the Green Bay Packers and an NFL assistant coach for twenty-nine years.

Who was chosen? One thirty-four-year-old with eleven years of coaching experience, two of which were as offensive coordinator, and a forty-two-year-old with four years of experience as an NFL assistant coach and one year as a college head coach. Each of these men had been an assistant coach under Sherman Lewis, who was passed over. Also chosen as head coaches were a former head coach whose previous four years produced records of 8-8, 7-9, 7-9, and 2-6, and ten men over the age of fifty-five with an average record of 6-10. Only one member of this latter "old boys' club" had made the playoffs the season before. All were white. It appears that race matters more than merit in hiring NFL head coaches.

According to a report released in October 2002, African Americans in the NFL are the last hired as head coaches and the first fired.[77] Few of them, the report found, were involved in the interview process. Since 1920, the league has hired more than four hundred head coaches and, as of the end of the 2002 season, eight of them (2 percent) have been African American. "When you see a Denny Green fired after the record he has built and then not get a new job," said attorney Cyrus Mehri, "or Marvin Lewis coach the best defense ever, win a Super Bowl and two years later not have a head job, you know that something is wrong."[78]

A similar pattern is apparent in baseball careers. A study of lifetime pitching and batting averages by sports sociologists at Northeastern University shows that black players have to out-hit and out-pitch their white counterparts by substantial margins to win and keep their jobs. Mere journeymen can have long and profitable careers as long as they are white, but among African Americans, only stellar and above-average players will succeed.[79] Perhaps this explains why there are so few black managers in major league baseball. Baseball typically hires managers, coaches, and front office personnel from the echelon of "good but not great" players. Because most of these players just happen to be white, black ballplayers have difficulty becoming coaches.

Professional sports are not atypical in this regard. In a national project examining the hiring practices of large law firms, Harvard University legal scholar David Wilkins observed that, as in baseball, black applicants with average grades are less likely to be hired than whites with the same records. Black partners are much more likely than whites to be Harvard or Yale graduates. The "black superstar" requirement is most obvious at the most prestigious firms. As one partner at an elite Chicago firm told the researchers, his firm sets "higher standards for minority hires than for whites. If you are not from Harvard, Yale, or the University of Chicago, you are not adequate. You're not taken seriously."[80]

As these examples indicate, race counts very heavily in the ways Americans are treated. Being white, as Chris Rock's fictional one-legged busboy recognized, has its advantages, and being nonwhite has its disadvantages. The problem of race in America is not that people come in different colors; the problem is that people are treated differently according to their color. The most important feature of being white, then, is not pigment, melanin, or skin color. It is, rather, the very close connection between being white and having improved economic opportunities and life chances.

FROM WHITE ADVANTAGE TO RACIAL SUBORDINATION: THE RECIPROCAL NATURE OF RACISM

The experiences of white and nonwhite Americans are intimately connected. The benefits of being white are related to the costs of being nonwhite. White Americans are privileged because they benefit from the present social order. As individuals and as a group, they derive advantages from the ways in which race limits the lives of people of color, whether they know it or not.

Because critics of color-conscious policies measure the decline of racism by the absence of crude personal prejudice, they do not recognize or take account of these potent realities. White coaches benefit from the higher standard to which black coaches are held. White Americans' chances of receiving loans are significantly enhanced when competition from people of color is reduced. When white men can buy new cars at markups one-third to half those offered to black men and women, their advantage (estimated at a collective $150 million annually by Yale professor Ian Ayres) is underwritten by race. In an era of cost pressure and scarcity in health care, the white advantage could be said to extend to the gift of life itself.

When economic and political resources are scarce, as most are, the relationship between whites and nonwhites may be zero-sum. Many white Americans are sure their children will lose when people of color demand their fair share of admission to elite universities or professional schools. For them, simply having to compete without the hidden benefits of being white is a significant hardship. Jennifer Hochschild articulates this concern elegantly: "As the number of contestants for a fixed number of prizes increases," she writes, "the chances of winning decrease. The arithmetic is simple: As blacks gain chances, whites lose certainty."[81]

Wins and losses look quite different from opposite sides of the racial divide. They also look different depending on time frame and basis of judgment. Sometimes whites fear that an outcome is zero-sum even if it may not truly be. Access to education looks like a zero-sum game, at least in the short run, as prestigious universities allocate limited places. But in the long run, failure to include people of color will harm everyone by limiting economic growth as well as by intensifying racial strife. Wins and losses can be calculated for a large group to which one belongs (like a race), for one's subsegment of the American population (such as an occupation), or for an individual. These different ways of judging who wins and loses, along with fear and mutual suspicion, make it difficult to assess outcomes consistently. Although they may not recognize it, whites and blacks sometimes find themselves in a lose-lose relationship. No one benefits, for example, when black youths go to jail because of a failure to invest in community social support systems. And if race was recognized and its consequences assessed instead of being ignored, perhaps policies with win-win results could be forged more often.

Whatever might be possible in a better future, today's race hierarchy is a powerful force. Thus whites, aware or not, misguided or not, typically resist change because their privileged status comes with (unearned) advantages. White Americans who believe they will lose if blacks gain are prone to oppose policies designed to reduce racial inequalities. Donald Kinder and Lynn Sanders point out that "insofar as interests figure prominently in white opinion on race, it is through the threats blacks appear to pose to whites' collective well-being."[82] Perhaps this explains why so many white American men think only of their short-term group interests and therefore oppose affirmative action policies. Because affirmative action eliminates the special advantages they have enjoyed historically, many white men believe they have something to lose when these policies are adopted. They believe this even though there is little evidence that white men lose jobs due to affirmative action.

Racism is related not only to actual privilege. It also entails a commitment to maintain *relative group status*. What matters is the magnitude or degree of difference that white Americans have learned to expect and maintain in relationship to people of color. A telltale illustration of this occurred when federal officials were trying to desegregate southern hospitals in the 1960s. A southern senator convinced officials in the Office of Equal Health Opportunity to create an exception to the desegregation policy. The exemption he created allowed doctors to place white patients in segregated rooms if physicians were willing to certify that integration would be detrimental to the patient's medical condition. Although very few doctors took advantage of this opportunity, the policy was tantamount to creating a new disease that afflicted whites: racism.[83]

Housing segregation is another, more pervasive, instance of whites establishing status differentials based on race. One expert reported

"Whites prefer and are willing to pay more for segregation than blacks are willing [or able] to pay for integration."[84] White people's apprehensions about living in racially mixed neighborhoods underscore this investment in relative group position. A large number of white Americans believe that property values decline as blacks move into a neighborhood. According to a *Newsday* poll, 58 percent of Long Island's whites felt this way, and another survey found that 40 percent of Detroit's white population also subscribed to this notion.[85] Because a home is viewed not only as a major investment but also as a symbol of one's worth, Massey and Denton contend "these views imply that whites perceive blacks to be a direct threat to their social status."[86] Stanley Greenberg's study of working-class white voters in Michigan confirms this interpretation. "Blacks constitute the explanation for their vulnerability," he writes, "and for almost everything that has gone wrong in their lives: not being black is what constitutes being middle class; not living with blacks is what makes a neighborhood a decent place to live."[87] Bobo and Zubrinsky provide a dramatic example of this expression of racism. Using data from a large multiethnic survey in Los Angeles, they found that, "as the affective difference that whites prefer to maintain between themselves and members of minority groups rises, so does the level of opposition to racial residential integration."[88]

THE POLITICS OF RACISTS AND NONRACISTS

Because white privilege is invisible, it is common to describe "racists" and "nonracists" as very different kinds of people. Racists are characterized by the Thernstroms and other racial realists as deeply prejudiced individuals who express "raw racism," "people who can and will do horrendous things."[89] Nonracists, on the other hand, are said to accept the principles of the civil rights movement and display few, if any, traces of prejudice. In this view, racists today are the exception and nonracists the rule. White Americans may disagree with blacks about appropriate civil rights policies—46 percent of whites, for example, think government should "ensure fair treatment of blacks," compared to 90 percent of blacks—but supposedly their opposition has nothing to do with racism.[90] Instead, as Paul Sniderman and Thomas Piazza insist, these differences are understood as a matter of principle. "The politics of race," they write, "now has a moral bite to it that it previously lacked; for it is no longer simply a matter of rejecting prejudice in favor of the [American] creed but of rejecting key elements of the creed itself."[91]

Conservatives like the Thernstroms make nonracism the norm and racism the exception. But drawing any sharp line between racists and nonracists is a slippery business. No doubt some racists are a disturbed bunch of people whose crude talk about people of color (as well as about women, Jews, and homosexuals) is repulsively frightening. What is striking, though, is the similarity between the behavior of those who voice blatantly racist sentiments and the so-called nonracist discourse and politics of self-styled conservatives and centrists. Putative nonracists often act like racists. Until recently, for example, former Senate majority leader Trent Lott (R-Miss.) and Congressman Bob Barr (R-Ga.) were closely associated with the Council of Conservative Citizens, a right-wing, prowhite political group. Before the *Washington Post* exposed this group's racist views, Lott told its members, "The people in this room stand for the right principles and the right philosophy."[92] This was not the first nor the last time Lott expressed sentiments that blurred the distinction between conservatism and not-so-subtle racist appeals. But a later statement cost him his position as Senate majority leader. "I want to say this about my state," Lott said, at a celebration of Senator Strom Thurmond's one hundredth birthday in December 2002. "[When Thurmond] ran for president we voted for him. We're proud of it. And if the rest of the country had followed our lead, we wouldn't have had all these problems over all these years, either." What was Lott so proud of and to which problems was he referring? Senator Thurmond left little to the imagination in his 1948 campaign against Harry Truman. "On the question of social intermingling of the races," Thurmond declared, "we draw the line. And all the laws of Washington and all the bayonets of the Army cannot force the Negro into our homes, into our schools, our churches and our places of recreation and amusement."[93] Lott is hardly the only respectable Senate conservative who smudges the line between racists and nonracists. Asked in 1994 by one of his Montana constituents, "How can you live back there [in Washington, D.C.] with all those niggers?" Senator Conrad Burns recalls he told the rancher it was "a hell of a challenge." Three years earlier the senator invited a group of lobbyists to join him at an auction. Asked what was being auctioned, he answered, "Slaves." Nor does one need to be white to conflate the meaning of racist and nonracist. "Supporting segregation need not be racist," black conservative Ward Connerly is quoted as saying. "One can believe in segregation and believe in equality of the races."[94]

Because politicians use coded language, the assumed differences between bigots and nonbigots are sometimes difficult to locate. It was not Klansmen who put an anti-immigrant initiative on the ballot in California. It was so-called moderate Republican men. And Republican politicians have repeatedly succumbed to the temptation to run race-baiting campaigns. It was not George Wallace who poisoned the 1988 presidential campaign with the notorious Willie Horton ads but an establishment Republican. And it was not a member of the KKK who defended the Confederacy to the *Southern Partisan*, a neo-Confederate magazine. It was John Ashcroft, the current United States Attorney General.[95] People who do not show up as bigots in attitude surveys sometimes behave like bigots.

When a theory assumes bigots and nonbigots are quite different but does not distinguish between them very well, how should one differentiate between "racists" and "nonracists"? Does one focus on the differences between racists and nonracists, or on their similarities? Does one define racism as virulent antiblack sentiments and a pathological hatred of African Americans or, to use Melanie Kaye-Kantrowitz's words, as "a system that normalizes, honors, and rewards whiteness"?[96] Does one treat racists as exceptional or normal? Does one treat "racist" accounts of white supremacy as lunacy, or merely as expressions of American self-portraiture from another era?[97] One approach finds racism in only a tiny remnant of the white population who explicitly endorse prejudiced beliefs; the other casts a wider net, finding expressions of racism among corporate executives, national politicians, and university regents.

Arguments that demonize racism and treat it as the exception lose sight of the complicated and subtle workings of being white in America. A focus on obvious bigotry, crude verbal performance, and political practices may make American "nonracists" feel better about themselves. But it also produces a false sense of security. Because it ignores culturally acceptable sophisticated forms of racism, this perspective is unable to detect the "nonracist" ways that being white works to the advantage of European Americans. Opponents of policies that undermine white people's privileges do not use Klan ideology to justify their opposition. Instead, they invoke the principles of American political beliefs. Not everyone who opposes color-conscious policies does so with the intention of defending white privilege. But one cannot assume, as all too many critics of color-conscious policies do, that opposition to affirmative action is based entirely on the principles of fair play and individual merit. Much of the opposition is based on resentment toward blacks, and this resentment is driven by a fear (conscious or not) that the interests of whites as a group are jeopardized by color-conscious policies.[98] Because color-blind policies are cast as a defense of individualism, the group interests at stake are concealed. But this move poses a more insidious problem than the raw racism of bigots. People voicing virulent antiblack sentiments are an easy target, but restricting *racism* to them leaves the institutionalized benefits of being white invisible and untouched.

RACISM AND LAW: THE MAINTENANCE OF WHITE PRIVILEGE

The law and legal institutions normalize white advantage by articulating and enforcing cultural norms, which help to maintain racial hierarchy in the United States. At first, this seems odd. After all, in the 1950s and 1960s, federal courts helped dismantle state-sanctioned racism. The courts, however, have been ineffective in addressing contemporary racial inequality because equal protection doctrine treats individual bigotry as the core of racism. The law's insistence that intention is the sine qua non of race discrimination matches the opinion of many Americans. But this search for individual blame is psychologically naïve, and it obscures the complex sources and relationships that produce racial inequality. As Angela Harris explains,

> Translated into constitutional law, this model ... works to identify intentional wrongdoers ... but leaves untouched unconscious racism, everyday cognitive bias and institutional structures that faithfully perpetuate patterns of racial subordination. As the legal structures that continue to disadvantage people of color become increasingly "race-neutral" in a constitutional sense, the moral model of discrimination facilitates both the denunciation of bigotry and *the maintenance of existing distributions of wealth and power*.[99] (Footnotes omitted; emphasis added.)

The face of racial subordination today is residential segregation, unequal loan policies, differential police stops, divergent medical care and schooling, variation in criminal sentencing, and disparate administration of the death penalty. Absent a smoking gun of intentionality, constitutional challenges to these forms of racial inequality are impossible.

In addition to the intention requirement, the Supreme Court's response to proposed remedies for racism poses another formidable obstacle to meaningful change. When private or public organizations set out to correct historic racial disparities, they typically institute some raceconscious remedial plan. But because such plans classify people based on race, the courts routinely strike them down. Even though these race-conscious plans aim to help subordinated groups, the courts believe they constitute reverse discrimination.[100] Under the resulting colorblind norm, lawyers rarely succeed in justifying affirmative action plans that seek to remedy actual racial disparities and societal discrimination. As Reva Siegel points out, the result is that "doctrines of heightened [judicial] scrutiny function primarily to constrain legislatures from adopting policies designed to reduce race and gender stratification, while doctrines of discriminatory purpose offer only weak constraints on the forms of facially neutral state action that continue to perpetuate the racial and gender stratification of American society."[101]

The irony is palpable: how did the Court arrive at a position where the antiracism doctrines of fifty years ago are now the barriers that protect racial inequality? Angela Harris explains it as fear and unwillingness to "contemplate large-scale projects of political, economic and cultural redistribution and the dramatic transformation of social institutions and practices that would result from a complete renunciation of American white supremacy."[102] Reva Siegel argues that the Court got into this trap because, like the proverbial generals, society always directs moral outrage at the previous forms of subordination. Tracking her thesis through the entire history of American race law, Siegel suggests that this "past-wars" approach encourages moral smugness about earlier eras while ignoring problems in the present.[103]

Siegel exposes serious inconsistencies in the Court's reasoning about race. When it strikes down race-conscious remedial plans, the Court employs what she calls a "thin" conception of race (race-as-morphological-accident, race-as-analogous-to-blood-type). Using this thin understanding of race, the Court rejects the arguments advanced by advocates of diversity and affirmative action who employ racial classification as a proxy for differences in history, culture, and experience. It sees those arguments as impermissibly stereotyping racial groups. But when minority plaintiffs challenge state policies that create or support racially disparate outcomes in housing, employment, criminal justice, and schools, this same Court uses a "thick" conception of race to justify leaving those outcomes undisturbed.[104] For example, in the *Croson* case the Court characterized the small number of minority contractors as the "natural" result of different occupational preferences among racial groups. This thick view of race allowed the Court to conclude that the differences in racial proportions were unobjectionable.[105] The Court's inconsistent use of these thick and thin conceptions of race, Siegel argues, creates a lose-lose world for advocates of racial equality.

COLOR-BLIND OR COLOR-CODED LAW?

In rejecting race-conscious classifications or remedies, the Court adheres to a jurisprudence of color-blindness that made sense in the 1950s and 1960s when segregation was legal and was based on a rigid system of racial classification. Color-blindness undermined and transformed that system. But fifty years later when state-sanctioned racial segregation is illegal and people of color have still to achieve truly equal opportunity with white Americans, the color-blind ideal actually impedes efforts necessary to eliminate racial inequality. Formal color-blindness fails to recognize or address the deeply rooted institutional practices and long-term disaccumulation that sustains racial inequality. Color-blind ideology is no longer a weapon that challenges racial inequality. Instead, it has become a powerful sword and a near-impenetrable shield, almost a civic religion, that actually promotes the unequal racial status quo.[106]

The law and legal culture remain critical tools for dismantling racial inequality. But the law today does not speak from a genuinely color-blind vantage point. Despite having completed the vital task of eliminating Jim Crow racial classifications, legal institutions still operate with a perspective that remains perceptually, analytically, and functionally color-coded. The color is white.

Some examples can illustrate how the justice system remains color coded. Taken-for-granted white privilege explains how one unusually public-spirited citizen could refuse to vote for someone she saw as an extraordinarily qualified young black attorney who was running for judge in a community whose population is more than half minority but whose sitting judges and magistrates were white. What was the citizen's reason? She feared the candidate would be "biased toward the community."[107] The fact that all the sitting judges were white was "normal" and therefore invisible to this white voter. The candidate's black skin and the majority-black community, on the other hand, were palpable.

Selection of grand jurors is another example. Law professor Ian Haney-Lopez found that even though Mexican Americans numbered one of every seven persons in Los Angeles County during the 1960s, they amounted to only one of every fifty-eight Los Angeles County grand jurors.[108] Using judges' sworn testimony about their practices for nominating grand jurors, Haney-Lopez found that "nine out of ten nominees came from within the judges' own social circles—83 percent of nominees were friends, neighbors, family members, spouses of acquaintances, or comembers of clubs, organizations, or churches, and [a few were recommended] by someone within those same circles or a fellow judge."[109] The judges emphatically denied that discriminatory intent had anything to do with their choices, and this is most likely true. Nevertheless, regardless of their intentions, the judges' unselfconscious bias produced a degree of racial apartheid in the grand juries. Superior court judges in Los Angeles County nominated 1,690 grand jurors between 1959 and 1969; only 47 of the nominees were Mexican Americans. And of the 233 nominees who were actually seated, only 4 were Mexican Americans.[110] The number of Mexican American grand jurors trebled to more than 6 percent of the total by the 1990s. By then, however, Latinos made up almost 41 percent of Los Angeles's population.[111]

Invisible white advantage also explains how a white "gum-chewing, tennis shoe wearing" clerk in an exclusive Manhattan shop could feel it was appropriate to refuse to "buzz in" an elegant African American law professor doing her Christmas shopping.[112] The editors of the journal that published the law professor's shopping story insisted on omitting all references to personal traits like skin color. Their grounds? They believed that not mentioning race (being color-blind) was necessary to being objective. The irony, of course, is that the story made no sense unless the parties' races were identified.

Other examples show that the experience, perspective, and privilege of white Americans permeate substantive law and policy. Lawyers, particularly influential lawyers, are overwhelmingly white.[113] The law these (mostly white) lawyers have created has important strengths, but it also reflects their (mostly white) perspective on the world. From criminal to constitutional law, from federalism to family law, from immigration to original intent doctrine, the law reflects and endorses the views, needs, and advantages of the "normal" white perspective.

White perspective is not the product of skin color but of culture and experience. We speak of the white perspective because it is the perspective most often held by whites and the institutions they construct and dominate. It is the perspective of the namers, the controllers, the holders of "natural" privilege and invisible power, those who can take for granted the advantages of the status quo. Through experience and disciplined reflection, some whites expand, if not escape, the perspective of whiteness. For reasons of identification or advantage, some nonwhites may embrace it. Both, however, are exceptions to the typical taken-for-granted, normal and unreflexive white perspective.

Lawyers articulate and apply concepts like *reasonableness, harm, culpability, desert,* and *merit*. While their perspectives on these important ideas are shaped in part by their experience, that experience is filtered through the lens of their white perspective. This standpoint shapes their view of what voting arrangements are fair.[114] It shapes the analysis and criteria of relevance for just administration of the death penalty.[115] It shapes the priority accorded to hate speech as compared to "fire-crying" or national security under free speech law.[116] It shapes whether accented speech undermines job qualifications.[117] These modern examples are as much a result of an unarticulated white perspective as was the historical conclusion that when a white person was mistaken for being black, a serious compensable injury had occurred, but when the opposite happened, compensation was not legally appropriate.[118]

White perspective sets the standards for *probable cause* or *reasonable suspicion*. It assesses institutional arrangements and personal behavior, deciding when confessions or consents to search are voluntary. It decides whether reasonable people feel free to refuse police requests and "go about their business."[119] White perspective weighs the appropriate responses of *reasonable persons* and the permissible latitude of *reasonable force*. It assesses the severity of crack cocaine offenses (which mostly involve poor blacks) as compared to crimes involving powder cocaine (which mostly involve middle-class whites). And it sentences offenders using crack to more time in prison than powder cocaine users, *even when they possess the same amount of cocaine.*

Some white lawyers, judges, and professors even erase race from the writing of the Constitution and the formation of the nation.[120] Some urge courts to measure constitutional rights by the "original intent" of the framers without acknowledging the founders' racism. Many of the founders, Rogers Smith has shown, understood themselves to be the "bearers of a superior culture or racial heritage [that] ... had obvious value in preserving the supremacy of the white, propertied, European-descended but largely native born male gentry who were the chief architects of the new governments."[121] Despite this history, commentators analyzing the constitutional framework of American federalism act as if these attitudes were unimportant when the nation's so-called neutral framework of rights and power was created. They neglect the powerful shaping force of slavery and race in the very structure of our government.

A final example comes from the heart of constitutional law. Constitutional lawyers and scholars attribute the origins of the foundational principle of judicial review to the Supreme Court's decision in *Marbury v. Madison.* But as federal appellate judge John Noonan observes, "[*Marbury*] was an empty declaration. The power asserted was not used. The power asserted was not used throughout Marshall's lifetime. For the next two generations the power asserted turned out to be mere huff and puff. ... *The first fruit of the great declaration was Dred Scott.*"[122] (Emphasis added.) The Court's decision in the *Dred Scott* case returned an escaped slave to his former owner. By upholding slavery, the Court asserted its authority to strike down federal laws, helping to precipitate the Civil War. Nevertheless, constitutional analysts downplay the role of slavery in the evolution of the principle of judicial review. Instead, they cite *Marbury*'s reputable and lofty rhetoric rather than the slavery-tainted *Dred Scott* decision—even when that means ignoring the case that first gave the doctrine some real bite.

COLOR-BLIND OR COLOR-CODED MERIT?

If racial perspective affects the law, then the process for choosing who will be lawyers is significant. Is the process that selects candidates for professional legal training color-blind? Admission to law schools claims to be based on merit. Merit, however, is not a freestanding or self-defining concept.[123] Merit must be merit in reference to something, for some purpose, based on some set of judgments and justifications. Traditionally, law schools have used Law School Admission Test (LSAT) scores and undergraduate grade point averages (GPAs) as proxies for merit. Schools choose these indicators because they correlate with law students' grades in the first year of law school.[124] Law schools use other kinds of information, but in mostly unstructured and discretionary ways. The academic indicators are by far the most decisive factors, with the LSAT playing a crucial role.[125] When merit is defined as excellence in test-taking, however, the selection process is not as color-blind as it claims to be.

Given their role as professional schools, it seems odd that law schools rely almost exclusively on academic measures of merit to choose students. Law schools train and credential lawyers. The mission of law schools is much more focused than that of colleges and universities. Law schools primarily prepare students for professional work. Only 2 to 3 percent of graduates from elite schools enter academic careers, but, ironically, law schools place more weight on academic indicators in admissions than academic departments do.[126]

Law school graduates hold jobs that require intellectual and analytic skills; they use and apply knowledge. Academic skills are important in professional performance, but they are not the only indicators of professional achievement. If legal rather than academic jobs are the aim of most law graduates, then some of the criteria of merit should measure the capacity for outstanding performance in legal work. But law schools do not even attempt to assess these capacities. There is reason to believe that this choice about how to define merit disproportionately excludes students of color.[127]

Decades ago, in *Griggs v. Duke Power*, the Supreme Court held that devices used to screen potential employees must be job related.[128] The Court recognized that where access to education was unequal, the workforce would be unnecessarily distorted by race if employers required applicants to hold academic credentials that had little or no demonstrated relevance to successful job performance. The situation of law school admissions is more subtle and complex, but it is closely related. Unlike the academic credentials required in *Griggs,* academic intellectual skills are related both to law school and to lawyering. But extending the *Griggs* reasoning, one might still ask whether academic credentials are the only ones related to being a good lawyer. Effective lawyers must also have abilities such as problem solving skills, people skills, persuasiveness, the capacity to inspire trust, communication skills, tenacity, and goal orientation. Using the approach taken by the Court in *Griggs*, then, one might object to law schools' heavy reliance on one relevant factor (academic potential) to the exclusion of others that are equally job related in determining which applicants merit admission.[129]

Seats in law schools are not jobs, but the links to jobs and *Griggs* are closer than they might first appear. Law is a state-licensed professional monopoly. The state delegates responsibility to the organized bar for certifying professional competence (through the bar exam and requirements for continuing education) and for maintaining professional discipline. These activities of the bar are important, but attaining a law school education is the pivotal step in becoming a lawyer.[130] Thus, law schools act as the primary screening device for the job of lawyer. If one applied the reasoning used in *Griggs*, it would be unjustified to focus almost exclusively on academic as opposed to job-related criteria in selecting students for this professional education.

This argument becomes compelling when the racial consequences of conventional admissions criteria are examined. Social science research shows that job success is correlated with a variety of factors. Even for jobs with significant intellectual content such as the law, "paper and pencil tests" of aptitude or achievement are not highly correlated with on-the-job success.[131] Performance on standardized academic tests does, however, correlate with race. Whites generally do better on paper and pencil tests and similar academic indicators than do blacks or Latinos. Successful performance on the job, however, is much more similar among racial groups. Therefore, reliance on paper and pencil tests will predictably create greater racial disparities in admissions than would a system that also adds in other types of predictors of successful job performance. Even though paper and pencil tests and conventional academic indicators deserve weight in measuring merit, *overuse* of those criteria and *underuse* of other important criteria produces racial disparities in selection that are disproportionate and unjustified. Christopher Jencks calls this type of racial unfairness "selection system bias."[132] Selection system bias pervades law school admissions practices. The result is that whites are advantaged at the expense of persons of color. Put another way, the processes of exclusion and inclusion used by law schools are not simply color-blind systems that measure "objective merit." Rather, law schools make choices about whom to admit on the basis of debatable criteria that are arguably color-coded. By using such limited criteria, law schools will fill their classes with white students and make it much more likely that the legal profession and the law will continue to reflect a white perspective.

BEYOND COLOR-BLINDNESS

In recent years, some whites have begun to recognize that they, too, have a race, that being white may not equal colorlessness, normality, or neutrality. Once their race becomes marked, whites will have the opportunity to observe what they could not see before: race and the pervasive patterns of stratification with which it correlates. The Thernstroms spend hundreds of pages asserting that racism is (nearly) dead, and that if only guilty whites and unreasonably angry blacks would stop ranting about race, color-blindness would be within our grasp. Yet toward the end of their book, even they admit that whites almost always notice *blackness:* "Whites are able to shed their racial identity. ... They had all the power. ... Part of the package of privileges that came with being white was the liberty to think in individual terms. Blacks ... were always black."[133] The Thernstroms note that whites have been racially invisible because they have had "all the power," but they do not recommend giving blacks power as a way to equalize racial invisibility. Instead, like other racial realists, they want formal, lip-service color-blindness without any shift in power. Would racelessness have the same meanings for blacks that do not have power as it does for whites that do? Not likely. It is power that confirms and normalizes the particular perspective of white Americans. It is dominance that allows racial invisibility. The ultimate benefit of racial power is the right to make one's advantages seem simply the natural order of things.

That unacknowledged perspective of white America radiates throughout contemporary color-blind racial discourse. The racial realist seeks to transcend racial conflict by banishing blackness and the consciousness of racial inequality that accompanies it. Racial realists could transcend racial conflict by naming whiteness and the privilege that accompanies it. But this possibility remains unexamined. Acknowledging and banishing white advantage is never considered. Nor do they propose that race be made less visible by redistributing white power, by diversifying white dominance of political, social, intellectual, academic, and economic institutions. Instead, racial realists urge color-blindness, which, in effect, "whitewashes" the racial status quo.

At the center of the debate over race in America is the question of what perspective we will use to define racism and the social policies necessary to end it. From what vantage point will problems be named and solutions found? Defining racism is not a semantic or theoretical issue. Narrowing the concept to purposeful individual bigotry is highly advantageous for whites. It locates racism in America's past. It labels black anger and white guilt as equally inappropriate. It renders most whites innocent. It blocks most governmental efforts to reduce racial subordination and isolation. And, most important, it protects and naturalizes the racial status quo. Advocates of color-blind policies do not address these issues. Nor do they admit that their conclusions mainly express the white perspective that comes naturally to them and to many other Americans. They ignore the possibility that different racial perspectives could exist. Yet only by acknowledging these profound differences in perspective can one begin to address the durable racial inequality of American society. To assume that a color-blind perspective is the remedy is to be blind to color. It is to lose sight of the reality that in contemporary America, color has consequences for a person's status and well-being.

The idea that racism is simply a collection of intentionally bigoted individual attitudes is fundamentally flawed, both theoretically and empirically. It uses assumptions that are not supported by empirical evidence, it ignores the collective dimensions of racism, and its conclusions are dictated by its vantage point. We have introduced an alternative concept of racism that rests on very different assumptions and looks to different sorts of empirical evidence to assess the persistence of racism in America. With this conception in place, a very different picture emerges of the state of racism in America.

In subsequent chapters we critically analyze the increasingly popular view that racism is obsolete and that the persistence of durable racial inequality is attributable to individual failure on the part of blacks, Latinos, and other people of color. We examine the unstated "domain assumptions" that guide the questions raised by this understanding, the data used to answer them, and the claims that follow. We show that optimistic reports of racial progress are overstated and hollow. Using our alternative understanding of racism to systematically investigate the persistence of inequality in labor markets, education, the criminal justice system, and politics, we arrive at very different conclusions. While less optimistic, our analysis is more accurate and, we think, more useful for constructing policies that reduce racial inequalities and find common ground to bridge the racial worlds that still divide America.

NOTES

1. Barbara Flagg makes this point in an illuminating and cogent way in "Was Blind, but Now I See: White Race Consciousness and the Requirement of Discriminatory Intent," *Michigan Law Review* 91 (1993): 953.
2. A recent study of racially and sexually harassing speech in public places found that 63 percent of African Americans reported hearing comments about their race every day, or "often." Only 5 percent of whites reported such comments. See Laura Beth Nielsen, "Situating Legal Consciousness: Experiences and Attitudes of Ordinary Citizens about Law and Street Harassment," *Law and Society Review* 34 (2000): 1068.
3. Thomas Nagel, *The View from Nowhere* (New York: Oxford University Press, 1986).
4. Richard Morin, "Misperceptions Cloud Whites' View of Blacks," *Washington Post*, July 11, 2001, p. A1. Three-fifths of whites think blacks have access to health care equal to or better than that of whites; in reality more than twice as many blacks lack health insurance. The study was conducted by the *Washington Post*, Harvard University, and the Kaiser Family Foundation.
5. Thernstrom and Thernstrom, *America in Black and White*, p. 177.
6. "Refocus Racism Conference Agenda," *San Francisco Chronicle*, August 13, 2001, p. A17.
7. Thernstrom and Thernstrom, *America in Black and White*, p. 500.
8. Thernstrom and Thernstrom, *America in Black and White*, p. 177; Dinesh D'Souza, *The End of Racism* (New York: The Free Press, 1995), pp. 253–54.
9. Thernstrom and Thernstrom, *America in Black and White*, p. 141. For example, the Thernstroms report survey data that show 83 percent of whites

in 1963 agreed with the statement "Negroes should have as good a chance as white people to get any kind of job."

10. Paul Sniderman and Thomas Piazza, *The Scar of Race* (Cambridge, Mass.: Harvard University Press, 1993), p. 46. Sniderman and Piazza asked whites whether they agreed with six common stereotypes of African Americans, for example, "Blacks need to try harder." Only 2 percent agreed with all six stereotypes.

11. We do not imply that everyone who uses this conception of race accepts the new orthodoxy on race.

12. Sniderman and Piazza, *Scar of Race,* p. 89.

13. Angela Harris, "Equality Trouble: Sameness and Difference in Twentieth Century Race Law," *California Law Review* 88 (2000): 1923, 2003.

14. See *Regents of the Univ. of Calif. v. Bakke,* 438 U.S. 265, 288 (1978); *Adarand v. Pena,* 515 U.S. 200, 217 (1995).

15. Alan D. Freeman, "Legitimating Racial Discrimination through Anti-discrimination Law: A Critical Review of Supreme Court Decisions," *Minnesota Law Review* 62 (1978): 1049.

16. See, for example, Paul Brest, "Foreword: In Defense of the Antidiscrimination Principle," *Harvard Law Review* 90 (1976): 1, 12–14; Owen M. Fiss, "Groups and the Equal Protection Clause," *Philosophy and Public Affairs* 5 (1976): 107–77; see especially pp. 118–29.

17. Reva B. Siegel, "Why Equal Protection No Longer Protects: The Evolving Forms of Status-Enforcing State Action," *Stanford Law Review* 49 (1997): 1131–35.

18. Ibid., p. 1137.

19. See *Griggs v. Duke Power,* 401 U.S 424 (1971). The Court retreated from this standard in a 1989 case, *Ward's Cove Packing v. Atonio* 490 U.S. 642, but Congress reinstated the disparate impact theory in the Civil Rights Act of 1991. Despite the pervasive racial disparities in employment and federal contracting, very few disparate impact claims succeed in today's courts.

20. Linda Hamilton Krieger, "The Content of Our Categories," *Stanford Law Review* 47 (1995): 1161, 1168, 1248.

21. *Alexander v. Sandoval* 532 U.S. 275 (2001).

22. Krieger, "Content of Our Categories," p.1171.

23. David B. Oppenheimer, "Negligent Discrimination," *University of Pennsylvania Law Review* 141 (1993): 899–972.

24. Hans Morgenthau, *Politics among Nations,* 4th ed. (New York: Alfred A. Knopf, 1966), pp. 225, 249.

25. Determining the state of mind of a defendant is vital to the assessment of culpability for most crimes. See *Model Penal Code and Commentaries: Official Draft and Revised Comments,* § 2.02 (Philadelphia: American Law Institute, 1985); Wayne R. La Fave and Austin W. Scott Jr., *Criminal Law,* 2d ed., §§ 3.4–3.7 (St. Paul, Minn.: West Publishing, 1982).

26. The exception is criminal cases charging a hate crime where specific intent is properly required.

27. Orlando Patterson, *The Ordeal of Integration* (Washington, D.C.: Civitas/Counterpoint, 1997), p. 61.

28. Donald R. Kinder and Lynn M. Sanders, *Divided by Color: Racial Politics and Democratic Ideals* (Chicago: University of Chicago Press, 1996), pp. 105–6. See also Donald R. Kinder and Tali Mendelberg, "Individualism Reconsidered," in David Sears, Jim Sidanius, and Lawrence Bobo, eds., *Racialized Politics* (Chicago: University of Chicago Press, 2000), pp. 44–74; and Lawrence Bobo and Ryan A. Smith, "From Jim Crow Racism to Laissez-Faire Racism," in Wendy Katkin, Ned Landsman, and Andrea Tyree, eds., *Beyond Pluralism* (Urbana: University of Illinois Press, 1998), pp. 182–220.

29. Reynolds Farley et al., "Stereotypes and Segregation: Neighborhoods in the Detroit Area," *American Journal of Sociology* 100 (1994): 756, fig. 3.

30. Camille Zubrinsky Charles, "Processes of Racial Residential Segregation," in Alice O'Connor, Chris Tilly, and Lawrence D. Bobo, eds., *Urban Inequality: Evidence from Four Cities* (New York: Russell Sage Foundation, 2001), pp. 233–37, 257–58.

31. Tom W. Smith, "Ethnic Images," *GSS Technical Report No. 19,* (Chicago: National Opinion Research Center, January 1991). Sniderman and Piazza claim that blacks express equally invidious stereotypes of other African Americans; see *The Scar of Race,* p. 45. It is not clear what conclusions one can draw from this evidence, however.

32. Howard Schuman, Charlotte Steeh, and Lawrence Bobo, *Racial Attitudes in America: Trends and Interpretations* (Cambridge, Mass.: Harvard University Press, 1985), pp. 74–75. See also Gerald D. Jaynes and Robin M. Williams Jr., eds., *A Common Destiny: Blacks and American Society* (Washington, D.C.: National Academy Press, 1989), pp. 137–38.

33. Paul Sheatsley, "White Attitudes toward the Negro," in Talcott Parsons and Kenneth Clark, eds., *The Negro American* (Boston: Beacon Press, 1966), p. 312.

34. Schuman, Steeh, and Bobo, *Racial Attitudes in America,* pp. 74–75, 106–7. See also Howard Schuman and Lawrence Bobo, "Survey-Based Experiments on White Racial Attitudes toward Residential Integration," *American Journal of Sociology* 2 (1988): 273–99.

35. Schuman, Steeh, and Bobo, *Racial Attitudes in America,* pp. 74–75.

36. Douglas Massey and Nancy Denton, *American Apartheid: Segregation and the Making of the Underclass* (Cambridge, Mass.: Harvard University Press, 1993), p. 63.

37. Ibid., pp. 77, 222, table 8.1. See also Reynolds Farley et al., "Stereotypes and Segregation: Neighborhoods in the Detroit Area," pp. 750–80.

38. Thernstrom and Thernstrom, *America in Black and White,* p. 217.

39. Kinder and Sanders, *Divided by Color,* p. 63.

40. Herbert Blumer, "Race Prejudice as a Sense of Group Position," *Pacific Sociological Review* 1 (1958): 3–7. See also, among other works, Harold Baron, "The Web of Urban Racism," in L. Knowles and K. Prewitt, eds., *Institutional Racism* (Englewood Cliffs, N.J.: Prentice-Hall, 1969), pp. 134–77; Robert Blauner, *Racial Oppression in America* (New York: Harper and Row, 1972); Thomas Pettigrew, ed., *Racial Discrimination in the United States* (New York: Harper and Row, 1975); Charles R. Lawrence III, "The Id, the Ego, and Equal Protection: Reckoning with Unconscious Racism," *Stanford Law Review* 39 (January 1987): 317–23; Alexander Aleinikoff, "The Case for Race-Consciousness," *Columbia Law Review* 91 (June 1991): 1060–80; David Roediger, *The Wages of Whiteness* (New York: Verso, 1991); David Wellman, *Portraits of White Racism,* 2nd ed., rev. (New York: Cambridge University Press, 1993).

41. George Lipsitz, *The Possessive Investment in Whiteness: How White People Profit from Identity Politics* (Philadelphia: Temple University Press, 1998), p. viii.

42. Cheryl I. Harris, "Whiteness as Property," in Kimberle Crenshaw et al., eds., *Critical Race Theory* (New York: The New Press, 1995), p. 288.

43. See Stephanie M. Wildman, *Privilege Revealed: How Invisible Preference Undermines America* (New York: New York University Press, 1996).

44. Michael Quint, "Racial Disparity in Mortgages Shown in U.S. Data," *New York Times,* October 14, 1991, p. A1; Michael Quint, "Racial Gap Found in Mortgages," *New York Times,* October 21, 1991, p. C1.

45. Ian Ayres, "Fair Driving: Gender and Race Discrimination in Retail Car Negotiations," *Harvard Law Review* 104 (1991): 817.

46. Diana B. Henriques, "Review of Nissan Car Loans Finds That Blacks Pay More," *New York Times,* July 4, 2001, p. A1.

47. Lena Williams, "When Blacks Shop, Bias Often Accompanies Sale," *New York Times,* April 30, 1991, p. A1.

48. Joe R. Feagin and Melvin P. Sikes, *Living with Racism: The Black Middle-Class Experience* (Boston: Beacon Press, 1994), p. 34.

49. Marian E. Gornick, Paul W. Eggers, and Gerald F. Riley, "Understanding Disparities in the Use of Medicare Services," *Yale Journal of Health Policy, Law, and Ethics* 1 (2001): 135; Lorna Scott McBarnette, "African American Women," in Marcia Bayne-Smith, ed., *Race, Gender and Health* (Thousand Oaks, Calif.: Sage Publications, 1996), pp. 51–52.

50. Sally Squires, "Cancer Death Rate Higher for Blacks," *San Francisco Chronicle,* January 17, 1990, p. A5.

51. T. J. Powell, "Prostate Cancer and African American Men," *Oncology* 11 (1997): 599–605. Although in the period 1990–95 the rate of prostate cancer among white men was 24 per 100,000 people, the rate for black men was double, 55 per 100,000. For breast cancer, there were 26 cases per 100,000 for white women and 31.5 cases for African American women. Among whites of both sexes the figures for lung cancer were 49 per 100,000 for whites and 60 cases per 100,000 for blacks. See Phyllis Wingo et al., "Cancer Incidence and Mortality, 1973–1995: A Report Card for the U.S.," *Cancer* 82 (1998): 1197– 1207.

52. Richard Cooper and Brian E. Simmons, "Cigarette Smoking and Ill Health among Black Americans," *New York State Journal of Medicine* 85 (1985): 344–49.

53. M. U. Yood et al., "Race and Differences in Breast Cancer Survival in a Managed Care Population," *Journal of the National Cancer Institute* 91 (1999): 1487–91. Even when access to health care is comparable, African Americans are diagnosed at a later stage and are 1.2 times more likely to die of breast cancer as whites.

54. Peter B. Bach et al., "Racial Differences in the Treatment of Early State Lung Cancer," *New England Journal of Medicine* 341 (Oct. 14, 1999): 1198.

55. McBarnette, "African American Women," p. 51.

56. Elizabeth White, "Special Report: Public Health Racial and Ethnic Disparities," *Health Care Policy Report* 9 (February 26, 2001), p. 315.

57. Michael Klag et al., "The Association of Skin Color with Blood Pressure in U.S. Blacks with Low Socioeconomic Status," *Journal of the American*

Medical Association 265 (February 6, 1991): 599–602. See also David Perlman, "High Blood Pressure in Blacks Blamed on Economic Stress," *San Francisco Chronicle,* February 6, 1991, p. A4.

58. M. B. Wenneker and A. M. Epstein, "Racial Inequalities in the Use of Procedures for Patients with Ischemic Heart Disease in Massachusetts," *Journal of the American Medical Association* 261 (1989): 253–57.

59. Shimon Weitzman et al., "Gender, Racial, and Geographic Differences in the Performance of Cardiac Diagnostic and Therapeutic Procedures for Hospitalized Acute Myocardial Infarction in Four States," *American Journal of Cardiology* 79 (1997): 722–26. See also Eric Peterson et al., "Racial Variation in the Use of Coronary-Revascularization Procedures: Are the Differences Real? Do They Matter?" *New England Journal of Medicine* 336 (1997): 480–86. After controlling for age, gender, disease severity, comorbidity, smoking status, insurance, type of admitting medical services, and year of procedure, Peterson and his colleagues found that blacks were 32 percent less likely to have had coronary bypass surgery and 35 percent less likely to have had any revascularization procedure. Peterson's study was conducted in a major university medical center.

60. Eugene Oddone et al., "Race, Presenting Signs and Symptoms, Use of Carotid Artery Imaging, and Appropriateness of Carotid Endarterectomy," *Stroke* 30 (1999): 1350, 1353–54. The study controlled for factors such as age and other medical conditions.

61. Marian E. Gornick et al., "Effects of Race and Income on Mortality and Use of Services among Medicare Beneficiaries," *New England Journal of Medicine* 335 (1996): 791–99. (Blacks have lower-limb amputations almost four times as often as whites.)

62. Marian E. Gornick, Paul Eggers, and Gerald Riley, "Understanding Disparities in the Use of Medicare Services," *Yale Journal of Health Policy, Ethics and Law* 1 (2001): 138.

63. Angus Deaton and Darren Lubotsky, *Mortality, Inequality and Race in American Cities and States,* National Bureau of Economic Research Working Paper 8370 (Cambridge, Mass.: National Bureau of Economic Research, July 2001), p. 9.

64. We address this issue in detail in chapter 2.

65. "Minority Physicians' Experiences Obtaining Referrals to Specialists and Hospital Admissions," *Medscape General Medicine,* August 9, 2001, <http://www.medscape.com/view article/408160> (accessed February 27, 2002). The study also found that 12 percent of black and 15 percent

of Latino physicians reported difficulty in obtaining specialty referrals compared to 8 percent of white doctors.

66. See *Crystal M. Ferguson et al. v. City of Charleston et al.*, 532 U.S. 67 (2001) (procedure for hospital screening and reporting to criminal authorities regarding population of largely minority women held unconstitutional). See also Dorothy Roberts, *Killing the Black Body: Race, Reproduction, and the Meaning of Liberty* (New York: Pantheon Books, 1997); Dorothy Roberts, "Punishing Drug Addicts Who Have Babies: Women of Color, Equality, and the Right of Privacy," *Harvard Law Review* 104 (1991): 1419–82; Marjorie M. Shultz, "Charleston, Cocaine, and Consent," *Journal of Gender Specific Medicine* 4 (2001): 14–16.

67. Janet Rich-Edwards et al., "Maternal Experiences of Racism and Violence as Predictors of Preterm Birth: Rationale and Study Design," *Paediatric and Perinatal Epidemiology* 15 (2000, Suppl. 2): 125.

68. K. Schulman et al., "The Effect of Race and Sex on Physicians' Recommendations for Cardiac Catheterization," *New England Journal of Medicine* 340 (1999): 618–26. The finding of racial disparities in this study was controversial. See Lisa M. Schwartz, Steven Woloshin, H. Gilbert Welch, "Misunderstandings about the Effects of Race and Sex on Physicians' Referrals for Cardiac Catheterization," *New England Journal of Medicine* 341 (1999): 279–83. All agreed, however, that blacks, particularly black women, were less often referred for aggressive treatment of cardiac symptoms than whites with identical symptoms and history. Schulman et al. reported an odds ratio of 40 percent less for blacks, p. 618; Schwartz et al. reported a probability of 7 percent less, p. 280.

69. Schwartz, Woloshin, and Welch, "Misunderstandings about the Effects of Race and Sex." On other traits, blacks and whites scored more similarly, or the differences ran in the opposite direction. For example, black males and females were judged to be happier, friendlier, and less likely to sue than their white counterparts.

70. Linda J. Krieger, "The Content of Our Categories," p. 1161.

71. Lawrence, "The Id, the Ego, and Equal Protection," p. 317.

72. M. Gregg Bloche, "Race and Discretion in American Medicine," *Yale Journal of Health Policy, Law and Ethics,* 1 (2001): 95.

73. Richard Lapchick and Kevin Matthews, *Racial Report Card: A Comprehensive Analysis of the Hiring Practices of Women and People of Color in the National Basketball Association, the National Football League, Major League Baseball, the NCCA and Its Member Institutions*

(Boston: Northeastern University, Center for the Study of Sport in Society, 1997).

74. *Racial and Gender Report Card* (Boston: Center for the Study of Sport in Society, Northeastern University, 2001).

75. Ibid.; Lapchick and Matthews, *Racial Report Card.*

76. Sarah Nelson, "Racial Discrimination in the NFL" (unpublished paper written for Department of Community Studies, Saint Cloud State College, 2001, photocopy).

77. Janice Rule, "Black Coaches in the NFL: Superior Performance, Inferior Opportunities," (Department of Economics, University of Pennsylvania); quoted in Thomas George, "NFL Pressured on Black Coaches," *New York Times,* October 6, 2002.

78. Quoted in George, "NFL Pressured on Black Coaches." Lewis was hired as a head coach after the 2002 season.

79. Cited by Brent Staples, "When a Law Firm Is Like a Baseball Team," *New York Times,* November 27, 1998, p. A42.

80. Ibid.

81. Jennifer Hochschild, "Race, Class, Power and the American Welfare State," in Amy Gutmann, ed., *Democracy and the Welfare State* (Princeton: Princeton University Press, 1988), p. 178. Kinder and Sanders found that whites who believed their children's admission to colleges and universities was jeopar-dized by racial preferences were strongly opposed to race-conscious policies. See Kinder and Sanders, *Divided by Color,* pp. 62–63.

82. Kinder and Sanders, *Divided by Color,* p. 85.

83. David Barton Smith, *Health Care Divided* (Ann Arbor: University of Michigan Press, 1999), p. 138.

84. Richard Muth, "The Causes of Housing Segregation," in *Issues in Housing Discrimination: A Consultation/Hearings of the United States Commission on Civil Rights,* vol. 1 (Washington, D.C. The Commission, November 12–13, 1985), pp. 3–13; quoted in Lawrence Bobo and Camille L. Zubrinksy, "Attitudes on Residential Integration: Perceived Status Differences, Mere In-Group Preference, or Racial Prejudice?" *Social Forces* 74 (1996): 887.

85. Reynolds Farley, Susanne Bianchi, and Diane Colasanto, "Barriers to the Racial Integration of Neighborhoods: The Detroit Case," *Annals of the American Academy of Political and Social Science* 441 (1979): 97–113.

86. Massey and Denton, *American Apartheid*, p. 94

87. Stanley B. Greenberg, *Report on Democratic Defection* (Washington, D.C.: Analysis Group 35, 1985), pp. 13–18. Cited in Massey and Denton, *American Apartheid*, p. 94.

88. Bobo and Zubrinsky, "Attitudes on Residential Integration," pp. 892, 887.

89. Thernstrom and Thernstrom, *America in Black and White*, p. 503.

90. Kinder and Sanders, *Divided by Color*, p. 17.

91. Sniderman and Piazza, *Scar of Race*, p. 26.

92. Bob Herbert, "Mr. Lott's 'Big Mistake,'" *New York Times*, January 7, 1999.

93. Quoted by Adam Clymer, "Republican Party's 40 Years of Juggling on Race," *New York Times*, December 13, 2002.

94. Quoted by Bob Herbert, "Weirder and Weirder," *New York Times*, December 19, 2002.

95. Neil A. Lewis, "Senate Committee Back Bush Choice for Justice Dept.," *New York Times*, January 31, 2001, p. A14. The Republican party has used implicit racial appeals to attract white voters for the last thirty years. For a compelling account of this, see Tali Mendelberg, *The Race Card: Campaign Strategy, Implicit Messages, and the Norm of Equality* (Princeton: Princeton University Press, 2001).

96. Melanie Kaye-Kantrowitz, "Jews in the U.S.: The Rising Costs of Whiteness," in Becky Thompson and Sangeeta Tyagi, eds., *Names We Call Home* (New York: Routledge, 1996), p. 124.

97. From 1790 to 1952, only a "white person" could become a naturalized citizen. See Ian Haney-Lopez, *White by Law: The Legal Construction of Race* (New York: New York University Press, 1996), p. 1.

98. Kinder and Sanders, *Divided by Color*, pp. 106–9, 263. See also Lawrence Bobo and James R. Kluegel, "Opposition to Race-Targeting: Self Interest, Stratification Ideology, or Racial Attitudes," *American Sociological Review* 58 (1993): 443–64; Jim Sidanius, Felicia Pratto, and Lawrence Bobo, "Racism, Conservatism, Affirmative Action, and Intellectual Sophistication: A Matter of Principled Conservatism or Group Dominance?" *Journal of Personality and Social Psychology* 70 (1996): 476–90.

99. Harris, "Equality Trouble," pp. 2003, 2011.

100. In theory, affirmative action is still possible but under highly restrictive conditions. For example, to be permitted under Title VII, an affirmative

action plan "must not unduly trammel the rights of non-beneficiaries." *United Steelworkers v. Weber*, 463 U.S. 193, 208 (1979). In effect, this means the plan must not interfere with the legitimate settled expectations (including seniority rights) of incumbent majority members, typically existing white male employees. It would be hard to find a better illustration of the thesis that current law maintains the existing distribution of advantage.

101. Siegel, "Why Equal Protection No Longer Protects," p. 1143.

102. Harris, "Equality Trouble," p. 2002.

103. Siegel, "Why Equal Protection No Longer Protects," p. 1143. Angela Harris describes a similar outcome, showing that the Court currently emphasizes discrimination as "differentiation" (classification) rather than discrimination as "disadvantage." Harris, "Equality Trouble," p. 2003.

104. Reva B. Siegel, "The Racial Rhetorics of Colorblind Constitutionalism: The Case of *Hopwood v. Texas*," in Robert Post and Michael Rogin, eds., *Race and Representation: Affirmative Action* (New York: Zone Books, 1998), pp. 44–45.

105. *City of Richmond v. J. A. Croson Co.*, 488 U.S. 469 (1989).

106. The literature discussing the pitfalls of color-blind ideology is large. See generally Neil Gotanda, "A Critique of 'Our Constitution Is Color-Blind,'" *Stanford Law Review* 44 (1991): 1; Kimberle Crenshaw, "Race, Reform and Retrenchment: Transformation and Legitimation in Anti-Discrimination Law," *Harvard Law Review* 101 (1988): 1331; Lawrence, "The Id, the Ego, and Equal Protection."

107. One of the authors' personal conversation with a voter during a 1994 judicial campaign.

108. Ian Haney-Lopez, "Institutional Racism: Judicial Conduct and a New Theory of Racial Discrimination," *Yale Law Journal* 190 (2000): 1728.

109. Ibid., p. 1736.

110. Ibid., p. 1742.

111. Ibid., pp. 1756–57.

112. Patricia Williams, *The Alchemy of Race and Rights: Diary of a Law Professor* (Cambridge, Mass.: Harvard University Press, 1991), pp 45–51.

113. In 1997, the legal profession was 2.7 percent black and 3.8 percent Hispanic. *Statistical Abstract of U.S.* (Washington, D.C.: U.S. Government Printing Office, 1998), p. 417. More significant, perhaps, for the development of legal perspectives, only one of the Supreme Court's law clerks

was African American in the fall of 2001. None was Hispanic or Native American. Four were Asian. Tony Mauro, "Number of Minority Law Clerks for Supreme Court Justices Declines," *American Lawyer Media*, October 29, 2001. Supreme Court clerks play crucial roles in the discussion and drafting of Supreme Court opinions.

114. We address this question in chapter 6.

115. *McCleskey v. Kemp*, 481 U.S. 279 (1987); David C. Baldus, Charles A. Pulaski, and George Woodworth, *Equal Justice and the Death Penalty: A Legal and Empirical Analysis* (Boston: Northeastern University Press, 1991). In chapter 4 we examine the argument that there are no serious racial disparities in the administration of the death penalty.

116. Charles R. Lawrence III, "If He Hollers Let Him Go: Regulating Racist Speech on Campus," *Duke Law Journal* (1990): 431; Charles R. Lawrence III and Mari J. Matsuda, *Words That Wound: Critical Race Theory, Assaultive Speech, and the First Amendment* (Boulder, Colo.: Westview Press, 1993).

117. Mari J. Matsuda, "Voices of America: Accent, Anti-Discrimination Law and a Jurisprudence for the Last Reconstruction," *Yale Law Journal* 100 (1991): 1329.

118. Cheryl Harris; "Whiteness as Property," in Kimberle Crenshaw et al., eds., *Critical Race Theory* (New York: The New Press, 1995); Haney-Lopez, *White by Law*.

119. *Florida v. Bostick*, 501 U.S. 429, 437 (1991). The U.S. Supreme Court reversed a Florida Supreme Court ruling that a specific police search had been coercive. Quoting from *Michigan v. Chesternut*, 486 U.S. 567 (1988), the justices ruled that coerciveness depends on whether a "reasonable person [would have felt that] he was not at liberty to ignore the police presence and go about his business." The court held that under this reasonable person test, several black youths confronted by police at the back of a crowded bus should have had no trouble in believing they could terminate the encounter without consenting to the requested search. Therefore, their consent was voluntary. David Cole calls the Bostick test "patently fictional." See *Equal Justice: Race and Class in the American Criminal Justice System* (New York: New Press, 1999), pp. 17–22

120. We draw the themes in this paragraph and the next from Dirk Tollotson, "Constitutional Eracism," Boalt Hall School of Law and the Center for the Study of Jurisprudence and Social Policy, University of California, Berkeley (photocopy available from authors).

121. Rogers Smith, *Civic Ideals: Conflicting Visions of Citizenship in U.S. History* (New Haven: Yale University Press, 1997), p. 101.

122. John T. Noonan Jr., "Comment on R. Kent Newmyer, 'John Marshall, Political Parties, and the Origins of Modern Federalism,'" in Harry N. Scheiber, ed., *Federalism: Studies in History, Law, and Policy: Papers from the Second Berkeley Seminar on Federalism* (Berkeley: University of California, Institute of Government Studies, 1988), p. 25.

123. Admissions decisions, particularly in public law schools, are not simply scholastic contests. They involve distributional equity, the allocation of scarce, tax-supported opportunities, access to a historic avenue of upward mobility, and opportunities for leadership in government. Consequently, admissions policies affect racial equity.

124. The correlation is moderate but greater than other indices that have been evaluated. Phil Shelton, president of the Law School Admission Council, acknowledged the narrow focus of the LSAT, saying, "All the LSAT was ever intended to predict was performance on property, contracts and torts essay questions. That's all. Period." See Michael Rooke-Ley, "Correction on Law School Admissions," *SALT Equalizer*, December 2001, <http://www.saltlaw.org> (accessed January 27, 2003). In focusing on correlates of first-year grades, admissions practice does not consider whether bias within law schools may influence law school grades. The first-year curriculum is still designed by overwhelmingly white law school faculties, and parallels what was taught nearly a century ago, when blacks were not even admitted. The greater alienation that students of color feel in law school has been widely documented and may affect their academic performance. See Kimberle Crenshaw, "Toward a Race-Conscious Pedagogy," *National Black Law Journal* 11 (1989): 1; Garner K. Weng, "Look at the Pretty Colors: Rethinking Promises of Diversity as Legally Binding," *La Raza Law Journal* 10 (1998): 753, 795–805; Claude M. Steele and Joshua Aronson, "Stereotype Threat and the Intellectual Test Performance of African-Americans," *Journal of Personality and Social Psychology* 69 (1995): 797.

125. In 1998, for applicants to Boalt Hall School of Law, UC Berkeley, who had GPAs of 3.75 or more, a 5-point difference in LSAT score cut the chance of admission from 89 to 44 percent; for the same year at UCLA, the chance of admission dropped from 66 to 10 percent. See William C. Kidder, "The Rise of the Testocracy: An Essay on the LSAT, Conventional Wisdom, and the Dismantling of Diversity," *Texas Journal of Women and the Law* 9 (2000): 193.

126. Because professional schools deal with enormous numbers of applicants, they are drawn to quantifiable indices that can be applied quickly and with apparent impartiality. Professional schools have traditionally been insecure about their intellectual credentials and legitimacy, perhaps tempting them to overemphasize test scores. Popular rankings of schools emphasize median scores of a school's students. Finally, professors themselves did extremely well on conventional academic indicia and may be especially prone to believe in their validity.

127. When the University of California eliminated affirmative action from admissions decisions, reliance on traditional numerical indicators sharply reduced the number of minority students admitted to law schools. At three of California's public law schools (Boalt, UC Davis, and UCLA), white enrollments rose from 60 percent of all first-year students to 72 percent, while black and Latino enrollments plummeted and Asian American enrollments were largely unchanged. William C. Kidder, "Situating Asian Pacific Americans in the Law School Affirmative Action Debate," *Asian Law Journal* 7 (2000). The one study of how law school admissions would change nationally if affirmative action were eliminated estimated a 53 percent decline in the number of students of color admitted and a 90 percent decline in the number of black students admitted. See Linda F. Wightman, "The Threat to Diversity in Legal Education: An Empirical Analysis of the Consequences of Abandoning Race as a Factor," *New York University Law Review* 72 (1997): 1.

128. *Griggs v. Duke Power*, 401 U.S. 424 (1971), held that employers may use screening tests that yield racially disproportionate outcomes only if those tests are "reasonably necessary to job performance." Chapter 5 discusses conservative criticisms of the case.

129. Some courts have rejected efforts to apply *Griggs* to the bar exam. See, for example, *Tyler v. Vickery*, 517 F.2d 1089 (5th cir. 1975), cert denied 426 U.S. 940 (1976). Although the bar exam is a closer analogue to employment selection than school admissions decisions are, the few decisions may be anomalous; they are persuasively criticized in Cecil J. Hunt, "Guests in Another's House: An Analysis of Racially Disparate Bar Performance," *Florida State University Law Review* 23 (1996): 721.

130. Without a law school diploma, only a very few lawyers gain entry to the bar. Overwhelming majorities of graduates from the elite law schools, whose admissions practices are under discussion here, pass the bar exam, usually on the first try, and enter the profession.

131. See N. Schmidt et al., "Adverse Impact and Predictive Efficiency of Various Predictor Combinations," *Journal of Applied Psychology* 82 (1997): 719–30.

132. Christopher Jencks and Meredith Phillips, eds., *The Black-White Test Score Gap* (Washington, D.C.: The Brookings Institution Press, 1998), pp. 57–58.

133. Thernstrom and Thernstrom, *America in Black and White*, p. 544.

DISCUSSION QUESTIONS

1. How do you think differently about the existence of racism in America?

2. How is racism commonly defined?

3. Identify and explain how the benefits of being white are directly related to the costs of being nonwhite.

4. How does racism continue to affect African American lives?

5. Why are race-neutral policies not necessarily race neutral?

PART TWO

➤ *RECLAIMING AFRICA'S HISTORY*

Afrocentrism and Historical Models for the Foundation
of Ancient Greece
MARTIN BERNAL

RECLAIMING AFRICA'S HISTORY

*O*ne of the great myths and principle supports of racial prejudice and bias is the ill-informed belief that the people of Africa and her descendants have never contributed anything noteworthy to the advancement, development, and expression of human culture and civilization (Herskovits). With the discovery of the existence of *Africanisms*—i.e., remnants of African culture that had survived the trauma of slavery and have been preserved in African American cultural practice and expression—Dr. Melville Herskovits disproved centuries of myths about African identity, as well as proved that people of the African diaspora were like any other people: they had preserved portions of their cultural identities.

Melville Herskovits, Carter G. Woodson, Alexander Crummell, W. E. B. Du Bois, and numerous other scholars at the beginning of the 20th century professed the need to provide people of African descent with a more accurate reflection of their past as well as the potentiality of their future by restoring their history. Each would challenge the Eurocentric perspective of written history as a distorted misrepresentation of blacks, perpetuated by racial stereotypes and myths which served to assist the privileging of whites while discrediting blacks. Dr. Martin Bernal would later join the ranks of scholars who challenged accepted notions and beliefs of black inferiority by publishing the first volume of his controversial work *Black Athena* in 1987.

Bernal, like his predecessors, believed that the way to end racism was by restoring the truth of the past.

❧ *SELECTED READING:*

Afrocentrism and Historical Models for the Foundation of Ancient Greece
BY MARTIN BERNAL

Afrocentrism and Historical Models for the Foundation of Ancient Greece

Martin Bernal

*T*his chapter deals with two distinct versions of the early history of Greece, which I have called the Ancient and the Aryan Models. The difference between the two Models turns, in part, upon Egypt's geographical location on the African continent and European preconceptions regarding the capabilities of African populations. According to the Aryan Model, which is still generally dominant today, Classical Greek civilization was the result of a conquest of present-day Greece from the north by the 'Hellenes'. These were Indo-European speakers, or 'Aryans'. The indigenous population of the Aegean, whom they conquered, are simply labelled by modern scholars as 'Pre-Hellenes'. All that proponents of the Aryan Model 'know' about the 'Pre-Hellenes' is that they were Caucasian—definitely not Semitic speakers or Egyptians—and they did not speak an Indo-European language. This last point is necessary because less than 40 per cent of the Greek vocabulary and very few Greek proper names can be explained in terms of other members of the Indo-European linguistic family.

The Aryan Model was only developed in the 1830s and 1840s. Until the beginning of the 19th century, scholars had accepted the ideas of writers of the Classical, Hellenistic and Roman periods (500 BC–250 AD) on Greece's distant past. This overall view, which I call the 'Ancient Model', was that the ancestors of the Greeks had lived in idyllic simplicity until the arrival of Egyptian and Phoenician leaders. These had acquired cities and introduced the arts of civilization, specifically 'Greek' religion, irrigation, various types of weapons and the alphabet. Ancient writers maintained that Greeks had continued to learn from the Egyptians, through study in Egypt, and that many, if not most, of the greatest Greek statesmen, philosophers and scientists had visited the Nile Valley.

I have two concerns here. The first of these—to which *Black Athena Volume I* (Bernal 1987) is devoted—is historiographical; that is to say, it is concerned with the writing and philosophy of history. The second is historical, setting out what I believe to be the least unlikely picture of what actually happened in the past.

The focus of my historiographical work has been on the shift from the Ancient to the Aryan Model, between 1780 and 1840. I am convinced that the first stage of this process, the abandonment of the Ancient Model, was not the result of scholarly developments, or 'internalist' factors. Rather, it was caused by changes in the general intellectual atmosphere, or for 'externalist' reasons. To put it crudely, I see four major forces as having effected the change. These were: (1) the establishment of the paradigm of progress; (2) the triumph of Romanticism; (3) the revival of Christianity after the French Revolution; and more important than all the others, (4) the application of racism to considerations of the relationship between Ancient Egypt and Ancient Greece.

No one has ever doubted that Ancient Egypt was much older than Ancient Greece. In Classical Antiquity and the Middle Ages the long-term passage of time was generally seen to be one of decline. Therefore, the Egyptians were not only seen as the teachers of the Greeks but as their moral and intellectual superiors. This image was reversed with the onset of the idea of progress which became dominant in Europe in the late 17th century. The historical process was now seen as one of improvement. Accordingly, the later Greeks had the advantage over the earlier Egyptians.

Romanticism, which also grew up in the 18th century, is essentially a view of the inadequacy of reason and the need to take sentiment or feeling into account. Romantics longed for small, dynamic communities with their inhabitants bonded by emotion. Therefore, they preferred the squabbling Greek city states to stable, long-lasting empires ostensibly ruled by reason, including Rome, China and Egypt, that were admired by the thinkers of the Enlightenment.

There was a great Christian revival throughout Europe and North America after the French Revolution and the defeat of Napoleon in 1815. Many in the newly Christian upper classes hated Freemasonry. Freemasonry was seen not only as the ultimate conspiracy within the Enlightenment, but also as having been behind the French Revolution itself. They also developed a loathing of Ancient Egypt, which they saw as being a central foundation of Freemasonry (but see Hamill and Mollier 2003).

Racism became an obsession in northern Europe by the end of the 17th century, with the establishment of racial slavery in America. As Europeans were treating Africans inhumanely, they tried to dehumanize them both actually and conceptually. Thus, Central and West Africans were portrayed by northern Europeans as animals or devils and as the epitome of barbarism. The role of Egypt as the foundation of western civilization was difficult to fit into this picture as Egypt was inconveniently situated on the African continent. There were two solutions: one, that of the Enlightenment and the Freemasons in particular, that Egypt was civilized and white (Hamill and Mollier 2003); the second, that of the Romantics, was to hold that it was uncivilized and black. However, there was also a third view.

THE ANCIENT EGYPTIANS AS BLACKS AND AS THE FOUNDERS OF WESTERN CIVILIZATION

At the end of the 18th century, this third vision began to be advocated. According to this the Ancient Egyptians were both African and the founders of western civilization. The probable—and improbable—beginning of this intellectual trend came from the works of the intrepid Scottish traveller James Bruce. In the 1760s and 1770s Bruce travelled through Egypt and spent several years in Ethiopia (Bruce 1790). He was a conservative and at times advocated the beneficial effects of slavery. At the same time, however, he saw connections between the civilizations of Ethiopia and Egypt, and believed that the Ethiopian form was the older. For Bruce, the source of the (Blue) Nile was the source of civilization. Bruce finally published the descriptions of his travels in 1790. Fifteen years before that, however, he had many meetings with notables in both England and France on the eve of the French Revolution. It was in the heady atmosphere of this period that the idea that the ancient Egyptians were both civilized and black Africans took shape.

The two men who established this concept were Charles François Dupuis and Constantine Chasseboeuf dit Volney. Dupuis was an erudite scholar of antiquity and a brilliant inventor. He was also a supporter of the Revolution and an organizer of the anti-Christian 'Religion of Reason' promoted by Jacobin leaders of the Revolution, which incidentally used many Egyptian symbols. Dupuis argued that Egyptian astronomy, which he believed to be the fundamental science, came to Egypt from the south (Dupuis [1795] 1822: 73). It was a conversation with Dupuis that inspired the younger Volney to write his mysterious and immensely popular prose poem *The Ruins of Empires*, first published in 1792. This included, near its beginning, the famous passage,

> There a people, now forgotten, discovered, while others were still barbarians, the elements of the arts and sciences. A race of men now rejected from society for their *sable skin and frizzled hair*, founded on the study of the laws of nature, those civil and religious systems which still govern the universe.

> (Volney [1804] 1991: 16–17; emphasis added)

Volney's explicit linkage of 'Negroes' to the origin of western civilization provided a powerful weapon for abolitionists. In France the great abolitionist, Reverend Grégoire, in his book *An Enquiry Concerning the Intellectual and Moral Faculties, and Literature of Negroes*, devoted the first chapter to Volney's arguments, emphasizing that the Ancient Egyptians were 'Negroes' and concluding, "Without ascribing to Egypt the greatest degree of human knowledge, all antiquity decides in favour of those who consider it as a celebrated school, from which proceeded many of the venerable and learned men of Greece" (Grégoire [1810] 1997: 25).

Grégoire's work, published in 1808, was translated into English in Brooklyn in 1810, and as early as 1814 it was giving more confidence to educated African Americans (Hodges 1997: xix–xx). The theme that Black Egyptians had founded civilization was taken up in two powerful pamphlets published in 1829. One, *The Ethiopian Manifesto, Issued in Defence of the Black Man's Rights in the Scale of Universal Freedom* was by Robert Alexander Young. The other, which was still more influential, was Walker's *Appeal to the Coloured Citizens of the World*. Walker argued that Egyptian enslavement of the Israelites had been far less onerous and demeaning than that of Africans in the United States (Walker [1829] 1993: 27–30, 39). Despite this attempt at reconciliation, there was a tension among African Americans between identification with the glories of Ancient Egypt and empathy with the Israelites, suffering under, then escaping from, Egyptian slavery (Champion: 167–168). The late St Clair Drake plausibly drew a distinction between 'Free Negroes' especially in the north, who emphasized their descent from the Egyptian civilization, and those under slavery in the south, among whom an identification with enslaved Israel was predominant (Drake 1987: 130–131).

THE RISE OF THE ARYAN MODEL

There is no reason to suppose that the European scholars who created the new field of *Altertumswissenschaft* (the Science of Classical Antiquity) knew of such writings. They were acutely aware, however, of Dupuis, Volney and Grégoire. Volney's *Ruins* was first translated into German by Georg Forster, the German Jacobin. Forster was the son-in-law of Christian Gottlob Heyne, who dominated ancient studies at Göttingen for the 50 years (1760–1810) in which *Altertumswissenschaft* was developed at that university.

Connop Thirlwall, the first writer—in either English or German—of a history of Greece in the 'new' mode, wrote of the Ancient Model in the 1830s,

> It required no little boldness to venture even to throw out a doubt as to the truth of an opinion [the Ancient Model] sanctioned by such authority and by the prescription of such a long and undisputed possession of the public mind, and perhaps it might never have been questioned, if *the inferences drawn* from it had not provoked a jealous enquiry into the grounds on which it rests.
>
> (Thirlwall 1835: 63; emphasis added)

The major inference here would seem to be the idea that the Egyptians were black and that therefore blacks had been the originators of 'white' civilization. This was not only distressing, but for 'progressive' European intellectuals it was 'unscientific'. In the 19th century, racial 'science' made it clear not merely that 'whites' were now better than 'blacks', but also, according to the idea of permanent racial essences, that they had always been so. Therefore Greek historians must have been mistaken and suffering from the mysterious diseases of 'barbarophilia' or 'Egyptomania' when they stated that 'Semitic' Phoenicians and African Egyptians had civilized Greece.

Karl Otfried Müller (1820–1824), one of the first products of Humboldt's new educational system, made the first attack on the Ancient Model. The first volume of his *Geschichten Hellenischer Stämme und Städte* (History of Hellenic Tribes and Towns) was published in 1820. In it Müller argued that the legends upon which the model was based were inconsistent and that there was no *proof* that any Egyptian or Phoenician colonizations had taken place. I am convinced that it is useless to expect proof in such areas and that, in any event, it is strange to demand it of those who maintain the ancient tradition, while waiving the requirement of proof for those who challenge it. Nevertheless, Müller was remarkably successful both because of the new ideological conditions outlined above and because his book on the subject was published in 1820 on the eve of the Greek War of Independence. This war became the one liberal cause it was possible to support in an age of extreme reaction. The Philhellenes who went to Greece were only the tip of the iceberg of a mass student movement for whom Hellas became an object of veneration.

German scholars very quickly denied the role of the Egyptians in the formation of Greece, and French and British scholars fell into line in the following decades. It is sometimes argued that it was the great 19th century advances in knowledge of ancient languages and archaeology that led to this change. However, the Egyptian half of the Ancient Model was destroyed before the languages of Mesopotamia, written in cuneiform, were understood, and well before Heinrich Schliemann discovered Mycenaean material culture. While it is true that Champollion deciphered hieroglyphics in the 1820s, his results were not accepted by German classicists for another 30 years, after Lepsius had substantially improved the decipherment. Thus, Champollion's breakthrough cannot have played a role in the destruction of the Ancient Model. Therefore, the only way in which one can explain the abandonment of the Ancient Model is through the general ideological changes described above.

By contrast, there was an important internalist cause behind the establishment of the Aryan Model. This was the working out of the Indo-European language family and the establishment of Greek as a member of it. If, as seems reasonable, one supposes that there was once a single people who spoke the ancestral language, or Proto-Indo-European, and that this people lived somewhere to the north and east of the Balkans, one must postulate that the Aegean basin received some substantial influence from the north. This could have taken a number of different forms, but given the ethnic predispositions of the mid-19th century, it was immediately seen as a conquest by a master race of Hellenes, whose vigour had been steeled by ethnic formation in the cold of Central Asia or the Steppe.

For several decades, the new image of Greek origins co-existed uneasily with the traditional belief that Phoenicians—though not the Egyptians—had played a significant role. This view was attacked in the 1890s but survived until the 1920s. Following Astour (1967) and others, I associate this historiographic downplaying of the Phoenicians—who were seen as the Jews of Antiquity—with the rise of racial, as opposed to religious, anti-Semitism at the end of the 19th century. This reached a paroxysm after 1917 with the perceived and actual association of Jews with Bolsheviks in the Russian Revolution. Conversely, I attribute the revival of interest in the Phoenicians to increasing Jewish self-confidence after the foundation of the State of Israel. Since the 1960s, Jewish scholars have led the gradual rehabilitation of the Phoenicians' central role in the formation of Greek civilization. The restoration of the Egyptian facet of the Ancient Model has been slower. The leading champions of the Ancient Egyptians have been black Americans, who have been much further from the academic establishment than Jewish professionals.

SUSTAINING THE ANCIENT MODEL

To return to the impact of Dupuis, Volney and Grégoire, both black and white abolitionists continued to use their arguments after academics were abandoning the Ancient Model. For instance, John Stuart Mill (1850: 29–30) wrote:

> It is curious withal, that the earliest known civilization was, we have the strongest reason to believe, a negro civilization. The original Egyptians are inferred, from the evidence of their sculptures, to have been a negro race: it was from negroes, therefore, that the Greeks learnt their first lessons in civilization; and to the records and traditions of these negroes did the Greek philosophers

to the very end of their career resort (I do not say with much fruit) as a treasury of mysterious wisdom.

This was a response to Thomas Carlyle's notorious article, 'On the Nigger Question' (see Bernal 2001: 457 n. 76). The purity of Mill's position on this issue is somewhat tarnished by his own commercial interests. Mill held a position as a high official in the East India Company, a long-term foe of its rival, the slave-owning West Indian planters.

Such views favouring the Ancient Model faded among people of European descent after the abolition of slavery in the United States in 1865. They continued, however, among African Americans. Intellectuals such as Frederick Douglass and scholars such as W. E. B. Dubois and St Clair Drake were uncertain about the 'Blackness' or 'negro physiognomy' of the Ancient Egyptians but they had no doubts about the 'Africanity' of Ancient Egypt or the size of the Egyptian contribution to Greek civilization (Drake 1987; Dubois 1975: 40–42, 1976: 120–147).

Among the group now known as 'Afrocentrists' there is little or no doubt about black African origins of European civilization. It should be emphasized that, as many of the leading writers in this group write for a popular audience and are without the resources available to academics, they make many mistakes in detail. In their main concern, the 'blackness' or 'Africanity' of Ancient Egypt, they belong to a scholarly tradition going back to the 1770s. The Afrocentrists continue the late 18th century 'black' version of the Ancient Model described above, although they are in general less interested in the contributions of Egyptian civilization to Greece. It is the academic establishment and European champions of the Aryan Model, not the Afrocentrists, who have made a fundamental break with tradition.

Until recently, the ideas of the black scholars have been unknown to non-blacks. Even today, their views tend to be seen as 'special pleading' or 'therapy rather than history'. This is indeed an important aspect of black 'vindicationalist' scholarship and it can certainly distort their conclusions. Nevertheless, I am convinced that it is not helpful to view Afrocentric writers on these topics merely in terms of socio-pathology, as is frequently done (Appiah 1993; Howe 1998). Indeed, it is totally inappropriate for European and Euro-American scholars to do so when the Aryan Model itself serves the same therapeutic function for many Europeans and Euro-Americans.

ATTEMPTING REVISION

Even though I see the Aryan Model as having been 'conceived in sin or even error', I do not believe that this in itself invalidates it as a useful historical tool. However, despite heavy criticism (as highlighted in Lefkowitz and Rogers 1996), the collation of studies in archaeology, Bronze Age documents and mythology, published in *Black Athena Volume II* (Bernal 1991), lead me to conclude that the ancients were right when they emphasized the centrality of Egyptian and Levantine cultures in the formation of Ancient Greece. I maintain that 40–45 per cent of Greek words and a higher proportion of proper names can be shown to have Egyptian or Semitic etymologies. Thus, there is no need for a substantial 'Pre-Hellenic' substratum to explain the non-European bulk of the Greek vocabulary.

The fact that these sources support the Ancient Model does not, however, mean rejecting all work carried out within the framework of the Aryan Model, or a complete return to the Ancient Model. There is no doubt that some crucial new factors, most notably the knowledge that Greek is fundamentally an Indo-European language, must be taken into account. Thus, I argue for the establishment of a 'Revised Ancient Model'. According to this, Greece has received repeated outside influences both from the east Mediterranean and from the Balkans. It is this extravagant mixture that has produced this attractive and fruitful culture and the glory that *is* Greece.

DISCUSSION QUESTIONS

1. According to Bernal, why did European intellectuals reject the Ancient Model of the origin of Western civilization?

2. Why did black and white abolitionists continue to use the Ancient Model after academia abandoned it in favor of the Aryan Model to explain the rise in Greek civilization?

3. How does the Aryan Model serve Europeans in the same way that the Ancient Model would serve Africans?

4. Why does Bernal believe that the Ancient Model can withstand academic scrutiny? What evidence exists that suggests Egyptian influence upon Greek culture? What evidence does Dr. Diop use to claim Egyptian influence upon West African culture and civilization?

5. How might a Revised Ancient Model provide a more accurate reflection of history as well as knowledge of the cultural influences of Africa upon Western civilization? How might this debunk the notion of European superiority and reveal the ethnocentric biases of written histories?

PART THREE

CONSTRUCTING AN AFRICAN AMERICAN IDENTITY

*A*frican Americans formed their cultural identity through a shared common history as the descendants of slaves, whose African ancestry and cultural ties were taken through force and lost through time, and whose notion of self-worth and identity was determined not as individuals, but collectively through the constraints of American society, which deemed by law, practices, and policies their "place." Resistance was the means by which both enslaved and free African Americans not only survived, but redefined themselves and constructed new identities based on the religious practices and social philosophies they embraced within their segregated communities. While blacks initially hoped that through the granting of their freedom they would achieve social acceptance and equality, racial prejudice prevailed throughout the postbellum era, causing many blacks to look to Africa as a locus for identity and as the source for a new homeland. The attitude that "we are not wanted here in America and we can never be fully realized as black people here in America" planted the seeds for the rise of black separatism and nationalism—i.e., a nation within a nation—and provided the platform for the study and examination of the ideology behind Afrocentric essentialism.

SELECTED READING:

Africa and the Challenges of Constructing Identity
BY TUNDE ADELEKE

Africa and the Challenges of Constructing Identity

Tunde Adeleke

*I*n *The Roots of African-American Identity* (1997), Elizabeth Raul Bethel identifies two critical events that shaped black American consciousness and identity in the nineteenth century. The first was the Haitian revolution of 1791–1804, which resulted in the overthrow of French plantocratic hegemony by black slaves. The revolution represented, for blacks in the United States and elsewhere, both a "model of political agency and racial achievement" that was denied to them and the potency and possibilities of nationalism in the context of New World experience. It consequently nurtured optimism on the prospect of transcending enslavement.[1] The second was the 1807–8 federal legislation prohibiting ships flying under the United States flag from engaging in the importation of slaves. Blacks welcomed this as signaling an end to the long sufferings brought upon Africans by enslavement and the transplantation process. This enthusiastic and joyous response betrayed a growing consciousness of affinity with Africans. The legislation thus induced optimistic expectations about the future of Africa and her descendants abroad, and many blacks began to envision eventual reunification with a lost African identity.[2]

The two developments, according to Bethel, "provided fertile psychosocial environments in which memories of the past intersected with realities and opportunities of the moment."[3] This intersection induced ambivalent nationalist consciousness, which in turn nurtured an equally ambivalent conception of identity. Blacks saw the anti-slave-trade legislation as a positive development that they hoped would terminate the nightmarish experience of dislocation and dehumanization that enslavement and transplantation entailed. The Haitian revolution exemplified the ultimate potential of New World nationalism. Celebrating these positive

Tunde Adeleke, "Africa and the Challenges of Constructing Identity," *The Case against Afrocentrism*, pp. 23-58, 191-194. Copyright © 2009 by University Press of Mississippi. Reprinted with permission.

developments, however, entailed coming to grips with an existential problem of self-definition—"Am I an American or am I a Negro? Can I be both?"[4]

Consciousness of African ancestry combined with the exigencies of the American experience to present, in the words of Bethel, "a continuing challenge to identity for African Americans, and it never would be entirely resolved."[5] This challenge mirrored a critical dilemma, that is, double consciousness, which many critics have since identified as the hallmark of black American identity. This dilemma involved critical existential inquiries into the very nature and character of the black American experience designed to ascertain the extent to which the American experience could be deemed positive and satisfying. The critical inquiry is as follows—To what degree has the American experience satisfied the yearnings by blacks for acknowledgment as full-fledged citizens of America, with their interests, aspirations, and values represented, articulated, advanced, and defended within the framework of the larger society? Put differently, has the American experience been positive and satisfying enough to nurture and sustain in blacks a faith in, and a sense of identity with, the larger society? The absence of a correspondence, the reality of divergence, between the aspirations, interests, and values of blacks, and those of the larger society, has been a defining character of black history and has informed conceptions and perceptions of black identity. There is, however, an added factor of equal importance in shaping black American identity—the denial and denigration of the black historical experience, ancestry, and heritage. This perceived lack of correspondence between black values, interests, and aspirations, and those of mainstream white society, has consequently configured and complicated the identity problem.

Blacks manifested double consciousness on identity from the very earliest of times. Many retained memories of Africa, while struggling to be acknowledged as Americans. Rationalizing the identity question, "Who am I?", consumed the attention of blacks, and Bethel is right in suggesting that the question may never be satisfactorily answered. Attempting to answer the question has provoked some of the most contentious debates in the annals of the black experience. The credit for identifying the focus of the modern context of the debate belongs to W. E. B. Du Bois, whose formulation captured the essence of the identity dilemma. His statement that "one ever feels his two-ness,—an American, a Negro: two souls, two thoughts, two unreconciled striving; two warring ideals in one dark body" underscores the status of the black American as a product of complex historical and cultural experiences.[6]

Du Bois, however, portrayed both experiences as vital to the formation of identity and cautioned against sacrificing one for the other, for each possessed intrinsic essence and validity. As he contended, the Negro "wishes neither the older selves to be lost." The Self (Negro) and the Other (America) are intrinsically and inherently essential, each with unique contributions to the world.[7] Du Bois thus conferred both historical reality and permanence to the double consciousness. He soon immersed himself in the struggles to validate both identities: the struggle for the integration of blacks into the United States as full-fledged citizens and the struggle by blacks to contribute to the defense and furtherance of the interests of Africa. The civil rights movement of the 1960s also exemplified this double consciousness as black Americans fought for integration (that is, American citizenship), while culturally and politically embracing and identifying with the struggles and challenges of the African continent.

The historical validation of the notion of double consciousness has not won universal acclaim and acceptance. It remains the subject of intense controversy among scholars, precisely because of its bearings on the identity question. The notion of double consciousness is central to modern discourses on black American identity, and responses to it betray conflicting interpretations of identity. A few years back, Gerald Early, former chair of African American Studies at Washington University in Saint Louis, Missouri, invited a select group of scholars to respond to the Du Boisean duality paradigm. Published as *Lure and Loathing: Essays on Race, Identity, and the Ambivalence of Assimilation* (1994), their responses betray the complexity and conflicting perceptions of identity among black Americans. A few respondents rejected the duality paradigm, denying its historical potency, while strongly counterpoising a monolithic identity construct grounded in African cosmology. Some accepted and validated the notion of double consciousness and thus acknowledged the legitimacy of the Afro and African American construction of identity. Some others embraced a more neutralist formulation and attempted to situate identity within a cosmopolitan and universal construct—humanity, western civilization, and so forth. Advocates of this "universal" construct perceive black identity as neither essentially

African nor essentially American but as the product of a broader and complex human experience. Finally, there are those who situate black identity squarely within a Euro-American cultural context.[8]

The above conflicting conceptions suggest fundamental differences on the significance and relevance of Africa. Historically, Africa had constituted a challenge to black Americans, precisely because in order to define themselves, they had to deal with the reality of their African background.[9] The fundamental challenge has been to establish whether blacks are Americans who had completely shed all trappings of their African ancestry, or Africans, residents in an alien and hostile environment, who somehow managed to retain their Africanness, despite centuries of separation from Africa and acculturation in a New World environment. The responses have been diverse and conflicting. Afrocentric scholars such as Molefi Asante, Maulana Karenga, and Marimba Ani (aka Dona Marimba Richards) proclaim the centrality of Africa to the construction of black American identity and insist upon identifying black Americans as quintessentially Africans.[10] These scholars deemphasize the transforming consequences of New World transplantation and acculturation, suggesting a certain shallowness and superficiality to Euro-American cultural impact and, as one critic put it, affirming the "purity, homogeneity and primordiality of African cultural influences among Afro-Americans."[11] The essentialization of Africa in Afrocentric essentialist thought therefore represents a rejection of the Du Boisean duality construct.

The true Afrocentrist is supposedly someone who is rid of double consciousness. Afrocentrism presumes the possibility of expelling or submerging one of the warring ideals—the Euro-American. Marimba Ani has no scintilla of doubt that blacks in the Diaspora are Africans. The retentions of Africanism in music, religion, family structure and norms, and burial practices clearly separate blacks from whites ethnically and culturally. As she put it, "Africa survives in our [i.e., black Americans'] spiritual make-up; that it is the strength and depth of African spirituality and humanism that has allowed for the survival of the African-Americans as a distinctive cultural entity in New Europe; that it is, our spirituality and vitality that defines our response to European culture; and that response is universally African."[12]

In Afrocentric epistemology, however, Africa is much more than an identity construct. Affirming African identity also represents a strong statement of protest. The late Amos Wilson unambiguously proclaimed this protest dimension. To assert the "Afrikan" identity, he argued, is to assume a radical posture against injustice. As he proudly declared, "I love the challenge of being Afrikan in today's world; it's wonderful! I love digging in my heels against the impossible odds of being black in America. What greater challenge could we have in life today than to be Afrikan?"[13] Africa thus acquires a utilitarian function far beyond representing identity. Critics deem the zero-sum stance on the African identity of black Americans that Afrocentrists maintain as grossly reductionistic and absolutist. W. D. Wright, for instance, does not believe that blacks are "hundred percent" African in character. He acknowledges the complex cultural, national, and ethnic factors involved in forging the black American identity.[14]

The Afrocentric absolutist stance on the African identity of black Americans has provoked a countervailing school that totally rejects Africa and posits instead slavery and the American experience as more substantive foundations for constructing the black American identity. Attempts to impose a racial and color line in the social, academic, political, and cultural spheres provoked widespread resentment that compelled interrogation of the complexity of the American and black Diaspora experiences. Many blacks object to being stamped with a racial label or being confined behind a racial boundary line. The monolithic Afrocentric construction of black history, identity, and culture provoked challenges from black politicians, academics, community activists, entrepreneurs, artists, and athletes, who rejected the simplifying and confining character of race and embraced a more complex and mainstream construction of identity. In the universities, and in the field of education in general, there are calls for a nuanced and representative paradigm that captures the complexity of the African and black Diaspora experiences. Many have come to realize the artificiality of race and its social and political character. This slavocentric or Americentric perspective has been articulated and defended more recently by the black American playwright Douglass Turner Ward, and former *Washington Post* Africa bureau chief, Keith Richburg. Among the most recent proponents of the anti-Afrocentric identity paradigm, Turner and Richburg, in different contexts, called for deemphasizing Africa and situating black American identity instead within the context of slavery. In his provocative book, *Out of America: A Black Man Confronts Africa*, Richburg rejects African identity and strongly implores black Americans to turn inward to their American experience to validate their identity.[15] In a keynote address to the Southern Conference on Afro-American Studies in Baton Rouge, Louisiana, in February of 1995, Ward boldly proclaimed himself a slavocentric and urged blacks to locate their identity in the enslavement experience. Between the two extremes of Afrocentrism and slavocentrism lie other perceptions on identity, ranging from the universalistic and humanistic to the existentialist. Essentially, these other perspectives represent attempts to anchor identity to some supposedly neutral ideals and values that are deemed neither essentially African nor essentially American.[16]

The differences and controversies generated by these conflicting perspectives are played out fairly regularly in the media and in scholarly publications and debates. Consequently, this chapter will not delve deeply into the modern debate. Rather, I hope to highlight something glaringly missing in contemporary discourses on black American identity—the historical context. Since Africa is critical to modern configurations of the identity debate among black Americans, it is pertinent to ascertain the depth and strength of the African consciousness of black Americans by examining how they historically responded to, and defined, their African connection. Did Africa occupy a central place as Afrocentric epistemology suggests, or was Africa subordinated to a greater identity? How crucial was Africa to black American conception of identity? What role did blacks assign Africa in their struggles, and how did they define themselves in the contexts of the struggles? Answering these questions would require a critical examination of the historical antecedents of the current controversies on identity.

I have chosen two critical historical epochs during which black Americans grappled with the identity question. The first is the moral suasion epoch (1830–1849), which was essentially integrationist in aspiration, and the second is the emigration phase (1850–1864, 1878– 1880s), which has been characterized as essentially a separatist and nationalist phenomenon. The first is associated with the phase of organized black abolitionism, the second with an organized quest for an independent black nationality abroad. Both epochs provide insights into the construction of identity and considerations of the place and relevance of Africa to the process. In the moral suasion phase, the more neglected of the epochs, the focus will be on the debate and controversies generated by the adoption of moral suasion as abolition strategy by leading blacks in the 1830s.

Moral suasion has often been characterized as a conservative movement whose purpose was to reconcile blacks to mainstream American values and, in the process, attain the rights and privileges of American citizenship.[17] Although it is true that the moral suasion crusade envisioned integration, the debate it unleashed entailed spirited arguments on identity. The debate centered around attaining some consensus on the identity of blacks and, most significantly, on how best to affirm and realize that identity. This debate revealed that though advocates of moral suasion shared a consensus on identity, they disagreed sharply on strategies. The African identity did not feature at all in the debate. On the other hand, the emigration phase focuses on the ideologies, policies, and schemes of leading black nationalists. Africa featured prominently in this latter phase. Emigration has been defined and analyzed almost exclusively in the context of nationalism and Pan-Africanism.[18] While this is true to a significant degree, black American nationalist consciousness, especially in the emigration phase, was also about the quest for self-definition and identity. The impulse for emigration developed out of the anguish felt over the intractable problems of identity and self-knowledge. Out of the emigration debate grew and developed a self-definition that shaped, and continues to shape, the identity discourse today. As an ideology of the abolitionist crusade, moral suasion assumed prominence in the 1830s. Since the motivation and underlying impulse for moral suasion developed against the backdrop of the enslavement experience, a brief examination of slavery and its bearings on identity is pertinent at this juncture.

SLAVERY AND THE CHALLENGE OF IDENTITY

To understand the fascination of black Americans with Africa, and the ambivalent and contradictory consciousness Africa provoked, and continues to provoke, among them, one needs to examine the very foundation of hegemony that slaveholders constructed. Enslavement and acculturation in the New World entailed a conscious and systematic process of simultaneous deconstruction and construction of identity.[19] Sometime in the early 1700s, a "slave owner Willie Lynch" addressed fellow slave owners on how best to tame and transform blacks into docile and perfect slaves. Widely publicized as "How to Make a Slave," "Lynch's" speech, which supposedly began circulating in 1712, described in great detail how slave owners could break the spirit and obliterate the humanity of their slaves. "Lynch" had no qualms about his barbaric, inhuman admonitions, for in his schema, slaves belonged alongside horses. He offered planters a strategy of stripping slaves of a sense of worth or any quality that might pose a threat to the smooth functioning of the South's "peculiar institution." The speech was indeed a recipe for deconstructing whatever identity slaves had and imposing in its place an identity that was amenable to slavery. Widely circulated today among black scholars, the authenticity of this document is indeed questionable. It is not dated, and there is no information on the publisher. In other words, the document could well be a hoax, and I am convinced it probably is. This notwithstanding, its basic premise of the need to transform blacks into perfect slaves, from human to subhuman identity, is consistent with a practice that, according to modern scholars, was prevalent among antebellum southern planters. As a North Carolina planter once admitted, "It is a pity that agreeable to the nature of things Slavery and Tyranny must go together and that there is no such thing as having an obedient and useful slave, without the painful exercise of undue and tyrannical authority."[20] Frederick Douglass, the famous "graduate of the *peculiar institution*" gave eloquent testimony to the brutalities and inhuman character of slavery in his epic autobiography.[21] On the authority of historian Ira Berlin, we do know that in 1727, some fifteen years after "Lynch's" document supposedly surfaced, one Robert "King" Carter, considered the richest planter in Virginia, purchased a handful of African slaves from a trader who had been trading on the Chesapeake. The transaction was a familiar one to the great planter, Berlin suggests, because "Carter owned hundreds of slaves and had inspected many such human cargoes, choosing the most promising from among the weary, frightened men and women who had survived the transatlantic crossing."[22] Writing to his overseer from his plantation on the Rappahannock River, Carter explained the process by which he initiated Africans into their American captivity; "'I name'd them here & by their names we can always know what sizes theyr are of & I am sure we repeated them so often to them that every one knew their name & and would readily answer to them.' Carter then forwarded his slaves to a satellite plantation or quarter, where his overseer repeated the process, taking 'care that negros both men and women I sent ... always go by the names we gave them.'"[23]

This process of renaming, according to Berlin, "marked Carter's initial endeavor to master his new slaves by separating them from their African inheritance."[24] Clearly, the deconstruction of the African identity and background was central to the acquisition of mastery over the slaves, and it began with the practice of stripping slaves of their African names and renaming them. This loss of name was only the beginning of "the numerous indignities Africans suffered at the hands of planters."[25] The process of de-Africanization entailed skills and language. According to Berlin, "Since many of the skills Africans carried across the Atlantic had no value to their new owners, planters disparaged them, and since the Africans' 'harsh jargons' rattled discordantly in the planters' ears, they ridiculed them." Thus began "the slow, painful process whereby Africans became African Americans."[26]

The capture and enslavement of Africans and their forcible transplantation to the New World were traumatic experiences that would transform many of these slaves into chattels, items of commerce, property to be bought and sold. Olaudah Equiano gave a vivid and captivating rendition of this trauma and transformation in his epic autobiography.[27] But we also see the essence of his Igbo identity as he takes us into the inner workings of his society—the values, norms, and institutions that defined identity and personhood, and how these were trampled upon and destroyed by slavery. For Equiano, and the thousands, if not millions, of slaves taken from Africa, enslavement struck at the very root of existential consciousness. The auctioning of the slaves and the "scrambling" by planters in Barbados underscored for Equiano and many others a critical stage in the process of deconstructing and reconstructing identity. The deliberate mixing of slaves of different ethnicities during the Middle Passage constituted a telling stage in the deconstruction of the captives' ethnicity. This would continue in the New World. As the likelihood of meeting, and being in the midst of, one's ethnic kin grew slimmer, slaves found themselves among strangers, with no means of effective communication. Suspended in this condition, the slave's gravitation from ethnicity to race began. The only language of communication with other slaves was embedded in the institution of shared misery—the violence and dehumanization of slavery built solely on the color of the skin.

Denied the familiarity, comfort, and reassurance of indigenous ethnicity by being kept among strangers with whom there was little verbal communication, slaves inadvertently gravitated toward, and embraced, the familiarity and comfort offered by color. Shared trauma, violence, and dehumanization became the glue that sustained and impressed upon slaves the practicality of color as the basis of identity. But this process was not just mechanical and uncoordinated, neither was it completely a choice that the slaves freely made. In fact, the Europeans themselves coordinated and choreographed the process of singling out color as the new identity for blacks by defining the very nature and qualities of blackness.

When Europeans made the epochal decision to turn to Africa for slave labor, it was a conscious decision that would entail negating the identity and humanity of a people in order to impose a new identity tailor-made for the drudgery of enslavement. Though the slave raids, capture, and enslavement traumatized the captives, these experiences represented the first stage in what would become a complex process of transformation and transmutation from Igbo, Wollof, Mandinka, Fante, Yoruba, Asante, Hausa, and so forth, into something negative and distasteful: a slave, black, nigger, and so on. The dehumanizing experiences of the Middle Passage pushed these slaves further along the path of deconstructing their indigenous identities. Such deconstruction was deemed essential to the success and future of slavery, for the institution could thrive best upon a people completely traumatized and stripped of a sense of worth and identity, of the unity, comfort, and reassurance that indigenous values represented and offered. In the judgment of slave owners, this is the only condition that would enable blacks fully and responsibly to embrace their new roles as slaves. Slavery thus constituted an affront on the personality and identity of slaves—two crucial existential factors. The rupture of capture and transplantation was the first telling blow on the personality. The imposition of slave status completed that depersonalization process as enslavement, in theory and practice, reduced the slave to something less than human.

Thus, the making of a slave society was also the unmaking and remaking of a people's consciousness of self. Slaves came to America not as "Africans" but as Mandingo, Fulani, Yoruba, Fulbe, Asante, Fante, Hausa, Ibo, and so forth. They became "Africans" in the New World. As James Campbell underscores, in the eighteenth century, Africa was the basis of collective identity for blacks. In fact, since colonial times, "African" was an accepted term for referring to blacks in North America.[28] Blacks accepted this collective identity. It was from the onset a problematic identity, however, constructed and conferred for a specific purpose—for a more effective management and control of slaves. The construct "Africa" gave blacks a collective identity, in an environment where one was desperately needed. From the beginning, therefore, it was clear that the only unifying attribute blacks possessed, aside from race, and perhaps because of it, was shared misery and oppression. Becoming "African" exemplified this collective identity of negation and negativism. In a curious way, what masters constructed as a collective identity for effective control eventually became, for slaves, a counter-vailing construct for affirming a collective identity that would facilitate group solidarity and survival. However, from the master's point of view, the African identity exemplified negative and debilitating qualities such as backwardness, inferiority, and primitivism. For blacks, on the other hand, being African exemplified unity, albeit within a collective identity of negation, shared miseries, failures, objectification, and depersonalization. Thus, even as Africa served as the basis for group solidarity and survival for blacks, it was a troubling and troublesome identity.

From the very beginning, therefore, the experience of slavery underscored the need for collective self-definition and self-affirmation. It also entailed an existential challenge to negotiate and affirm an identity that became a foundation for group survival. In their daily ordeal, blacks continually confronted certain existential questions: Who are we? Why are we treated differently? These questions arose logically out of the dehumanizing experience they were subjected to. They searched for answers to these questions, convinced that such answers would not only explain their ordeal but also point the way to a clearer knowledge of identity. Knowing and affirming identity was considered critical to the success of the struggle for freedom. Enslavement was thus a constant struggle over a contending, complex, and troublesome consciousness of identity. There was a conscious effort on the part of the slave masters to purge blacks of any sense of positive identity, especially one that would negate and compromise the structure and foundation of the institution of slavery.[29] Whether blacks arrived in the New World with their indigenous values and identities intact, or lost them in the process of transplantation and enslavement, the experience that they were subjected to on the plantations raised crucial questions of identity. Slavery was built on a denial and negation of whatever collective existential ethos these slaves brought with them. Blacks were enslaved, according to pro-slavery ideology, because they were primitive and inferior. Slavery thus assumed the character of a civilizing process. The African identity (that is, being black) was considered evil, an identity to be shunned and avoided.[30] The acculturation process that slavery entailed became a medium of being "civilized" in European values. For slaves, therefore, enslavement became the foundation for a new identity. Though overwhelmed and challenged by this experience and consciousness, many blacks stuck to positive memories of Africa, and often invoked "Africa" in crucial moments of their struggles. Thus, Africa became a rallying point, and the basis of self-definition. In the late eighteenth and early nineteenth centuries, free blacks in Ohio, Pennsylvania, New York, and Massachusetts adopted the name "African" for their institutions—churches, schools, and fraternal societies.[31] This is indicative of a consciousness of affinity with Africa. This expression of African consciousness served as the framework for the advancement of the black struggle for freedom and equality.

Slavery nurtured in blacks what Samuel Dubois Cook termed "a tragic conception of history," contrived to destroy any desire for self-fulfillment.[32] The de-tribalization or de-Africanization process began on the slave ships of the Middle Passage. Through a deliberate process of intermingling slaves of different ethnic and linguistic origins, slavers hoped to prevent the emergence of any corporate sense of identity that would threaten the stability of slavery. As Eric Lincoln describes it, "History was suspended, and that part out of which all status and all relationships derive, and which constitutes the only sure reality in African cosmology, was summarily denied or leached away. American slavery offered 'no place to be somebody.'"[33]

The process of discrediting and nullifying the African heritage and inducing self-abnegating consciousness in blacks intensified on the plantations. Pro-slavery ideologists unleashed a barrage of negative propaganda aimed at controlling the slave's consciousness. As Leon-ard Curry surmised, "White superiority—and, hence, the 'innate' inferiority of Negroes—was … a concept requiring neither scientific nor theological justification, nor documentation by evidence. It was a given, a timeless verity applicable to all societies in all ages."[34] To solidify the institution of slavery, slaves must first be made both to acknowledge the poverty and nullity of their backgrounds and to internalize consciousness of help-lessness and vulnerability that would render them totally dependent on the masters for almost anything, including self-definition and identity.[35]

Slavery thrived on what Charles Mills aptly terms a "racial contract"; one that "establishes a racial polity, a racial state, and a racial juridical system, where the status of whites and nonwhites is clearly demarcated, whether by law or custom. And the purpose of this state ... is, *inter alia*, specifically to maintain and reproduce this racial order, securing the privileges and advantages of the full white citizens and maintaining the subordination of nonwhites."[36] Fortunately, or unfortunately (depending on your status), this "partitioned social ontology," this "universe divided between persons and racial subpersons"[37] (to borrow Charles Mills' descriptions) did not function as expected. Masters never achieved the total domination they sought over slaves. Despite the efforts of the slave owners to attain total control and regulation of slave lives, slaves were able to develop their own world that "was influenced but by no means totally controlled by the Slaveholders' regime."[38] Though some blacks internalized self-abnegating values and became "good slaves," many others rebelled, becoming what Kenneth Stampp termed "troublesome property."[39] For the latter, the challenge of self-definition, of asserting and affirming one's identity, became a daily preoccupation.

In their struggles to transcend the boundaries of enslavement and counteract imposed and debilitating conceptions of identity, many blacks espoused emancipatory, counterestablishment ideas and developed positive self-conceptions. Examples of such counterestablishment and positive conceptions of the self abound in the numerous Nat Turners, Denmark Veseys, Gabriel Prossers, David Walkers, Paul Cuffees, and Lott Carys that the institution of slavery nurtured.[40] By 1830, however, the year blacks inaugurated the convention movement and the begin-ning of organized black abolitionism, it had become clear to perceptive blacks that violence, or any radical confrontational approach to slavery and racism, was at best suicidal. The brutal and savage responses of southern whites to slave insurrections, both real and imagined—the surge of anti-black violence and pogroms, beginning in Cincinnati in 1829, and spreading to other northern cities—clearly demonstrated the depth and virulence of racism. They also underscored the relative pow-erlessness of blacks.[41] Leading blacks confronted a dilemma. On the one hand, they perceived the specter of a nation rife with racism and bigotry, and seemingly determined to keep blacks permanently degraded. On the other hand, the surge of reform movements in the North compelled attention and inspired hope and optimism in many blacks. In the Second Great Awakening, from 1825 through 1835, liberal and reform-minded whites in New York and New England unleashed religious evangelical crusades aimed at radically transforming society into a better place for all, with slavery coming under close scrutiny and criticism.[42]

Utilizing the weapon of moral suasion, these reformers, the rank of which included Charles G. Finney of New York, Benjamin Lundy of Baltimore, James Birney of Alabama, and Lyman Beecher of New England, endeavored to change society for the benefit of all, regardless of race or ethnic backgrounds, convinced that societal evils resulted not from any innate deficiencies or inabilities but from moral failures—failures that, in their judgment, individuals possessed the moral capacity to undo.[43] As one authority put it, they "believed in a new, more immediate relation between man and God and man and his fellow creatures—one that emphasized perfectibility rather than inability, activity rather than passivity, benevolence rather than piety."[44] The reformers had strong faith in the individual's capacity both to attain perfection and actively and positively to transform society. They consequently conferred on the individual a moral responsibility to partake in actually changing and redressing societal wrongs.[45] Rejecting orthodox Calvinism, they "minimized original sin and preached instead the doctrine of free will. Sin was voluntary, and thus every individual could do good and become good."[46]

The surge of religious evangelism inspired hope and optimism in blacks. Instead of folding their arms in resignation, or succumbing to fatalistic ethos, or even escaping to Canada or some safe haven abroad, blacks portrayed themselves as a people with the capacity to assist in transforming America. As white abolitionists including William Lloyd Garrison, the Tappan brothers, Arthur and Lewis, Simeon S. Joycelin, Benjamin Lundy, and John Greenleaf Whittier armed themselves with the weapon of moral suasion and nonviolence, and mounted frontal attacks against slavery, blacks felt encouraged to invoke the long-tried tradition of self-help, cooperative activities, and economy that had shaped the reform efforts of eighteenth-century free blacks in New York and Pennsylvania. They officially launched the convention movement and proclaimed moral suasion as their guiding principle. Since the prevailing ideology exalted the individual, blacks, individually and collectively, became actively energized and projected themselves as active agents of change. They hoped to accomplish this, however, by first changing themselves and their communities with the weapon of moral suasion. Moral suasion thus became the underlying ideology of the black convention movement, and the convention itself provided the forum for further enunciation of, and debate on, moral suasion. In moral suasion, blacks found an ideology that, they hoped, could reform their communities, while peacefully and nonconfrontationally convincing whites to accept them as full-fledged citizens of the United States. The moral suasion debate was thus inspired by the need to affirm and secure a cherished identity—becoming full-fledged American citizens. Blacks, according to James Oliver Horton, saw themselves as "special Americans, dedicated to the spirit of American liberty as few others were. They were not alienated Americans even though for them American society was alienating. They were not discouraged Americans, even though the racial restrictions were discouraging. They were committed Americans, determined to improve the country's treatment of its people."[47]

MORAL SUASION

The moral suasion phase witnessed the origin and development of organized black abolitionism. For the first time, free blacks took the momentous step to organize and deliberate on how to change their condition. The need for organized efforts by blacks could in fact be traced to John Ruuswurm's clarion call to blacks in the founding edition of his *Freedom's Journal* in 1827. Ruuswurm was Jamaican-born and the first black to graduate from an American college (Bowdoin College). *Freedom's Journal* became the first black newspaper published in the United States. Its first editorial stressed the importance of blacks assuming more active roles in articulating and projecting their cause. As the editorial put it, "We wish to plead our own cause. Too long have others spoken for us."[48]

Although Ruuswurm and his coeditor Samuel Cornish talked in terms of journalistic representation, by the late 1820s, the rising tide of anti-black sentiments and pogroms would induce other black leaders to recognize the urgency of organized movement. The immediate factor was the outbreak of anti-black violence in Cincinnati, Ohio, in 1829.

Alarmed by the sudden increase in the free black population of the city, whites decided to enforce the provisions of the Ohio Black Code, which required free blacks to post a bond of five hundred dollars as guarantee of good behavior and providence. Violence erupted, compelling many free blacks to flee the city.[49] The resurgence of violence, not only in Cincinnati but in other cities such as New York, Philadelphia, Boston, Charleston, Pittsburgh, Washington, Baltimore, and Providence, impressed on blacks the need for organized response, thus inaugurating the convention movement in 1830.[50] Between 1830 and 1835, blacks met in five different conventions to deliberate on how best to bring about positive changes in their experiences of racism, marginalization, and rejection.[51] Not being acknowledged as fullfledged members of the American polity was a major motivation. The denial of the American identity was, therefore, a key factor in the rise of organized black abolitionism.

Several studies underscore the centrality of identity to the convention movement. Bethel describes it as "the first mass civil rights movement in the United States."[52] By the 1800s, the vast majority of the black American population was American-born, with little recollection of Africa. Whatever knowledge or consciousness of Africa that existed was colored by pro-slavery propaganda and values, which served to alienate many blacks from, rather than endear them to, the continent. Africa was not a place to cherish or with which to desire identification. Many blacks perceived themselves as "negative Americans" or "aliened Americans," people denied any positive self-definition and knowledge.[53] The need to define and assert an identity, therefore, became a central focus of the black abolitionist crusade.

Though brought together by the desire to organize and fight back in the face of overwhelming adversity, the platform that black abolitionists produced betrayed a deep sense of wanting to be acknowledged as Americans. These early conventions clearly revealed a strong integrationist consciousness.[54] Though some blacks embraced emigration and colonization as avenues of escaping the ugly and harsh realities of their lives, the vast majority refused to give up. Delegates overwhelmingly rejected and condemned colonization and invoked passages of the Constitution and Declaration of Independence in justification of their claims to American citizenship. For most blacks, colonization or permanent relocation to another country was anathema. It was tantamount to a voluntary relinquishing of identity.

The rising tide of anti-black violence notwithstanding, many blacks retained strong faith in the potency of moral suasion to bring about meaningful change. The ambition of every black person was to transcend the boundaries and limitations created by slavery and racism and be identified as an American citizen with all the accompanying rights and privileges. For example, in Philadelphia, the city with the largest concentration of free blacks in the country, blacks remained "convinced that although the path to acceptance and accomplishment in America was strewn with obstacles, it was the road to be taken."[55] To achieve this end, however, blacks had to subscribe to, and inculcate, values and goals that the mainstream society had identified as constituting the distinguishing characteristics or essence of being American—industry, thrift, economy, education, and moral uprightness. These values became the constituent elements of moral suasion. As they enthusiastically declared at the second convention in 1832, "We yet anticipate in the moral strength of this nation, a final redemption from those evils that have been illegitimately entailed on us as a people. We yet expect by due exertions on our part ... to acquire a moral and intellectual strength, that will inshaft the calumnious darts of our adversaries and present to the world a general character, that they will feel bound to respect and admire."[56]

The first five Negro national conventions, therefore, embraced these moral suasion values, convinced that the cultivation of these values would open wide the gate to full America citizenship. Moral suasion was a crusade for identity. Blacks were denied American identity in Constitution and in practice. They were either slaves or free blacks, but not citizens, not Americans. Being a slave, or not being one, defined their identity. The establishment in effect imposed a slavocentric construction of identity on blacks. Blacks were good only as slaves, or in subordinate positions. In fact, many pro-slavery preachers affirmed that blacks had been chosen and set aside by providence to be slaves.[57] Getting out of this restrictive slavocentric mold became the preoccupation of the early black conventionists. Black abolitionism, therefore, was a search not just for freedom but also for a sense of identity. Even if free, the life experience of blacks was still very much shaped by the fact of belonging to a race for whom enslavement was deemed appropriate. Moral suasion was aimed at breaking out of this slavocentric identity and establishing the basis for the affirmation of American identity. What is unique about this period was the consensus among blacks on the desirability of the American identity. There was hardly any black person who did not envision or desire to become an American citizen in the practical sense of it. Moral suasion was essentially the strategy devised for attaining this goal. It set the guidelines or framework for the realization of a cherished identity.

Prominent leaders such as William Whipper and the Reverend Lewis Woodson spearheaded the moral suasion crusade. They strongly asserted their claim to American identity. In consonance with the dictates of moral suasion, they acknowledged that the primary reason for the denial of the American identity to blacks was largely shortcomings in the black condition, that is, situational deficiency, and declared a commitment to addressing those deficiencies. Race was not considered a significant factor. In defining themselves, therefore, black leaders espoused an ideology that emphasized the possibility of attaining American identity. They projected themselves as Americans held back and down by deficiencies in their condition, deficiencies that could be remedied through moral suasion.

Although oppressed, alienated, and marginalized, blacks felt they shared a lot in common with whites and, therefore, worked hard to bridge the gap. In defining themselves as Americans, these leaders invoked certain universalistic ideals that they claimed united them with whites. The crusade for moral suasion symbolized an affirmation of American identity, a determination to be fully American, a demonstration of compatibility with classic American traditions and values. Moral suasion was consequently as much an explanation for black subordination as an affirmation of identity. It was an integrative and optimistic ideology, influenced by faith in the potency of universal values, values that supposedly impacted humanity regardless of race. Advocates therefore defined progress as the result of the triumph of those values. The proliferation of those universal values would eventually acquire for blacks the long-denied American identity.

The first three conventions were held in Philadelphia, Pennsylvania. The proceedings and declarations emphasized the primacy and efficacy of moral suasion. Blacks pledged to be industrious, economical, thrifty, and morally upright.[58] Controversy surfaced at the fourth convention in 1834 in New York. According to one source, disagreement developed between the New York and Pennsylvania leadership over moral suasion.

The more radical and race-conscious New York leadership began to question the efficacy of moral suasion. To prevent a radical change in the focus of the convention, the venue was quickly moved back to Pennsylvania the following year. The 1835 convention, the last of the early national conventions, established the American Moral Reform Society, the framework for propagating moral suasion.[59] The founding of this society underscored the determination of blacks to become fully American through peaceful character reform, and William Whipper became the prime mover and spiritual leader of the moral suasion crusade.

Information on Whipper's early life is sparse. Born in 1804 in Little Britain, Lancaster County, Pennsylvania, by 1828 he had settled comfortably in Philadelphia, Pennsylvania, and become one of the most successful black businessmen in the state. Though victimized by the prevailing climate of racism, Whipper, undoubtedly influenced by his economic success, developed strong faith in the potency of industry to break through racial barriers. Imbued with a strong sense of identity as an American, Whipper believed that the denial to blacks of American citizenship was only temporary and that with the success of moral suasion they would become fully integrated. He assumed the responsibility of providing blacks with the ideological guidance, and he believed that character reform would satisfactorily resolve the problem of black identity.

For Whipper, the resolution of the question of whether blacks were Americans or not lay in certain divinely given universal ideals. Though human destiny and the relationships between individuals and among groups are shaped by the functioning of those ideals, one's identity also has a lot to do with behavioral inclinations. In essence, blacks had a choice in determining how they defined themselves and how others responded to and perceived that self-definition. Underlining his universalistic inclination, Whipper fully embraced the Garrisonian precept, "My country is the world, my countrymen are all mankind."[60] He presented himself as color-blind, one who saw every human being as brethren. With this outlook, Whipper defined black subordination as the failure of blacks to live up to the dictates of moral suasion and, in consequence, the failure by the entire society to fully embrace and live according to those universal ideals.[61] Once these deficiencies were remedied, the problem of black identity would become resolved, as the barriers separating the races would disappear and whites would recognize and acknowledge blacks as fellow citizens. Whipper proclaimed, "God's moral ethics" as the foundation on which to build the black struggle, the legitimizing factor against which to measure demands by blacks for citizenship and equality.[62]

The notion of "God's moral ethics" underlined his belief in a universal standard, based upon the idea of one God, one humanity. Black leaders accepted the notion of the existence of an overriding divine moral order, one that mandated a uniform standard of morality for humanity, regardless of race or geographical location. As a strong believer in universalism, Whipper maintained that "virtues" and morality, rather than the color of the skin, or some other primordial factor, should differentiate people.[63] These moral and virtuous qualities resulted from adherence to those divinely established universal moral standards. One concept dominated his thought: *reason*. He described reason as "the noblest of all goals that brings man closer to God." *Reason* allows human beings to rise above, and transcend "physical inflictions that are offspring of passion"—for example, pains and grief resulting from racism and slavery. *Reason* was, in effect, a weapon for neutralizing the painful and crippling effects of slavery. It generates stoical quality in human beings, enabling them to transcend, and consequently ignore, earthly pains and suffering. It also motivates people to seek solutions in "something higher than human power"—God's moral power.[64]

Whipper challenged humanity to perfect its reasoning capacity, and move closer to God, a situation that instantaneously neutralizes all physical pains and suffering associated with slavery, racism, societal inequities, and other forms of man's inhumanity to man. Once *reason* predominates, government actions and policies are transformed as they bear the imprints of divinity, resulting in universal peace and love.[65] Consequently, though Whipper acknowledged the existence of discrimination, his explanation of its causes pointed not to race, or policies of particular individuals, but to humanity's deviation from the path of *reason*. To be guided by reason, he opined, is to be propelled by love, eventuating in universal peace and harmony.[66]

Color became irrelevant as a factor in the denial to blacks of American citizenship. Since the key problem emanated from moral failures, the proffered solution tended to deemphasize race. Racial distinction and prejudices originated, according to Whipper, "in the spirit of selfishness, cultivated and sustained by a religious and moral delinquency in principle, in utter disregard of the divine will ... and every element that is calculated to cement the interest of society in one universal brotherhood."[67] He consequently rejected the notion of a racially exclusive movement. Once *reason* prevailed, blacks would attain American citizenship. The doctrine of universal brotherhood would prevail in the aftermath of the reign of *reason*. Society would become color-blind, and black identity as Americans would be an acknowledged fact.

Whipper's ideas and convictions provoked angry response from blacks who felt that race and racism occupied prominent places in the struggle for identity. Since blacks and whites shared separate paths and experiences, the black struggle ought to reflect this separation. Those who espoused this view urged blacks to adopt clearly a conception of the self that reflected divergence from whites. Blacks were not Americans and could never become fully American until universalism was abandoned and the distinct experience and identity of both races were acknowledged. In order to become fully American, blacks must first begin by acknowledging racial and cultural distinctiveness. In essence, the struggle for universalism and the American identity must first be waged on a racially distinct platform. Those who advocated this separatist perspective belonged to the more "radical" New York leadership group, including the likes of Samuel Cornish, William Hamilton, and Samuel Hardenberger. Despite their desire for reform, these leaders rejected Whipper's universalism.

Cornish called upon the Moral Reform Society to evolve a clear and definite plan, identify concrete goals, and develop a definite strategy for attaining them, rather than engaging in what he perceived as a spurious and deceptive universalism that was "destined to influence nobody."[68] The problems of "the poor, proscribed, down-trodden and helpless people" deserved more time and efforts. Societal reality revealed, Cornish observed, that some people occupied comfortable positions, sustained by the exploitation and subordination of others. Universalism blurred both this reality and its fundamentally racial character.[69] Cornish's paper, *The Colored American*, therefore pushed for a racially exclusive strategy and ideology. Whipper objected, and denounced separatism as a measure destined to erode the moral legitimacy of the reform movement. He implored blacks, as members of the human family, who are also susceptible to universal values, to join forces with, rather than oppose, whites in the quest for a better society.[70]

Cornish disagreed, and accused the Moral Reform Society of assuming national responsibilities instead of zeroing in on critical black problems. Putting it bluntly, he charged Whipper with endeavoring to "elevate whites to the neglect of blacks" and also make blacks "beasts of burden" by placing the entire nation on their shoulders. He proposed a redefinition of the society's mission to emphasize issues pertaining solely to "the proscribed colored people."[71] It should be emphasized that Cornish was not opposed to the American identity. He equally cherished this identity and believed that blacks were as entitled to it as whites. He disagreed, however, with Whipper on strategy, that is, the means for attaining that identity. Given what he perceived as the depth and pervasiveness of racism, Cornish considered universalism unrealistic. In order to attain the citizenship status of whites, blacks, in Cornish's view, had to adopt, and proceed on, a separatist platform. In other words, Cornish urged blacks to situate their quest for the American identity on a solid foundation of racial distinctiveness.

Thomas Sidney, another respondent to the moral suasion debate, quickly declared his opposition to universalism. "In an effort for freedom," he argued, "there are several important and indisputable qualifications, which the oppressed alone possess." He identified two interrelated qualifications as the most critical. First, a sense of actual suffering and, second, a determination to end suffering. Sidney insisted upon a convergence of both the feeling (that is, consciousness) and the purpose (that is, reaction) of those who suffer in order to effect any meaningful and effective strike for freedom. Put differently, to struggle effectively and legitimately against oppression, one had to have experienced oppression. Consequently, in the estimation of Sidney, blacks alone possessed the moral legitimacy to organize against slavery. Underlining the necessity for a racially exclusive movement, Sidney linked the elevation of a people to "the inward rational sentiments which enable the soul to change circumstances to its own temper and disposition." It "is not measured by dependent upon external relations" (or forces). In his view, "the relative position and the relative duties and responsibilities of the oppressed and the oppressors" constituted the only ground upon which to predicate any argument for or against "complexionally distinctive organization." Whenever a people are oppressed peculiarly, he noted, "distinctive organization or action is required on their part to destroy oppression." Creating a distinct identity was crucial to Sidney, and he implored blacks to adopt the name "Colored American," a term Whipper had vehemently opposed on the ground that it undermined universalism, favoring instead the appellation "Oppressed American." Sidney, like Cornish, advocated a racially distinctive platform.[72]

Whipper was not the only focus of the moral suasion controversy. Another contributor, whose views perhaps generated even more heat, was the Reverend Lewis Woodson. A fugitive from Virginia, Woodson rose rapidly through the ranks of Philadelphia black leaders. His was equally a success story. He owned several barber shops and assisted in establishing and running the only colored school in Philadelphia. As a member of both the religious community and the elite black intelligentsia, Woodson would have had difficulty isolating himself from the controversies surrounding moral suasion. Furthermore, his deep commitment to the black struggle rendered such an isolationist posture unlikely. His approach seemed, in the estimation of contemporaries, critical of Whipper. On closer examination, however, his ideas tended to complement Whipper's. In a seven-part series titled, "Moral Work For Colored Men," he underlined the peculiarity of blacks and the need for special attention and strategies: "The relation in which we have for generations been held in this land, constitutes us a distinct class. We have been held as slaves, while those around us have been free. They have been our holders, and we the held. Every power and privilege have been invested with them, while we have been divested of every right. The distinction of our classification is as wide as freedom and slavery."[73] He too approved of the moral reform efforts, strongly believing that blacks were miserably deficient in education, morality, and industry and, therefore, needed to be elevated in order to justify any claims of American citizenship. Writing under the pseudonym "Augustine," Woodson acknowledged black deficiencies but stopped short of endorsing a racially exclusive movement. Like Sydney, he too welcomed the sympathy and support of whites, while emphasizing the prime responsibility of blacks.[74]

In its totality, Woodson's strategy paradoxically seemed to steer blacks in the direction of Whipper's universalism. He praised whites and expressed faith and optimism in the inevitability of change. He perceived a flexible and malleable society, one that was susceptible to moral arguments. Colored persons of healthy state of morals, he observed, attracted the respect and admiration of whites and were encouraged, rather than discriminated against, thus underscoring the situational imperative of prejudice. In his words, "I have noticed that the intelligent Colored man of polished manners, and pleasing address, is always well received and well treated, while some others, who are even wealthy, but who had paid no attention to the cultivation of the manners and habits of polished society, were rejected." He too, like Whipper and many others, placed greater burden on blacks. To benefit from the reform impulse of American society, and attain the much sought after American citizenship, blacks had to demonstrate both the will to improve, and also take the first tentative steps in that direction.[75]

Woodson's most contentious views resulted from his notion of the dual character of humanity—that it was possible for blacks to succeed, even in the most prejudiced environment. The oppressive legal system was not the problem, he intimated, but the demeanor and condition of human beings, especially blacks. The most direct path to an inclusive society, therefore, remained the cultivation of pleasing manners and unquestionable integrity. However violent or virulent racism was, it would crumble once confronted by a colored man of a healthy state of morality. The immortal side of man, that is, his inherent divine nature, allowed him to live and escape the evil effects of cruel laws. Though every individual possessed this divine quality, it is, however, functional and effective only in those who invoke it, and invoking it entailed a conscious effort to live according to the tenets of moral suasion. Prejudice, consequently, was most pronounced, he believed, whenever blacks were immoral, corrupt, and illiterate. Such negative qualities induced mistreatment from whites and a disposition on their part against integration. He referred to his personal experience in justification of the notion that "condition and not color" was the major cause of prejudice. He outlined the following as the "qualifications" for the admission of blacks into "polished society": hard work, polished manners, and physical and material condition. When these qualifications are achieved, he suggested, "a man slides into his proper circle with ease."[76]

The subject of emigration featured prominently in Woodson's discourse on moral suasion. Since one of the goals of moral suasion was economic elevation, Woodson believed that the acquisition of land would best facilitate this objective. He thus urged blacks to emigrate from densely populated and racially tense environments to the "West," identified as comprising Indiana, Illinois, and Ohio, where, according to him, land and other avenues of economic advancement abounded. The West was the new frontier for blacks, with promises of a more comfortable and desirable life. Such economic development would facilitate integration.[77]

He envisioned America as a liberal and open society, compelled to engage in discriminatory practices by the deficiencies and failures of blacks. His strong objection to "political action," or actions aimed specifically at the repeal of repressive laws, underscored an unflinching faith in moral suasion. He deemed such actions misdirected efforts. Bad laws did not originate slavery and racism. The twin evils were, he argued, products of an unrighteous and corrupt mind, or, as he put it, of "the corrupt moral sentiment of the country."[78] Once the moral sentiment was purified, slavery and all accompanying evils would disappear. He thus elevated man's moral quality to a height of prominence—the key determinant of human action and societal condition. The condition of this moral impulse influenced societal values and institutions. This led him to yet another conclusion; "that a morally good man cannot do a physically bad deed," suggesting a correlation between morality and virtue. There is undoubtedly a strong element of Whipperian universalism in Woodson's moral interpretation of human actions. His ultimate goal, it seems, was to reform the "corrupting element" in the moral fiber of society, and slavery would cease as "the great source from whence it springs would be dried up."[79] Both he and Whipper saw blacks as the major source of the corrupting element. Overall, Woodson advanced a very optimistic philosophy. He saw American identity as very much within the grasp of blacks. He did not perceive any conspiracy or concerted efforts by whites to deny blacks access to citizenship. The problem, in his judgment, was that blacks had yet fully to explore and exploit all available possibilities.

The debate and controversies over the implications of moral suasion notwithstanding, blacks remained faithful to the basic premise that moral improvement would result in the realization of American citizenship. It is no exaggeration to suggest that in this early phase of the black abolitionist crusade, most blacks sought American nationality and identity and were optimistic that a gradualist, reform-oriented platform would lead eventually to the desired goal. Though blacks disagreed on the exact character of the platform, they shared a consensus on the goal— American citizenship. Moral suasion thus remained entrenched, even as blacks began to organize politically vocal state conventions in the 1840s. They hinged everything on the potency of reason, on man's presumed desire and inclination for progress, on the reality, and compelling force of universal values, and perhaps most significantly, on a strong faith in humanity, guided by universal, divine values. Given this faith in the inevitability of change, blacks jettisoned confrontation in favor of coop-eration. Even when they acknowledged extraneous circumstances, they often emphasized their own failures. Moral suasion was supposed to serve as a dynamic, intertwining ideology that would ultimately bridge what was deemed an ephemeral racial schism.

Paradoxically, it would take the success of moral suasion to reveal its deficiency as a reform strategy. By the late 1840s, the number of mor-ally upright and economically elevated blacks in Philadelphia and other parts of Pennsylvania had more than doubled. Evidence from other parts of the country—Boston, New York, Cincinnati—clearly revealed determined efforts on the parts of blacks to cultivate habits of thrift, in-dustry, economy, and temperance, and they achieved success measured by the wealth and economic successes of individuals and organizations.[80] Their rewards, however, came in the form of opposition, resentment, and increased anti-black violence. In his study of Philadelphia, Bruce Laurie underscores the economic efforts and accomplishments of the city's black population and the corresponding negative and violent reac-tions of whites.[81] Other studies reveal that this trend was not isolated to Philadelphia. In several northern cities, wherever blacks manifested the desire and determination to conquer economic poverty as a step toward political elevation, they encountered violent responses from whites. Perpetrators of violence targeted wealthy blacks and symbols of black economic power.[82] One study describes the Moyamensing riots of 1842 in Philadelphia as "one of the prime examples of whites denounc-ing blacks for their degradation while simultaneously destroying those institutions which sought to eradicate that degradation."[83] It dawned on many that the key factor was not *condition* but *race*, and, consequently, some blacks concluded that no matter how hard they worked to cultivate moral suasion, the chances of integration remained bleak. At a gather-ing in Harrisburg, Pennsylvania, these blacks voiced their frustration over the failure of moral suasion. According to them, "The barrier that deprives us of the rights which you enjoy finds no palliative in merit—no consolation in piety—no hope in intellectual and moral pursuit—no reward in industry and enterprise." They underlined the fact that they were denied opportunities of elevation "because we are not 'white.'"[84] Moral suasion then gave way to immediatist and political strategies.

The failure of moral suasion clearly impressed on blacks the problematic of identity. The upsurge of anti-black movements, violence, and policies suggested a stronger racial dimension to identity. This affected a shift in black consciousness. Many became fully aware of the place of race in the denial to them of the American identity. This did not, however, lead to a total abandonment of moral suasion. Moral suasion became part of a broader platform of protest. The conventions of the 1840s, both state and national, emphasized both moral and political agenda. Though moral suasion failed, blacks did not relinquish their claim to American identity. By all available criteria that whites had used to claim that identity, blacks continued to press their own claim.

A strong declaration of affinity with America and a desire to be acknowledged in theory and practice as Americans characterized the proceedings of the 1840s conventions.[85] Henry H. Garnet perfectly captured the feelings of other blacks in a speech delivered at the Seventh Anniversary of the American Anti-Slavery Society in 1840. After affirming that blacks had satisfied all criteria for American citizenship, he declared, "With every fiber of our hearts entwined around our country, and with an indefeasible determination to obtain the possession of the natural and inalienable rights of American citizen, we demand redress for the wrongs we have suffered, and ask for the restoration of our birthright privileges." He repeated the same theme in his epochal speech at the Buffalo convention three years later in which he told the slaves, "forget not that you are native-born American citizens, and as such, you are justly entitled to all the rights that are granted to the freest."[86] In an address to the people of the state of New York, black delegates to the state "Free Suffrage Convention" of 1845 declared, "We love our native country, much as it has wronged us ... *We are citizens*; this we believe would never have been denied, had it not been for the subserviency of the people of the free states to slavery" (emphasis added).[87]

Blacks were hopeful and optimistic that a combination of reform, petition, and peaceful protest would eventually convince whites to concede their citizenship rights and privileges. In the conventions of the 1840s, black leaders implored their respective communities and constituencies to continue to cultivate those same moral suasion ideals as keys to

American citizenship. The underlying objective was to demonstrate to whites that there was nothing inherently wrong with blacks and that, given the right conditions, blacks were fully capable of self-improvement. This, they believed, would facilitate integration.

By the late 1840s, however, it became clear that the combination of moral suasion and political activism had not changed white perceptions and dispositions and that the quest for citizenship and American identity remained as elusive as it had ever been. But the failure of moral suasion alone would not induce blacks to turn completely away from their aspiration of attaining American citizenship. Subsequent developments, however, underlined the centrality of race and impressed on many the futility of integrationist aspiration and the elusive character of the American identity. The Fugitive Slave Law of 1850 was one of such developments. Under the provisions of the law, the federal government pledged its resources and assistance to the apprehension and return of fugitive slaves. This law convinced many that racism was pervasive and perhaps even permanent, and that blacks had no safe haven from slavery. The hope of becoming American became even dimmer. The law sharpened the debate on identity and convinced many of the need for a new identity external to the American context. Emigration became an attractive option for some, and Africa became the obvious choice. It should be emphasized, at this juncture, that the moral suasion debate, this very critical discourse on black American quest for, and affirmation of, identity, did not feature Africa. The disputants disagreed on strategies, but there was never a dispute on their objective—American citizenship.

EMIGRATION AND NATIONALISM

Martin Delay, the acclaimed black nationalist and advocate of an independent black nationality and identity, was initially a staunch advocate of moral suasion. He had in fact been among the most forceful advocates of the ideology and had spent the years 1847–49 propagating the doctrine to free black communities in the North.[88] Delany strongly believed that blacks were as qualified as, if not more qualified than, whites for American citizenship. This optimism sustained the integrationist and moral suasion phase of his career. The passage of the Fugitive Slave Law in 1850, however, destroyed this optimism. The law revealed a radically different America than he had hoped for. It established America, in his judgment, as a land "for whites only" and stripped blacks not only of considerations for citizenship but, most critically, of any protection, thus rendering them vulnerable to perpetual subordination. He described the law as a violation of the constitution, saying it debased blacks "beneath the level of the recognized basis of American citizenship."[89] Blacks were now clearly an alien people. There was consequently an urgent need for a new identity. Delany assumed the responsibility of helping blacks map out strategies and modalities for realizing this new identity. In several publications, he defined this new identity as African and Pan-African.[90] The depth and pervasiveness of racism convinced him that blacks had no hope of attaining American identity. This conviction led him to a racial essentialist construction of the black struggle. For Delany, "a question of Black and White" became "the great issue, sooner or later," that would determine "the world's destiny."[91]

Delany exhorted blacks to reclaim their African heritage as the basis of a new identity. They were not only black but also Africans, and as Africans, they shared historical and cultural experiences with Africans on the continent. Since America was irredeemably racist, blacks could never be accorded their cherished American identity. Delany soon began to spearhead and galvanize the emigration movement. Between 1850 to the outbreak of the Civil War, he urged blacks to relinquish the never-ending search for the American identity. The creation of a new black nationality in Africa would serve as the solid foundation for a new black identity. His travels in Africa from 1859 to 1861 bolstered his faith in the possibilities and future of a black nationality and identity based on Africa. He returned in early 1861 and began to campaign vigorously for emigration. He proclaimed his resolve to relocate to Africa and urged wealthy and enterprising blacks to consider relocating and assuming the African identity.[92]

Opponents of emigration such as Frederick Douglass objected strongly to externalizing the struggle. Douglass portrayed emigration as a dangerous distraction. In fact, the struggle between Douglass and Henry H. Garnet on African nationality and emigration was, in essence, a debate on conflicting consciousness of identity.[93] Garnet, like Delany, advocated a new nationality in Africa based on the development of a cotton economy. Douglass strongly opposed emigration, which he viewed as tantamount to voluntarily relinquishing all claims to American citizenship. He reminded blacks of the role and sacrifices of their fore-bears in helping to develop the American wilderness. Consequently, Douglass insisted, blacks had as much right to nativity as any white person.[94] He emphasized the possibility of a cultural pluralistic America in which blacks could remain, and still maintain their distinct identity, values, and institutions. Few emigrationists shared Douglass's optimism. In fact, Delany maintained that it was impossible to have an America in which blacks would be integrated with their racial/cultural distinctive-ness intact. By the late 1850s, he had come to the conclusion that the quest for full integration and American identity jeopardized the racial and cultural essence of blacks.[95]

Emigration, a movement that developed in response to rejection and the failure to realize one identity, was soon redirected at the reaffirma-tion of another identity—the racial and cultural essence of being African. Preserving the racial and cultural distinctiveness of blacks became a matter of life and death for Delany. In his judgment, coexistence with whites threatened the racial and cultural heritage of blacks. In essence, the price of integration, if it was possible to become fully American, would be a sacrifice of one's African identity. In Delany's estimation, blacks would have to commit cultural suicide, cease being black and African, in order to be fully accepted as Americans. This was too high a price to pay for American citizenship.[96] Nothing, he insisted, was worth sacrificing his blackness and African identity for. He offered emigration to blacks as the key to remaining black and African. In his strong defense of, and articulation of the imperative of, the African identity, Delany set the tone for future Afrocentric discourse. Despite his sense of alienation and depth of nationalism, Delany soon abandoned his quest for, and advocacy of, the African identity. By 1863, with the progress of the Civil War, he saw prospects for the American identity and nationality in the war, and joined Frederick Douglass, Henry H. Garnet, and other black leaders in supporting the Union cause. He exhorted blacks to focus inward and strengthen their faith in American nationality and identity.[97]

The ease with which Delany abandoned emigration and the quest for the African identity underscored the strength of his American consciousness and desire for American identity. But his expectations and those of blacks in general would be disappointed. The revolution of rising expectations that the Civil War engendered soon collapsed. Though the war destroyed slavery, and the reforms of the subsequent

Radical Reconstruction era (1866–1876), particularly the Fourteenth and Fifteenth Amendments, conferred citizenship and the franchise on blacks respectively, including the promise of legal equality, implementation of these constitutional reforms and guarantees proved difficult. The vast political landscape that Reconstruction opened up for blacks soon shrank as conservatives and defenders of the antebellum status quo gradually and viciously fought their way back to positions of authority in the South. By the end of Reconstruction in 1877, blacks were citizens in name only. The rights and privileges they had won were compromised and revoked. In other words, the Civil War and Reconstruction failed to resolve the problem of black identity. By the late 1870s, it was obvious that blacks remained alien to the American nation and would be accommodated only in subservient and subordinate roles. The return to power in the South of members of the *ancient regime* in consequence of the Compromise of 1877 sealed the fate of blacks. The "redeemers," as they fondly referred to themselves, assumed power with a vengeance, determined to undo every vestige of radical Reconstruction and return blacks to the status they had occupied, and roles they played, before the war. This development brought to the fore, once again, the age-old question of black identity.

Blacks, many of them among the most optimistic of the civil war and Reconstruction era, turned outward in a desperate search for a separate and external identity. Again, many turned to Africa, including Martin Delany. But the activist phase of Delany's African identity search was over. It would be left to two other black nationalists to propagate and vigorously pursue the realization of the African/black nationality and identity in the post–Civil War epoch: Alexander Crummell and Henry McNeal Turner. Both men emphasized the urgency of developing a strong African identity.

After he and other blacks were forced out of the Georgia legislature by whites, Turner denounced his American identity and enjoined blacks to embrace Africa as a viable alternative identity.[98] He was very critical of integration-minded blacks such as Booker T. Washington, whose brand of nationalism suggested enduring faith and hope in the possibility of realizing the American dream and identity. Turner expressed the same degree of concern over the possibility of blacks losing their identity. He stressed the urgency of an independent black nationality, and a new African identity.[99] Like Delany, Turner envisioned a dark and gloomy future for blacks in America. Africa provided the basis for regeneration and for the construction and consolidation of a new nationality and identity. He made several trips to Africa in the 1890s in pursuit of his black nationality scheme.[100] In his own response, Crummell proposed a Pan-African Christian community of Africans and blacks in the Diaspora. He expressed pride in his African ancestry and declared a commitment to the development and redemption of Africa. His writings and public lectures underscored experiential and identity linkages between Africa and black Diaspora. He implored black Americans to become more actively involved in the elevation and development of Africans. He soon moved to Liberia, West Africa, and immersed himself in the spread of literacy, Christianity, and "civilization" among the indigenous people.[101] All three men (Delany, Crummell, and Turner), at different times, went to Liberia and traveled extensively in other parts of the west coast of Africa.

Thus, leading nationalists of the nineteenth century strongly affirmed their African identity. Being black and of African heritage mattered the most to them. They considered the African heritage and identity worth affirming and defending in the context of rejection and alienation in the United States. They all espoused a Pan-African construction of identity, which they believed unified all blacks, regardless of geographical location. This Pan-African identity became the means of combating the ever-threatening Eurocentric cultural hegemony. Prompted by the elusive character of the American nationality and identity, these black nationalists mobilized Pan-African consciousness and sought the realization of a new nationality and identity through cooperative endeavors between Africans and black Americans. In different ways, Delany, Crummell, and Turner, attempted to make Pan-Africanism the basis of responding to the challenges of blacks in Africa and the Diaspora.

A critical examination of the history of Pan-Africanism, particularly of the strategies devised by nineteenth-century black nationalists for actualizing the Pan-African ideal and solidifying African identity, reveals a deep cultural distance and alienation from Africa, a consequence, no doubt, of the acculturation process in the New World. While these nationalists declared interest in assuming African identity, once in Africa, their utterances and activities betrayed ambiguities with respect to the projected African identity. It became clear that the Pan-African construction of identity was not as deep-rooted and strong as the expressions and rhetoric suggest. In other words, there was a certain superficiality to the Africa identity construct. These nationalists manifested a much stronger attachment to their elusive and cherished American identity.

From the birth of organized abolitionism in the early nineteenth century to the present, Africa had always served black Americans as the basis of articulating identity and an inspiration in the struggle for freedom and survival. The tendency by modern Afrocentric scholars to inject some mutuality or consensual ethos into the historical relationship of Africans and blacks in Diaspora misrepresents the reality. Such tendency ignores the complexity of the relationship. A critical look at the crucial nineteenth century would illuminate the contradictions and disharmony within black American nationalist and Pan-African thought. While blacks in Diaspora espoused Pan-African ideals and expressed a desire to identify with Africans, their activities betrayed cultural alienation from Africa. Though they acknowledged being black and of African ancestry, culturally, Delany, Crummell, and Turner distanced themselves from Africa. Their expression of cultural identity was unambiguously Eurocentric. They opted for shaping Africa according to the Eurocentric images that had shaped their own acculturation.

Delany, Crummell, and Turner were in Africa in the crucial period from 1850 to the 1890s, when European relationships with Africa began to change from "cooperation" to confrontation and occupation, a change that led inevitably to formal colonialism. During this momentous epoch, Europeans debated what to do with Africa and how to go about implementing this new aggressive policy. Whether by design or not, these black nationalists embraced this new aggressive policy. During a visit to Britain in 1861, Delany advocated the use of force against Africans to stem the tide of what he presented as an endemic crisis among indigenous African states, a crisis that he insisted inhibited the orderly and peaceful flow of civilization. He urged European missionaries to resocialize Africans away from what he perceived as barbaric indigenous traditions and modes of living.[102] Similarly, Turner also characterized Africans as barbaric and backward people in need of the civilizing touch of external forces.[103] Crummell referred to Africans as barbaric, restless, violent, and crude people against whom the use of indiscriminate force was legitimate. Crummell advocated violence as a potent weapon for controlling what he characterized as the wild barbarism of indigenous Africa, and he implored the British not to be restrained by democratic considerations. In his view, no price was too

high for Africans to pay in return for the benefits of European civilization. He advocated systematic reeducation of Africans in Anglo-Saxon
values.[104] There was, therefore, a discrepancy between the rhetoric of
African and black confraternity, nationality, and identity that these
nationalists popularized, and their distant, condescending, and hegemonic attitudes toward Africans.

The implications of their contradictions and ambivalence for the notion of identity are clear. Visiting and living in Africa exposed all three
to realities that challenged the romanticized images and expectations
that undergirded their quest for African identity. Most significantly,
as I argued elsewhere, exposure to African realities revealed their un-
Africannesss. They saw and realized their own cultural difference and
distinctiveness.[105] They realized that, though of African ancestry, they
had become culturally different and that the acquisition of African
identity was more complex and problematic. In other words, exposure
to Africa confirmed their American and Anglo-Saxon essence. Though
driven by rejection and alienation to seek the African identity, these
nationalists soon realized that culturally they shared more in common
with Americans and Europeans than with Africans. They realized how
difficult it was to presume that simply relocating to Africa made one an
African. Though they initially proclaimed African and black identity, as
they became conversant with Africa, they soon realized that the basis
of their identity and affinity with Africa was purely *racial*, not *cultural*.
The realization of cultural distance from Africa and the feeling of alienation from African tradition and customs necessitated strengthening
and reaffirming the cherished but elusive Euro-American identity. With
renewed vigor, all three embarked upon the difficult task of reasserting
cultural affinity with Euro-America.

Without really saying it, their denunciations and negative characterizations of Africans revealed that they did not see themselves as wholly
African. They envisioned themselves as blacks with strong American,
European, and Anglo-Saxon cultural connections. But then, there was
a problem. What was the benefit of being black and Anglo-American in
an epoch when European imperialist ideology defined all blacks (that is,
peoples of African ancestry) as primitive and inferior? Delany, Crummell,
and Turner felt challenged to legitimize and justify their claim to Anglo-
American identity. To do this, it was necessary both to emphasize distance
from Africa and to close the cultural gap with Europe, a gap established

by the ideology of white supremacy. They found the answer in the very institution that had brutalized and dehumanized them—*slavery*. Invoking religious historicism, they theorized that the enslavement of Africans was divinely inspired and sanctioned as a foundation for the fulfillment of God's purpose for Africans. Enslavement brought many out of "dark" Africa into close proximity with Europeans. Socialized and acculturated in superior European values, these blacks would now return to Africa as bearers of light and civilization to those still languishing in barbarism. Furthermore, enslavement closed the cultural gaps with Europe. Consequently, black Americans could no longer be classed in the same cultural category with indigenous Africans. As Delany emphasized, though involuntary and evil, slavery bred an educated, enlightened, and civilized black American population destined for greater responsibility and greatness in Africa.[106] All three nationalists shared Delany's interpretation of slavery. For Crummell, slavery was the "Fortunate fall," an embodiment of positive experience.[107] In Turner's view, slavery was "the most rapid transition to civilization for the Negro."[108] He predicted that in the future the world would become more appreciative of slavery.[109] I have done a more exhaustive analysis of the religious historicist contents of nineteenth-century black nationalism elsewhere.[110]

Edward Wilmot Blyden was another nationalist who used Africa to propagate the myth of African inferiority and backwardness and also rendered a positive construction of slavery. In an address titled "The African Problem and the Method of Its Solution," which he delivered at the seventy-third anniversary of the Colonization Society in Washington, D.C., January 19, 1890, Blyden acknowledged the civilizational and historical accomplishments of Egypt, in contrast to the darkness and backwardness of the interior of Africa. He characterized indigenous Africans as backward and primitive people who have resisted the touch of superior European civilization. Blyden, who was then the principal of Liberia College, a post he assumed in 1880, urged black Americans to come to Africa and heed her cry for help. He then provided a providential rationalization of slavery. God sanctioned slavery largely for the preservation and civilization of a portion of Africa so that the preserved would return to uplift those left behind. According to him,

> The Negro race was to be preserved for a special and important
> work in the future. Of the precise nature of that work no one can

form any definite conception. It is probable that if foreign races
had been allowed to enter their country they would have been
destroyed. So they brought them over to be helpers in this country
and at the same time to be preserved. It was not the first time
in the history of the world that a people have been preserved by
subjugation to another. ... Slavery would seem to be a strange
school in which to preserve a people; but God has a way of salting
as well as purifying by fire.

Blyden's positive rendition of slavery was popular among black nationalists. Africa, Blyden continued, was enveloped in darkness and primitivism, while the Americas were opened and developed. The solution to
Africa's problem lay in colonization. In fact, Africans desperately called
for it in their cry, "Come over and help us." Further emphasizing the
need for colonization, Blyden declared, "It is a significant fact that Africa
was completely shut up until the time arrived for the emancipation of
her children in the western world." He presented himself as a messenger
sent by Africans to convince black Americans to come to Africa and help
rescue them from barbarism.[111]

Enslavement, therefore, was a necessary price to pay for the benefits
of western civilization. Though this redefinition of slavery was done
partly to bridge the cultural gap between Europeans and black American
nationalists, it was in essence an exercise in identity construction. Being
part of the enslavement experience amounted to a nullification of the
African identity they initially proclaimed affinity with. What was most
significant for Delany, Crummell, Turner, and Blyden was that slavery
had brought them closer to the American identity. What this reveals is
that despite their criticism of Euro-American values and influences, and
a determined search for a new identity, these nationalists failed to project any consistency on the crucial question of identity. Their nationalist
values and schemes betrayed cultural ambiguities. They were driven
by alienation in America to seek African identity, only to be driven by
revulsion and cultural alienation from Africa to assert and reaffirm their
Euro-American identity. They perceived themselves no longer as Africans
but as products of a historical experience mandated by slavery, an experience that had transformed them culturally into something different from
Africa. Delany, Crummell, and Turner exhibited a complex and troubling
consciousness of identity, exemplifying Du Bois's duality construct.

The search for a rational answer to the existential question "Who are
we?" preoccupied blacks. Their response was unambiguous: Americans.

Failure to achieve this identity, however, led many to embrace Africa. But their profession of affinity with Africa and Africans betrayed ambivalence and evoked conflicting passions of love, dislike, confraternity, and distance.

NOTES

1. Bethel, *Roots of African-American Identity*, 82.
2. Ibid., 81–82.
3. Ibid., 81.
4. Ibid., 82.
5. Ibid.
6. Du Bois, *Souls of Black Folk*, 3.
7. Ibid., 3–4.
8. Early, *Lure and Loathing*.
9. Bethel, *Roots of African American Identity*, 25–27.
10. Asante, *Afrocentricity*. See also his *Afrocentric Idea* and *Kemet*. Richards, *Let the Circle Be Unbroken*.
11. Howe, *Afrocentrism*, 233.
12. Richards, *Let The Circle Be Unbroken*, 1.
13. Wilson, *Falsification of Afrikan Consciousness*, 40–41.
14. Wright, *Black Intellectuals*.
15. Richburg, *Out of America*.
16. Early, *Lure and Loathing*.
17. Bell, "American Moral Reform Society." McCormick, "William Whipper."
18. Miller, *Search for a Black Nationality;* Kinshasa, *Emigration vs. Assimilation;* Moses, *Golden Age of Black Nationalism*.
19. Eyerman, *Cultural Trauma*.
20. Stampp, *Peculiar Institution*, 141.
21. Andrews and McFeely, *Narrative of the Life of Frederick Douglass*.
22. Berlin, "From Creole to Africa," 19.
23. Ibid.
24. Ibid., 19.
25. Ibid., 20.
26. Ibid.
27. Edwards, *Equiano's Travels*.
28. Campbell, *Middle Passages*.

29. Magubane, *Ties That Bind*, 15–88. Walvin, *Questioning Slavery*, 49–95. Oakes, *Ruling Race*, 3–34.

30. Tise, *Proslavery*. See also Genovese, *World the Slaveholders Made*.

31. Reed, *Platform for Change*, ch. 3. See also Horton, *Free People of Color*, 152–53. Nash, *Forging Freedom*, ch. 4.

32. Cook, "Tragic Conception of Negro History," 225–31.

33. Lincoln, *Coming Through the Fire*, 101.

34. Curry, *Free Black in Urban America*, 81.

35. Walvin, *Questioning Slavery*. Oakes, *Ruling Race*. Jones, *Born a Child of Freedom*, ch. 1.

36. Mills, *Racial Contract*, 13–14.

37. Ibid., 16.

38. Kolchin, *American Slavery*, 133. Also, Walvin, *Questioning Slavery*, 64–71.

39. Stampp, *Peculiar Institution*. Also, Kolchin, *American Slavery*; Walvin, *Questioning Slavery*.

40. Aptheker, *American Negro Slave Revolts*. See also his "Consciousness of Negro Nationality to 1900."

41. Adeleke, "Primacy of Condition."

42. Sorin, *Abolitionism*, 17–37, ch. 3. Mabee, *Black Freedom*. Stewart, *Holy Warriors*. Gienapp, "Abolitionism and the Nature of Ante-Bellum Reform."

43. Ibid.

44. Sorin, *Abolitionism*, 44

45. Ibid., ch. 3. Mabee, *Black Freedom*, 1–111. Gienapp, "Abolitionism."

46. Mabee, *Black Freedom*. Also, Simmons, "Ideologies and Programs of the Negro Anti-Slavery Movement."

47. Horton, *Free People of Color*, 158.

48. Aptheker, *Documentary History of the Negro People in the United States*, vol. 1, 82.

49. Bethel, *Roots of African American Identity*, 119–26.

50. Ibid. See also Curry, *Free Black*, 96–111.

51. Bell, *Survey of the Negro Convention Movement*. Pease and Pease, "The Negro Convention Movement," in Nathan I. Huggins, ed., *Key Issues in the Afro-American Experience*.

52. Bethel, *Roots of African American Identity*, 120, 130. Horton, *Free People of Color*, 158. Reed, *Platform for Change*, ch. 5.

53. Wright, *White Man Listen!* 16.

54. Bell, *Survey*. Reed, *Platform for Change*, ch. 4. Pease and Pease, "Negro Convention Movement." Quarles, *Black Abolitionists*. Horton, *Free People of Color*.

55. Nash, *Forging Freedom*, 103.

56. Bell, *Minutes of the Proceedings*, 34.

57. Tise, *Proslavery*, chs. 6, 10, 13. Walvin, *Questioning Slavery*, chs. 4–5.

58. Bell, *Minutes of the Proceedings*.

59. Ibid. See also Simmons, "Ideologies and Programs," ch. 2.

60. McCormick, "William Whipper."

61. Ibid.

62. *The Colored American*, July 29, 1837, 3.

63. Ibid., September 9, 1837, 3.

64. Whipper, "Address on Non-Resistance," 3.

65. Ibid.

66. Ibid.

67. *The Colored American*, March 29, 1838, 2.

68. Ibid., March 13, 1841, 3.

69. Ibid.

70. Ibid., September 9, 16, 1837, 3; February 10, 1838, 3; March 17, 1838, 3.

71. Ibid., September 9, 1837, 2; March 13, 1841, 3.

72. Ibid., March 6, 13, 1841.

73. Ibid., December 2, 9, 1837; January 13, 27, 1838; February 10, 1838.

74. Ibid., November 3, 1837, 2.

75. Ibid., February 16, 1839, 3.

76. Ibid.

77. Woodson, "West," *Colored American*, February 17, May 3, 1838; January 15, February 5, March 2, 16, July 15, August 31, 1839.

78. Ibid., January 15, June 15, August 31, 1839, 3.

79. Ibid.

80. Litwack, *North of Slavery*, ch. 5. Curry, *Free Black*, 37–48.

81. Laurie, *Working People of Philadelphia*, 53–66.

82. Litwack, *North of Slavery*, ch. 5. Richards, *"Gentlemen of Property and Standing," ch.* 2. Curry, *Free Black*, ch. 6.

83. Simmons, "Ideologies and Programs," 34.

84. Foner and Walker, *Proceedings of the Black State Conventions, 1840–1865*, vol. 1, 124.

85. Foner and Walker, *Proceedings of the Black State Conventions*. Bell, *Minutes of the Proceedings*.

86. Ofari, *"Let Your Motto Be RESISTANCE,"* 133–34, 149.

87. Foner and Walker, *Proceedings of the Black State Conventions*, vol. 1, 39.

88. Adeleke, "Race and Ethnicity in Martin R. Delany's Struggle."

89. Delany, *Condition, Elevation, Emigration and Destiny*, ch. 17, 154.

90. Ibid. See also Delany, "Political Destiny."

91. Rollin, *Life and Public Services*, 335.

92. Adeleke, "Race and Ethnicity."

93. Ofari, *Let Your Motto Be RESISTANCE*, chs. 6–7.

94. Foner, *Life and Writings of Frederick Douglass*, 202.

95. Adeleke, "Race and Ethnicity."

96. Ibid.

97. Sterling, *Making of an Afro-American*, chs. 20–22.

98. Coulter, "Henry M. Turner." Redkey, "Bishop Turner's African Dream."

99. Turner, "American Colonization Society," 44, 52–59, 83–84.

100. Redkey, "Flowering of Black Nationalism." Also, Redkey, "Bishop Turner's African Dream."

101. Rigsby, *Alexander Crummell*.

102. Delany, "Official Report of the Niger Valley Exploring Party," 102–6, 133–34.

103. Turner, "Emigration to Africa," 55, and his "American Colonization Society," 44.

104. Crummell, "Relations and Duty of the Free Colored Men," 215–84. See also his "Duty of a Rising Christian State," 87; "Progress of Civilization Along the West Coast of Africa," 107; "Our National Mistakes, and the Remedy for Them."

105. Adeleke, *UnAfrican Americans*.

106. Rollin, *Life and Public Services*, 351–56.

107. Rigsby, *Alexander Crummell*, 113.

108. Turner, "Question of Race," 74.

109. Turner, "Emigration Convention," 147.

110. Adeleke, *UnAfrican Americans*, ch. 6. See also his "Religion in Martin R. Delany's Struggle."

111. Ibid., 570–76, 580, 583.

DISCUSSION QUESTIONS

1. Identify the two critical events that shaped black American consciousness and identity in the 19th century, and explain how and why these events had such an impact on African Americans.

2. Why has Du Bois's notion of double consciousness come under scrutiny? What are the current arguments against it (the text identifies four)? Discuss and explain how and why people see identity construction so differently.

3. How do Afrocentrists perceive Africa in relation to identity construct? Why?

4. Discuss what is meant by the *slavocentric* or *Americentric* perspective of racial construction of identity. In what ways is this perspective anti-Afrocentric? How does this perspective represent the artificiality of race?

5. Discuss the role of slavery in deconstructing identity. Give examples of this depersonalization process and discuss what is meant by the "unmaking and remaking of a people's consciousness of self."

6. What is *moral suasion*? Discuss the role of free blacks in defining and expressing this movement.

7. Discuss and explain why Martin Delany revoked his stance on moral suasion to embrace a racial essentialist construction of black identity. Why would "Black and White" become "the great issue, sooner or later, that would determine the world's destiny?" Has this vision already come to pass?

QUESTIONING THE NEED FOR RACIAL ESSENTIALISM

W. E. B. Du Bois declared in his book *The Souls of Black Folk*, published in 1903, "that the problem of the twentieth century is the problem of the color line." By addressing the widespread impact of imperialism, colonialism, forced migration, slavery, and hegemony on descendants of Africans scattered throughout the world, Du Bois, like many other scholars and intellectuals of his time, raised the question "What does it mean to be black?" What is the essence of blackness? The question posed does not refer to any inherent characteristics, qualities, or behaviors associated with race that would characterize a Eurocentric perspective of "racism," but rather suggests a worldview that was conceived by blacks themselves that would reflect a "fundamental similarity with all members of the group and a fundamental difference from non-members" that was rooted in a spiritual connection as well as in the actual struggle against racism (Adeleke).

Is there some unifying quality, notion, or understanding at the core of one's identity that distinguishes one racial category from another? Can an entire race of people possess a "collective consciousness" of their blackness as a monolithic group, or does the acknowledgement of such a distinction further perpetuate, rationalize, and justify the psychological and physical barriers of the color line that assimilationist philosophy sought to deconstruct? Ultimately, can racial essentialism and Afrocentric essentialist thought—while playing a viable role in the uplift, development, and restoration of Africa's history and in the recognition of African American culture, history, and identity—provide

171

the basis or the necessary framework to address the increasingly complex and diverse issues that afflict the lives and progress of Africans on the diaspora in the 21st century?

SELECTED READING:

Afrocentric Essentialism
BY TUNDE ADELEKE

Afrocentric Essentialism

Tunde Adeleke

*I*n a lengthy presidential address delivered to the National Emigration Convention in Cleveland, Ohio, in August 1854, Martin R. Delany (1812–1885) emphasized the pervasiveness and virulence of racism in the United States and urged black Americans to consider immigrating to external locations such as Africa and the Caribbean, where they would have unfettered opportunities to develop and realize their full potentialities.[1] In Delany's judgment, race had become perhaps the single most critical factor in human relations, both within the United States and on the international scene. As he poignantly declared, "It would be duplicity longer to disguise the fact that the great issue, sooner or later, upon which must be disputed the world's destiny, will be a question of black and white, and every individual will be called upon for his identify with one or the other."[2] Accenting the color line, Delany proposed a Manichean construction of domestic and international relations—blacks against whites, Europeans against non-Europeans. Since, in his judgment, coexistence on the basis of equality and freedom appeared inconceivable, blacks needed their own domain of independence and nationality elsewhere, preferably in Africa. For Delany, the continued quest for integration in America had become a culturally destructive option that potentially could also jeopardize and possibly obliterate the African identity of blacks.[3]

To his nineteenth-century contemporaries, Delany was the quintessence of blackness. In Delany's makeup, according to a biographer, there was no compromise with whites. This reputation of Delany as uncompromisingly anti-white, and a consistent advocate of the color line is widespread and entrenched. Yet, Delany was not born and raised with this disposition. He started out a believer in the promises of the American Dream and fought

Tunde Adeleke, "Introduction: Afrocentric Essentialism," *The Case against Afrocentrism*, pp. 3-22, 190-191. Copyright © 2009 by University Press of Mississippi. Reprinted with permission.

fervently against separatism. By the early 1850s, however, he had come to a critical crossroads. Disillusioned with the lack of change and apparent invincibility of racism, he began to spearhead and galvanize the emigration movement. It was in this capacity as leader and president of the emigration movement that he convened the Cleveland convention of 1854. After the convention, he spent the next eight years crusading for emigration. In his writings and speeches, Delany drew attention to the ubiquitous nature of racism and to what he perceived as a more sinister and troubling reality: a conspiracy by American whites and those he referred to as their "Anglo-Saxon cousins" to subordinate, subjugate, and exploit Africans and blacks in the Diaspora ad infinitum.[4] Race became, in Delany's judgment, the engine dynamo of global development, with the white race occupying the top echelons of the societal ladder, a position that conferred benefits and privileges of immense proportion, while blacks, and people of color generally, were confined to a life of deprivation and degeneration. In Delany's judgment, the reality mandated racial solidarity on the part of oppressed blacks. In order to conquer oppression and escape perpetual subordination, blacks had to unite and forge a common front. He committed himself to the pursuit of black unity and separatism from 1852 until the outbreak of the Civil War in 1861 compelled him, once again, to reverse course and embrace integration.

Almost fifty years after Delany's speech, W. E. B. Du Bois published his seminal work *The Souls of Black Folk* (1903), in which he echoed Delany's racialized worldview by characterizing "the problem of the twentieth century" as "the problem of the color line, the relation of the darker to the lighter races of man in Asia and Africa, in America and the islands of the sea."[5] Du Bois's declaration proved prophetic. No issue dominated international relations in the twentieth century, and shaped the relationships between peoples in different parts of the globe, particularly in the regions he identified, as prominently as race. Many analysts have in fact ventured the prediction that, judging by the state of contemporary race relations, particularly the ascendance of ethnocentric and cultural jingoistic consciousness on a global scale, race and, ipso facto, the color line, would indeed become the substantive problems of the twenty-first century.[6] Although he too emphasized the color line, Du Bois cautioned against overemphasizing race, given his dualistic construction of the black American. He portrayed blacks as a people formed of the dual experiences and heritages of Africa and America, and constantly tormented by the conflicting values and ideals emanating from this duality. As he explained,

> One ever feels his two-ness,—an American, a Negro; two souls, two thoughts, two unreconciled strivings; two warring ideals in one dark body ... The history of the American Negro is the history of this strife,—this longing to attain self-conscious manhood, to merge his double self into a better and truer self. In this merging he wishes neither of the older selves to be lost. He would not Africanize America, for America has too much to teach the world and Africa. He would not bleach his Negro soul in a flood of white Americanism, for he knows that Negro blood has a message for the world. He simply wishes to make it possible for a man to be both a Negro and an American.[7]

Thus, Du Bois warned against sacrificing one identity and heritage for the other. Both possessed intrinsic essence and validity and should, therefore, be acknowledged and respected. Both Delany and Du Bois underscore the primacy of the color line as an essential dynamic of American history, but they had radically different considerations in mind. For Delany, separation was a major consideration: the creation of an independent black nationality in Africa. Du Bois was a little ambivalent. Although he too emphasized race and racial consciousness, the complexity and duality of the Negro was an equally compelling consideration. While race mattered to Du Bois, and he eventually became active in Pan-Africanism, his analysis took due cognizance of, and accented, the American dimension of the Negro identity.[8] Both Delany and Du Bois would go on to use their racial convictions to support paradigms that advanced Pan-African consciousness and movements designed to unify all blacks and peoples of African descent upon a platform of economic, social, and political struggle and regeneration.

The concept of the color line that Delany and Du Bois emphasized has a deep historical pedigree. Some scholars trace its origin back to the dawn of enslavement in the New World. In fact, color was the defining essence of the South's "peculiar institution" from its inception in the seventeenth century to its demise in the mid-nineteenth century. The color line defined and shaped the relationship between masters and slaves. It conferred human qualities and attributes to the former while depicting the latter as subhuman.[9] Despite its historical depth, the color line has, however, been conceived and understood essentially in terms of a demarcation paradigm, that is, a concept that validates racial boundaries. There have not been any serious attempts to probe its deeper ramifications. There are indeed critical but neglected dimensions and implications of the color line that significantly shaped the attitudes and orientations of those within the parameters of the line, especially in relation to others deemed external, and by implication hostile, to the racial group.

The concept of the color line implies the imperative of racial unity and consensus within the parameters of a distinctive racial category. Put differently, the color line is much more than acknowledging racial boundaries. It is also an affirmation of the pertinence of racial unity and consensus, of the need to further, within the racial group, monolithic and homogeneous values—a condition deemed fundamental to the struggles and survival of the race in what is perceived as a hostile world environment. Everyone within the racial group is therefore expected to subscribe to a particular worldview, to remain faithful to what are perceived to be the needs, interests, and aspirations of the group. This mandates avoidance of actions or utterances that would seem to compromise or erode racial solidarity. At all times, members are expected to contribute positively to furthering the corporate interests of the racial group, and to be prepared and willing to defend the race regardless of the issues and circumstances. In essence, the color line is premised on absolute allegiance and devotion to one's racial group. This dictates an orientation to society and reality defined by alienation, racial and ethnic exclusivity, and an almost paranoid disposition that dichotomizes society and reality into conflicting and irreconcilable entities.

Delany boldly and more forcefully proclaimed and defended this broader dimension of the color line in his writings and speeches than did Du Bois. His analysis of American and global relations in the late 1850s and early 1860s underscored a rigid racial demarcation and construction of social, historical, and political realities. Delany discerned a global order in which whites/Europeans sought black subordination. To escape this fate, he called for emigration and the creation of an independent black nationality.[10] In a letter soliciting support for his emigration scheme addressed to Dr. James McCune Smith, Delany wrote,

> The present state of the political affairs of the world more than at any period since the establishment of international policies among

Christian governments—which policies comprehend and imply all nations and peoples, whether civilized or heathen—call for and imperatively demand our attention as descendants of Africa in whole or part ... One of the most prominent features in the present conflicts, struggles, and political movements among the nations of the world seems to be: Which can reduce us to a condition the best adapted to promote their luxury, wealth, and aggrandizement, to which as a race, for centuries we have contributed more than any other race.[11]

Nothing was more important for Delany at this phase of his career than to convince blacks of the supreme importance of, and imperative for, constructing a countervailing platform of struggle based strictly on racial demarcation. To him, race mattered more than anything else, and he urged all blacks to unite in the spirit of his 1854 declaration.

The color line was, therefore, conceived not only to draw attention to the potency of race as a factor in determining public policies but also to underscore the necessity and establish modalities for racial solidarity. Equally significant, it was meant to affirm and defend a group's corporate identity built upon race and ethnicity. This broader dimension of the color line has, however, proven to be more idealistic and visionary. Though racism mandated the color line, its very essence and existence depended on the attainment of balance or harmony within a racial group. In other words, the color line doctrine affirms the indispensability of racial harmony and consensus to the sustenance, strengthening, and survival of the racial group.

History, however, has shown a consistent muddling of the color line. In order to sustain the line, its advocates suggest, blacks must exhibit cohesiveness built on shared feelings of love and confraternity. Some observers contend that the ascendance of racism and the problematic state of black America (measured by economic poverty, social and political subordination and marginalization, problems of drug addiction, teenage pregnancy, unemployment, the alarming rate of homicide, and so forth) accord legitimacy to the color line. In essence, these negative and destructive circumstances and factors have become unifying elements that authenticate the color line. It becomes incumbent on all blacks to rally behind the line. Actions or movements that seemed to efface the color line, or even compromise its authenticity, were often frowned at and vociferously opposed. For many, therefore, toeing the line, faithfully advancing, and defending, at all times and under all circumstances, the interests and problems of blacks became the litmus test of racial identity. It is this allegiance that establishes one's authenticity as a black person. It is also what distinguishes an authentic black person from an "Uncle Tom."[12]

The conviction of confraternity evokes anger and resentment toward those who, either through actions or utterances, appear to compromise or undermine the interests and aspirations of the race. Racism is presumed to be of such potency as to obviate any basis for disrupting or muddling of the color line. Intraracial problems and contradictions are expected to be kept within rather than made issues of public discourses that could potentially damage the image of the race and thereby provide the other group (that is, the racial enemy on the other side of the color line) ammunition with which to further malign and mistreat the race. The mandate of racial solidarity stands indissoluble, even in circumstances when the conditions and complexities of the racial group clearly demand critical introspection and self-criticism. In this respect, the color line accents racial censorship and discourages actions or comments that are critical of blacks, especially if such criticisms could become subjects of public discourse. Such self-criticisms, however justified, are discouraged because they present the outside world with the image of a black community in crisis and disarray, thus compromising the struggle at critical moments when the entire race was expected to stand together in harmony and unison. A good illustration is the responses of some black nationalists and scholars to the publication of Keith Richburg's *Out of America: A Black Man Confronts Africa*. Published in 1997, the book immediately provoked anger and resentment among black Americans and Africans. In radio and television talk shows and on network news, angry respondents lambasted Richburg, accusing him of maligning and misrepresenting Africa and of displaying ignorance of African history. Many called him a black racist, an Uncle Tom, someone who manifested profound self-hatred and confusion on identity.[13] Members of a group referred to as "mainstream African American middle class" dismissed Richburg as "a self-serving Uncle Tom looking to make good with his white bosses."[14] Former chair of the African American studies department, Temple University, Molefi K. Asante, found the book "offensive and obscene." He described Richburg as someone "caught in the spiral of psychic pain induced by ... 'Internal inferiorization.'"[15]

Although today the color line is not officially proclaimed as vehemently as in the past, it nonetheless remains a defining characteristic of the black American struggle. Black militants of the 1960s civil rights struggles—Black Muslims, the Black Panthers, and Black Power—embraced the color line. Black Power advocate Stokely Carmichael based his Pan-African philosophy on racial demarcation. The Black Panthers spearheaded a movement that emphasized racial divisions. This was and remains true of the Nation of Islam. In fact, Nation of Islam leader Elijah Mohammed and his successor Louis Farrakhan never made secret their advocacy of, and commitment to, the color line, justified largely on pathological and negative characterizations of whites. Mohammed's speeches are replete with calls for constructing and strengthening the color line. His "truth" about the black situation in America is unambiguously racial and racist. As he declared, "We, the Black men are of God. Our oppressors whoever they may be are of the devil. Their nature is evil! They are incapable of doing well."[16] Describing "the nature of the white man," Farrakhan, on the other hand, refers to, "the Caucasian" as "a vessel made for dishonor. He's like a vile olive branch grafted in. He ain't natural, he's not a natural branch, he's grafted in among the peaceful people. This is a graft that is a sucker."[17] The essentialization of race is not isolated to radical fringe elements within the black struggle. Racial essentialism or, more appropriately, the existentialization of color is an integral and critical component of revolutionary black idealism, the best example of which is Afrocentrism.

Molefi Asante, a leading advocate of the Afrocentric genre, articulates and advocates the color line in clearly unambiguous terms in his writings.[18] In one of his books, *Afrocentricity* (1989), Asante emphasizes the need for the development and defense of what he terms the "collective consciousness" of blacks. He stresses the importance of racial unity and harmony, for, in his judgment, blacks remain dogged and threatened by self-abnegating and destructive, hegemonic, Euro-centric values. As he warns, "There can be no effective discussion of a united front, a joint action, and a community of interest until we come to good terms with collective consciousness, the elementary doctrine of economic, political, and social action."[19] Underlining the essence of the collective consciousness, he writes, "Our collective consciousness must question writers who use symbols and objects which do not contribute meaningfully to our victory. *How could a black writer be allowed to use symbols which contradict our existence and we not raise our voice?*" (emphasis added).[20] In this last sentence, Asante clearly establishes the importance of intellectual vigilance on the part of blacks against black writers who betrayed the color line. As constructed by Asante, Afrocentricity represents the intellectual articulation of the color line in all its broader ramifications and implications. But Afro-centricity goes beyond authentication of the color line. Its broader intellectual premise or raison d'être was to challenge and deconstruct Eurocentric denial, and misrepresentations, of black/African history and culture. It advanced a construction of the black/African cultural and historical experiences designed to provide order, rationality, and essence where none had been acknowledged by Eurocentric historiography. It also sought to reverse the negative Eurocentric portraits and renditions of the black and African cultural and historical experiences. In consequence, Afrocentric scholars have made, and continue to make, certain claims about African/black history and culture that often ignore or compromise historical reality, assertions that are socially and therapeutically utilitarian but historically misleading and inaccurate.[21]

Historically, the human drive for essentialist ethos has resulted from, and reflected, the inequality of the human historical encounters. The doctrine of white superiority, affirmation of Eurocentric distinctiveness and distinction, European claims of special and dominant status, assertions of Anglo-Saxon purity and superiority, and advocacy of white solidarity are all part of the historical edifice and repertoire of European hegemony.[22] Over time, this hegemonic disposition reproduced its own contradiction and antithesis. Borrowing from and mirroring the tradition of the hegemonic class, subordinated, oppressed, and exploited groups soon develop "political" and "oppositional" consciousness.[23] In the black American context, this consciousness unleashed countervailing ethos of resistance that crystallized into some forms of essentialism—racial, cultural, or ethnic. Thus, the binary of hegemony-subordination, empowerment-powerlessness, eventually resulted in counterhegemonic essentialist ethos meant to validate and reflect the claims, aspirations, and values of the subordinated and powerless group. Therefore, it could be argued that hegemony is not the exclusive preserve of the dominant powerful class. Subordinated groups have the capacity to develop hegemonic and essentialist ideologies of self-promotion and racial and cultural validation. I focus in this book on the latter type of essentialism, offering an exposition and critique of the cultural, social, historical, and identitarian implications of the essentialist tradition in contemporary black cultural nationalist thought as theorized in Afrocentricity. This work is neither a history of Afrocentricity nor a discussion of the ideology. The focus is not on Afrocentricity per se. The last decade has witnessed outpourings of critical expository, revisionist, and neorevisionist writings on the subject.[24] What I offer is a critique and deconstruction of the social, cultural, historical, and intellectual ramifications and implications of Afrocentric essentialism. The term "Afrocentric essentialism" refers to the use of Africa to advance a monolithic and homogeneous history, culture, and identity for all blacks, regardless of geographical location. Race is a central defining element of Afrocentric essentialism. It is in fact the glue that binds other elements of Afrocentric essentialism such as culture and ethnicity. In Afrocentric essentialist thought, Africa is the embodiment of what are characterized as immutable identitarian elements that unite all blacks: race, ethnicity, and culture. These elements, especially culture and ethnicity, according to Afrocentric essentialist scholars, have not been fundamentally impacted by centuries of separation from Africa and acculturation in America. Put differently, "Afrocentric essentialism" refers to the monolithic construction of the black American and African Diaspora experiences, the location and interpretation of these experiences within a Pan-African historical and experiential paradigm. Though Afrocentric essentialism embodies racial essentialism, it is much broader. Race is just a key defining element, the glue that binds Afrocentric essentialism. Both racial essentialism and Afrocentric essentialism seem synonymous and interchangeable, but the latter is much broader. Algernon Austin provides this apt definition of racial essentialism:

> Racial essentialism means that groups are seen as possessing an essence—a natural, supernatural, or mystical characteristic—that makes them share a fundamental similarity with all members of the group and a fundamental difference from non-members. The essence is understood in racialist thinking as being immune to social forces. It does not change with time or social context. In essentialist thoughts, blacks in the United States share a fundamental similarity with blacks in the African nation of Malawi, for example, and blacks today share a fundamental similarity with blacks in ancient Nubia thousands of years ago.[25]

Austin's definition underscores this use of race to construct a monolithic identity across historical time and space with disregard for historical change. Afrocentric essentialist thought acknowledges the centrality of race. Owing to its problematic character as identitarian construct, however, leading Afrocentric scholars now deemphasize race and highlight ethnicity, broadly and vaguely represented by the concept "Africa." Africa became a much more reliable identitarian construct that embodies something that binds all blacks, something much more substantive than race—*culture*, which, despite centuries of separation, had supposedly survived almost intact among blacks in Diaspora. Being African (ethnicity) became the essential defining element around which to organize and combat Eurocentric hegemony. Hence, while some Afrocentric scholars acknowledge the social and political construction of race and thus its limited value and diminished status, and elevate Africa as the essential factor, Afrocentrism actually embodies race and nurtures racialist consciousness. Again invoking Austin:

> Afrocentrism is a racial ideology because it ideologically constructs a heritable essential difference among human populations.
> Within Afrocentric theory, people who are of the African Cultural system are presented as being fundamentally different from people outside this system. These differences are passed on to the descendants of people within this African Cultural System so that centuries later the descendants of Africans are said to be culturally African. Because these cultural differences are not influenced by social forces, they remain present in the same form over millennia.[26]

This continuity is best represented in Afrocentric depiction of continental Africans and all blacks in Diaspora as one people who share identical historical and cultural experiences. Afrocentric scholars consider this monolithic construction of the African and black historical and cultural experiences critical to survival and success in their historical and existential struggles against forces of white/European historical and cultural hegemony. They construct a historical continuum of shared interests, experiences, and challenges unifying Africans and blacks in Diaspora. This is evident in the works of Asante, Marimba Ani, Maulana Karenga, Nai'm Akbar, Amos Wilson, and John Henrik Clarke, among many others.

A defining characteristic of Afrocentric essentialism is the Manichean conception of history. Afrocentric scholars represent history as an arena of irreconcilable conflicts between diametrically opposed cultures—black versus white. They advance a racialized paradigm that delineates boundaries of historical and cultural conflict between blacks and whites.[27] Their affirmation of a uniform and homogeneous Africa and black Diaspora history and culture underscores certain critical cannons of Afrocentric essentialism: the development of a countervailing African epistemology as the modus vivendi for black empowerment and regeneration; the proclamation of a monolithic African identity for all blacks regardless of geographical location; the advancement of the cultural essence and superiority of black and African cosmology; the development and propagation of the "stolen legacy" thesis, a theory that attributes the core values of western civilization to the overriding influence of ancient civilizations of Africa, particularly Egypt. This theory has become an article of faith among Afrocentric scholars who have used it to advance what some critics depict as a hegemonic universal Afrocentric historiography.[28] Furthermore, Afrocentric essentialist thought underscores the historical depth and authenticity of a positive African consciousness among blacks. Finally, there is also a deemphasizing of New World (metropolitan) influences, consciousness, and acculturation among blacks; that is, the denial of the essence and validity of the New World (American) consciousness and identity among blacks.

To understand Afrocentric essentialism fully, it is imperative that the tradition is appropriately contextualized within the historical discourse of black alienation and resistance. From slavery to the present, blacks have had to struggle against the forces and manifestations of Eurocentric essentialism. Enslavement, racism, and segregation (Jim Crow) were all built on affirmations of white superiority and corresponding claims of black inferiority. As slaves, blacks were deemed subhuman, items to be owned, bought, and sold by whites. As free, they were deemed primitive and inferior, not deserving of close association with the "superior" white race. Historically, Eurocentric essentialism engendered misery, alienation, subordination, depersonalization, dehumanization, and subjugation. Whether in slavery or freedom, it nurtured in blacks alienated consciousness, provoking resistance and ultimately the development and articulation of a combative countervailing essentialist worldview: Afrocentric essentialism. The roots of Afrocentric essentialism can in part be traced to the nineteenth-century black resistant traditions of abolitionism, moral suasion, colonization, and emigration. Modern representations of Afrocentric essentialism are in the "militant" ethos and movements of the black struggle from Pan-Africanism to Black Power and Black Panthers. Modern attempts to revive Pan-Africanism is premised on the conviction that continental Africans and blacks in Diaspora are one people who share identical problems and challenges and are threatened by, and vulnerable to, the hegemonic machinations of the old racial enemy (whites/Europeans). This explains the racial/ Afrocentric essentialist construction of the struggle and the location of Africa as the foundation, the edifice of black resistance.

In modern times, early centralization of Africa abounded in Marcus Garvey's philosophy and movement, in the writings and speeches of the "radical" activists of the civil rights struggles such as Stokely Carmichael and Malcolm X, and in the writings and speeches of the late West Indian scholar-activist Walter Rodney. Rodney offered a sound knowledge of African history as a prerequisite for any meaningful and effective confrontation with Eurocentric historiography and worldview and emphasized the imperative of using historical knowledge to rescue blacks from cultural imperialism. African history became a weapon for combating and deconstructing what he termed "European cultural egocentricity."[29] At the roots of Afrocentric essentialism lie African history, African cosmology, African identity, and African epistemology. From the early slave resistance and anti-slavery abolitionism through nineteenth-century emigration movements to the present, the black struggles reflected and entailed efforts, directly or indirectly, aimed at deconstructing ethos of Eurocentric essentialism. This is reflected in the insurrectionary tradition of Nat Turner and Denmark Vesey; the quasi-historical efforts of the pioneers of black intellectual resistance such as William C. Nell, James W. C. Pennington, Robert Benjamin Lewis, James Theodore Holly, William Wells Brown, George Washington Williams, and Martin Delany; the moral suasion ethos of the early nineteenth-century black abolitionist movement spearheaded by the likes of William Whipper and Lewis Woodson; and the nationalist and colonization schemes of the nineteenth century. In different ways, therefore, these efforts constituted attempts to confront and challenge the hegemonic order that had been validated and legitimized by Eurocentric racial and cultural essentialist ethos. The doctrine of white supremacy that justified Europe's claim to cultural and civilizational supremacy also shaped the historical relationships of whites and non-whites and legitimized the subordination and dehumanization of the latter.

Over time, however, the failure of blacks to overcome the experiential impacts of Eurocentric essentialist ethos compelled many to invoke black and African essentialism in response. Thus, racism became a critical element in the development of essentialist ethos. The role of race in the construction of white essentialist ethos laid the foundation for the countervailing development of black and African essentialism. Although there were several occasions in the eighteenth and early nineteenth centuries when race appealed to blacks as a potential framework of constructing resistance and affirming and validating self/identity, the mid-nineteenth-century upsurge of black nationalist and emigrationist consciousness was a major point of maturation, and gradual crystallization, of Afrocentric essentialist consciousness.

Delany's epochal racial essentialist declaration of 1854 noted above was perhaps a critical turning point in the evolution of Afrocentric essentialism. The entire speech amplified the growing disillusionment of blacks with the failure of integration. Delany would go on in his writings and struggles to give greater substance and strength to "Afro-centric essentialist" values that future generations of black nationalists and activists would invoke. He emphasized the imperative of an African-centered epistemology and insisted on a trans-Atlantic nexus of struggle that united Africans and blacks across the Diaspora as people with shared history, culture, identity, challenges, and problems. He used race (that is, the fact of blackness) as the basis of delineating distinct boundaries of historical encounters and struggles and advanced a monolithic interpretation of black history, while also advocating an Africa-black Diaspora unity built on a common platform of struggle.

This book is a critical interrogation of the cultural and intellectual implications and ramifications of Afrocentric essentialism. As defined above, the concept "Afrocentric essentialism" refers to the monolithic construction of the black experience, the location and interpretation of the black experience within a Pan-African historical and experiential paradigm, and perspective, as a countervailing force against the hegemonic influences and impact of Eurocentric essentialism. Afrocentric essentialism is predicated largely on the convictions that "Afrocentric consciousness" is deep-rooted among blacks in Diaspora and that this consciousness of Africa had always been positive and endearing. From this came the Afrocentric call for Pan-African solidarity and for using Africa as the platform of commonality, identity, culture, and struggle. A major defining character of Afrocentric essentialism is the racialization and ethnicization of the black experience; however, the drive toward essentializing the black and African historical and cultural experiences resulted in what many describe as a dehistoricization process.[30] In other words, the need for a homogeneous and monolithic African and black Diaspora worldview led to deemphasizing of the historical process. Afrocentric scholars have found it necessary to deny or deemphasize the processes of historical change and transformation in America. They deem constructing an essentialist tradition of history and culture profoundly critical to group survival and empowerment in the context of what they perceive as the ever-present and potent threat of Eurocentric hegemony. Although in recent years there has been increased scholarly attention to Afrocentric historicism, little attention has been given to examination of the intellectual, social, and cultural ramifications and contradictions of its essentialist projection of black history, especially in relation to issues such as identity, Pan-Africanism, globalization, the historical process, and the historical representations and utility of Africa. For example, as already stated, Afrocentric essentialism projects Africa as a unifying framework for all blacks. The basis of this "African-centeredness" is the belief that blacks in the Diaspora had historically harbored a deep and positive consciousness of Africa and a strong desire to identify with the continent. It is this claim of historical depth and potency of African consciousness among blacks in the Diaspora that inspired a corresponding assertion of historical continuity and confraternity, and advocacy of reconnection with the continent and reactivation of Pan-Africanism. There are pertinent but often neglected paradoxical questions relating to Afrocentric amplification of the "African roots of, and African influence on, western civilization," and the supposed immutability of African culture, while denying or deemphasizing the acculturative influence of the New World: How is it possible that a people whose legacies, according to Afrocentric scholars, so profoundly shaped Western tradition, would remain uninfluenced by Western contacts? How were they able to retain the original African identity and culture intact (that is, remain essentially African)? These questions underscore the central paradoxical and philosophical problematic of Afrocentric essentialism—the claim of cultural originality and exclusivity in a context of historical and cultural contacts, exchanges, and hegemony!

Afrocentric essentialist scholars depict Africans and blacks in the Diaspora as a community of like-minded, historically and culturally congruent people, whose shared history and culture not only transcended space and time but also defied the process of change. The two are considered one, united by commonality of interests, aspirations, and challenges; a people whose shared identity had not been affected by the historical process of change and transformation, despite centuries of geographical and historical separation. Certain key essentialist ideas derive from such narrow racial, cultural, or ethnic construction of the black Diaspora and African experiences. First, the utility of race, blacks and continental Africans defined as one people united by racial identity and shared struggles; a people whose historical experiences were shaped by the fact of race (color), in consequence of the negative and dehumanizing experiences of their encounters with whites and Europeans. Second, the depiction of Africans and Diaspora blacks as a people of shared "African" culture, the reality of historical separation and transplantation notwithstanding. African cultural retentions in the New World are projected as historically rooted and, therefore, evidence of the permanence and indestructibility of the African essence. In Afrocentric essentialism, therefore, all blacks share one African identity regardless of historical experiences and geographical locations. Thus, historical *time* and *space* appear irrelevant and inconsequential. Here, Afrocentric essentialist scholars reject the Du Boisean duality construct and any suggestion of New World impact on identity. In their judgment, the American experience never significantly affected the identity and consciousness of the *real* African person. The Afrocentrist is not tormented or influenced by warring ideals.[31] The third is the construction of what I characterize as a *gloracialized* worldview against globalization. Advocates of Afrocentric essentialism reject globalization and the prospect of global cultural citizenship and affirm instead ethnic and racial identity and consciousness.[32] It should be noted, however, that Afrocentric suspicion of globalization is much older than the advent of globalization. It is rooted in what some of the pioneers of black historiography characterized as the hegemonic character of "universal history." It is rooted in their representation and rejection of universal history as Eurocentric and destructive to blacks, and in their Eurocentric construction of global history. The advent of globalization has only strengthened Afrocentric suspicion and provoked some of the most virulent anti-globalization ideas. Even as many applaud globalization as obviating and transcending the restrictive parameters of the nation state, thus affording greater opportunity for human interactions and intercultural communication, Afrocentric scholars portray globalization as anti-black. They perceive globalization as essentially an enlargement of the power of the hegemonic nation-state and therefore pernicious. This problematizes the conflict between globalization and the nation-state. In other words, the nation-state remains a problematic entity, the shrinkage of its traditional boundaries of political influence notwithstanding. Afrocentric essentialist scholars suggest that it is not possible to embrace globalization without first confronting and resolving the contradictions and limitations of the nation-state. In Afrocentric essentialist construct, therefore, the global arena is an extended domain of the problematic nation-state. Thus, in the Afrocentric genre, globalization reflects continuation of Eurocentric hegemony and essentialism, hence the need for a countervailing Afrocentric essentialist response and vigilance—which comes in the form of *gloracialization*. I define *gloracialization* as the consciousness of racial distinctiveness, developed and projected on a global scale, unifying all blacks, regardless of geopolitical location, drawn together by perceived threats emanating from European global cultural expansion. This highest and global expression of black racial consciousness is considered the most potent and formidable force with which to negate the cultural hegemonic implications of globalization.[33]

Ironically, Afrocentric scholars erect boundaries of distinct historical experiential performances within the larger context of American national historical performance, and often at odds with it. The hegemonic nature of the larger context of historical performance led blacks to search for, and construct, their own space within which they are able to perform and tell their own story, while highlighting the limitations and hegemonic character of the dominant space. This justified establishment of distinct epistemological and cosmological boundaries outside of the dominant domain. A major problematic is how blacks are able to construct and navigate distinct cosmological and epistemological spaces while living within a Eurocentric space. To understand black history and culture, Afrocentric scholars insist, one must do so within an African-centered epistemology to the exclusion of the acculturative impact of

New World geopolitical space. However, Afrocentric essentialism goes beyond just a platform. What makes it distinctive today is not the platform character but the use of the platform as the basis of constructing a homogeneous and monolithic worldview for all blacks and Africans regardless of geographical locations and historical and cultural experiences. As emphasized, Afrocentric essentialism underscores historical and experiential uniformity and conformity for Africans and all blacks across historical time and space, without due acknowledgment of the historicity of *time* and *space*. That is, both *time* and *space* are treated as static and ahistorical entities, and not the conduits of historical and cultural transformations. Africa is at the heart of Afrocentric essentialism; it is the very basis and foundation for a common identity, historical and cultural experiences and affinity, the substructure for constructing uniform and unifying experiential discourses of historical, cultural, and identitarian homogeneity.

This appeal and utilization of Africa as a weapon and the basis of struggle goes back to the early nineteenth century. Enslavement and dehumanization were based on the negative portraits and rendition of the African background and connection. Initially, this elicited rejection of, and alienation from, Africa. The early-nineteenth-century black abolitionist and moral suasion ethos were designed to affect distance from Africa and achieve full integration in America.[34] By the mid-nineteenth century, for many blacks, Africa was becoming an attractive and acceptable basis of constructing a countervailing platform of struggle. For key nineteenth-century black nationalists, Africa became the basis of a counteroffensive against Eurocentric hegemony. Though for them, the underlying objective of constructing a counter-identity and experience based on Africa was to reshape and reform the American condition.[35] Paradoxically, the essentialization of Africa reflected, in some sense, recognition of historical process and transformation. Even as they constructed a monolithic racial platform of struggle, the activism of nineteenth-century black nationalists mirrored ambivalence that itself implied some recognition of the historical process and transformation. In the postmodern context, however, the essentialization of Africa has come to mean deemphasizing and deessentializing of the historical process. Afrocentric essentialism underscores the fragile, porous, and shallow character of New World enculturation. To bridge the divide created by the historical process or transplantation, and New World acculturation, Afrocentric scholars felt it necessary to deemphasize the historical essence of both transplantation and acculturation. That is, transplantation, in Afrocentric genre, represents just a geographical act, not a culturally transforming process. Enslavement simply took Africans from one locale to another without any lasting transformation and impact. Afrocentric essentialism thus exhibits the following attributes: the tendency to impose uniform identity on all blacks, the tendency to advance uniform culture, regardless of geographical locations or historical experiences, and the tendency to locate all blacks within a monolithic epistemological and cosmological tradition. Afrocentric essentialists associate black Americans, cosmologically and epistemologically, with Africa, as opposed to the western epistemological and cosmological traditions. On the basis of the above, Afrocentric scholars advocate reaffirmation of Pan-Africanism as a viable platform and framework of constructing and demonstrating unifying experiential challenges. Thus, Afrocentric essentialism underscores the color line—black separation and alienation—even in the context of a broadening globalization of the human experience.

Although Afrocentric essentialism is deep-rooted in history, the emergence of Afrocentricity in the modern world represents its ideological maturation, the highest point of Afrocentric essentialism. The historical underpinning of contemporary Afrocentric essentialism is the perceived onslaught on blacks in the post-civil rights era, as in attacks on, and reversals of, the gains of the civil rights struggles. This has caused alienation, resulting in calls for strict delineation of the racial and cultural lines, affirmation of black distinctiveness and uniqueness, cultural conflicts, dissonance and divergence, as opposed to convergence and compatibility. The hegemonic character of mainstream historical experience led many blacks inexorably to affirmation of Afrocentric values and distinctiveness. Thus, rejection and negation led to affirmation of, and quest for validation in, Africa.

The hegemony-subordination binary within which the black American experience unfolded problematized the Self-Other identitarian nexus and consciousness. Afrocentric scholars reject the identity problematic that Du Bois represented in dualistic and conflicted terms. While Du Bois emphasized acknowledging the validity of the Self-Other dichotomy, Afrocentric scholars affirm the Self (Negro) while invalidating the Other (American). While Du Bois presented both in historical relational terms as mutually reflective and reinforcing, Afrocentrists present one as the negation of the other, both perpetually at odds. Du Bois described both as engrossed in a conflict of mutuality, with shared historical and cultural experiences. Afrocentrists underscore distinctiveness, conflict, and negating values.

In a recently published provocative study, Debra J. Dickerson attempts further deconstruction of the racial underpinning of the cultural black nationalist worldview. She wrote *The End of Blackness* (2004) in order to prove and promote "the idea that the concept of 'blackness,' as it has come to be understood is rapidly losing its ability to describe, let alone predict or manipulate, the political and social behavior of African Americans. Given its strictures and the limitations it places upon the growth and free will of those to whom it refers, it diminishes their sovereignty as rational and moral actors."[36] She advocates "updating" blackness so that blacks "can free themselves from the past," and stop "defining themselves out of America."[37] Dickerson underscores the depth of racialist consciousness and convictions among blacks and the degree to which such disposition has informed, and continues to shape, black American history and experience. She emphasizes the negative, constricting, and circumscribing influence of race-conscious disposition and how it is both limiting and undermining the possibilities and potentialities of blacks. Dickerson's "gauntlet thrown down to the black powers that be," echoes much of the strictures against the stranglehold of racialist consciousness among blacks. She articulates in profoundly effective and powerful terms the debilitating effect of racial thinking. Unfortunately, as powerful and potentially influential as Dickerson's work is, the fact remains that racialist consciousness has taken such a strong hold among blacks that it has become synonymous with the very survival and success of the race. Especially in the times of "compassionate republicanism," to be race conscious became a defining essence of being "a real black person." In other words, race consciousness and racial solidarity have become countervailing strategies of struggle and survival. There is nothing wrong with being race conscious. It is a manifestation of one's awareness and responsiveness to the realities of daily life. The problem, however, is in using such consciousness as the basis of existential aspirations and struggles; of allowing race to define and determine, and thereby limit, one's choices, aspirations, visions, and goals. It is ironic that a construct that is widely acknowledged for its fragility and artificiality was, and remains, key to defining the character of a people's conception of self and construction of history. It seems equally ironic also that at a time when many are questioning the utility of race, some blacks are heavily dependent on it as a unifying experiential construct and the basis of constructing boundaries and frameworks for existential struggles.[38] Undoubtedly, it is the virulence and potency of racism in America that has provoked and reinforced black people's affinity to race as a viable means of existential validation.

This book illuminates the social, intellectual, and political representations, challenges, and limitations of Afrocentric essentialist consciousness among black Americans. The many complex dimensions of essentialist ethos are identified and analyzed in relation to identity, historical memory, conceptions, and perceptions of Africa; relations between blacks in Diaspora and continental Africans; and the responses of blacks to the challenges and implications of the expanding terrain of human encounters and experiences. I interrogate the prominence of Africa as a construct and frame of historical and cultural reference in black essentialist ethos. I contend that very often the construction of Africa entailed a dehistoricization process that deemphasizes and diminishes the essence of history. Put differently, in order to construct and defend an essentialist construction of the black experience, Afrocentric essentialist scholars often ignore or deemphasize the dynamics of history. I have written this book, first, to develop and analyze Afrocentric essentialism as a comprehensive and dynamic agency in black history and, second, to probe its many-faceted representations in, and impacts on, black American history and consciousness. Most important, this book is meant to illuminate Africa's problematic, conflicted, and ambiguous role, underscoring the contradictions and limitations of Afrocentric essentialist thought. I aim to suggest that while theoretically Afrocentric essentialism seems like a logical response to alienation and the deepening crisis of black impoverishment, it remains historically weak as a means of understanding, or mirroring into, the historical realities of the black experiences in America and the entire Diaspora.

NOTES

1. Delany, "Political Destiny," 327–67.
2. Ibid., 337–38.
3. Ibid. See also Delany, "Political Aspect"; Delany to Professor M. H. Freeman; Delany, "Political Events."
4. Delany, "Political Events."
5. Du Bois, *Souls of Black Folk*, 13.
6. Holt, *Problem of Race in the 21st Century*. Barndt, *Understanding and Dismantling Racism*.
7. Ibid., 3–4.
8. Ibid.
9. Stampp, *Peculiar Institution*; Elkins, *Slavery*; Davis, *Inhuman Bondage*.
10. Delany, "Political Aspect," "Political Events." See also his "The International Policy of the World Towards the African Race."
11. Delany, "Important Movement."
12. Adeleke, "Color Line as Confining and Restraining Paradigm." See also Adeleke, "Black Americans and Africa."
13. Richburg, *Out of America*.
14. "Richburg Firestorm," 51.
15. *Journal of Black Studies*, September 1997, 129, 130–32. Also, Sackeytio, "For a Self-Denying 'African'-American Journalist," 53; Egbo, "Self-Denial and Retribution," 52.
16. Mohammed, *Fall of America*, 17.
17. Eure and Jerome, *Back Where We Belong*, 247.
18. Asante, *Afrocentricity* and *The Afrocentric Idea*; Kemet, *Afrocentricity and Knowledge*.
19. Asante, *Afrocentricity*, 30.
20. Ibid., 39.
21. Shavit, *History in Black*; Howe, *Afrocentrism*; Lefkowitz, *Not Out of Africa*.
22. Blaut, *Colonizer's Model of the World*.
23. Morris and Braine, "Social Movements and Oppositional Consciousness."
24. Shavit, *History In Black*; Howe, *Afrocentrism*. See also Walker, *We Can't Go Home Again*; Moses, *Afrotopia;* Ziegler, *Molefi Kete Asante and Afrocentricity.*
25. Austin, *Achieving Blackness*, 12–13.

26. Ibid., 128.

27. Shavit, *History in Black*; Walker, *We Can't Go Home Again*; Howe, *Afrocentrism*.

28. James, *Stolen Legacy*.

29. Rodney, "African History in the Service of Black Revolution," 51. See also Adeleke, "Guerilla Intellectualism."

30. Shavit, *History in Black*; Stowe, *Afrocentrism*; Lefkowitz, *Not Out of Africa*.

31. Asante, "Racism, Consciousness and Afrocentricity."

32. Ani, *Yurugu*.

33. Adeleke, "Gloracialization."

34. Adeleke, "Moral Suasion and the Negro Anti-Slavery Crusade."

35. Adeleke, *UnAfrican Americans*. See also his "Constructing a Dual Cultural Space."

36. Dickerson, *The End of Blackness*, "Introduction," 3.

37. Ibid., 4–5.

38. Graves, *Myth of Race*.

DISCUSSION QUESTIONS

1. What were the differences in the approaches of W. E. B. Du Bois and Martin Delany to dealing with racial problems concerning the color line?

2. Why did Delany feel that race mattered more than anything else?

3. Which approach do you most closely identify with, and why?

4. Define and discuss Molefi Asante's notion of the "collective consciousness."

5. According to Asante's theory, would a black artist be limited by his or her race in the construction and representation of his or her work of art? Why?

6. Discuss and explain how Afrocentric and racial essentialism can be both limiting and empowering. Why the existence of this dichotomy?

PART FOUR

DEVELOPING A RADICAL BLACK CONSCIOUSNESS

*I*t was the summer of 1966 when a young Stokely Carmichael stood before a crowd of poor, black Mississippi sharecroppers and yelled out to the crowd, "What is it that you want?" to which the crowd enthusiastically responded, "We want black power!" So marked the beginnings of the ideological rift that would later separate Carmichael from the Student Nonviolent Coordinating Committee, Dr. King, and the idealistic Freedom Riders—young activists who had traveled to Mississippi on buses from all over the United States to register black voters and encourage them to promote change. The seeds of black power were rooted in the writings of psychiatrist Franz Fanon, who penned the book *The Wretched of the Earth*, which "analyzed the psychology of the colonized and their path to liberation" (Fanon) and in the works of scholars and intellectuals like Harold Cruse, who, in 1967 released his book *The Crisis of the Black Intellectual*. Cruse's book questioned racial integration as a viable means to uplift black people, and in fact argued that it was a trap "because it required that blacks shed their culture and, in turn, accept the full set of values of the dominant society even though racial inequality persisted" (Cruse). The long-suffering pleas of Dr. Martin Luther King Jr. to be a nation at peace with itself and to engage in the practice of Christian humanism and passive resistance gave way to the forceful words of Fanon, immortalized through Malcolm X, to end colonialism and the effects of racial oppression "by any means necessary!"

The Cuban and other liberation movements ignited the flame that indicated a revolution of the people was imminent. The

Black Panther Party, organized in Oakland, California, to defend black citizens against police brutality in their neighborhoods, sent a clear, visual message to the world and all of America that black people were taking control of their own lives, finding their own voices, and controlling how they would be represented and defined through art, media, and in politics.

SELECTED READING:

"Black is Beautiful!" Black Power Culture, Visual Culture, and the Black Panther Party
BY AMY ABUGO ONGIRI

"We Waitin' on You": Black Power, Black Intellectuals, and the Search to Define a Black Aesthetic
BY AMY ABUGO ONGIRI

"Black Is Beautiful!"

Black Power Culture, Visual Culture, and the Black Panther Party

Amy Abugo Ongiri

One does not necessarily have to wait for a
revolutionary situation to arise; it can be created.

—Ernesto "Che" Guevara, *Guerilla Warfare*

LITTLE JOHNNY IN SCHOOL
Little Johnny says, "My brother was in Vietnam and got shot in the ass."
The teacher says, "Hey freeze, freeze. Don't say 'ass,' say 'rectum.' "
Little Johnny says, " 'Rect 'um?' Shit, it killed 'um!"

—Richard Pryor, *Bicentennial Nigger*

Guerilla Warfare Che Guevara's Armed Struggle and the Black Panther Party

*E*rnesto "Che" Guevara's simple formulation of the factors that enabled the 1965 revolution in Cuba and that could potentially enable
revolution throughout the world were widely read and highly influential
among all who considered themselves dispossessed and revolutionary
during the social and cultural upheaval of the mid-1960s to late 1970s.
In a 1968 film, *Black Panther,* created by the Third World Newsreel
Collective and the Black Panther Party to highlight their cause and the
situation of their imprisoned leader, Huey P. Newton, the camera pauses
didactically on a copy of *Venceremos,* a 1969 collection of Guevara's
speeches and essays, as Newton describes from his jail cell the goals of
the party and its possible sphere of influence by using the Cuban revolution as a metaphor for the possibilities for Black revolution in the West.

Amy Abugo Ongiri, "'Black is Beautiful!' Black Power Culture, Visual Culture, and the Black Panther
Party," *Spectacular Blackness: The Cultural Politics of the Black Power Movement and the Search
for a Black Aesthetic,* pp. 29-57, 196-199. Copyright © 2009 by University of Virginia Press.
Reprinted with permission.

Guevara greatly favored military action over political action, and most influential with the Black Panther Party was his claim that, rather than wait for revolutionary situations to arise as traditional Leninist Marxism demanded, the guerilla had a duty to create revolution through his own actions. This also transformed the configuration of revolutionary struggles for "land and freedom" not only throughout the agrarian economies of Latin America and Africa but also throughout the urban, industrialized United States and Europe.[1] Groups influenced by Guevara's concept of armed struggle included not only the Black Panther Party in Oakland, California, but organizations as diverse as the Red Army Faction in West Germany, the Red Brigade in Italy, and the Weather Underground, the Black Liberation Army, and George Jackson's incipient People's Army in the United States.

Throughout *Guerilla Warfare,* Che Guevara maintained a singular focus on revolution as a military possibility alone. However, his "*indispensable* condition" that "the guerilla fighter needs full help from the people of the area" had the unintended consequence of privileging symbolic as much as actual military action (4). This, combined with the Black Panthers' media-savvy approach and the explosion of interest in popular African American culture in the late 1960s and 1970s, expanded Guevara's model of revolution so that it could allow for victories the significance of which Guevara could neither have anticipated nor accounted for. The Black Panther Party would largely fail in its nearly fifteen years of existence at its final goal to "serve and liberate the colony, by the only means necessary—the GUN," as the first issue of the Black Panther Community News Service proclaimed (Foner, 8). In a seeming contradiction to Guevara's fundamental belief that the symbolic actions of revolutionaries, if effective, would necessarily create the conditions for revolution, the more the Black Panther Party seemed to fail in the actual armed struggle, the greater were its successes in convincing U.S. culture of the necessity not only for the party's own existence but for revolution itself. In the end, the Panthers' successes would lie more in the influence they wielded in the arena of popular culture than in military culture. This chapter explores the apparent contradiction between the party's cultural successes and its political failures, as well as its overall role in defining the parameters of postwar African American culture.

Guevara's *Guerilla Warfare* begins with a chapter titled "Essence" that lists "three fundamental conclusions" that "the Cuban revolution revealed": "1) Popular forces can win a war against an army. 2) One does not necessarily have to wait for a revolutionary situation to arise; it can be created. 3) In the under-developed countries of the Americas, rural areas are the best battlefields for revolution" (1). For urban self-styled guerillas like the Black Panther Party, the exact relationship between the "three fundamental conclusions" about the Cuban revolution and the possible contradictions between Guevara's call for a rural revolution and the actual urban industrialized conditions in which they existed were less important than Guevara's claim that revolutionary conditions could be created by small, committed groups bound together by certain strategic revolutionary aims. Guevara's theory, dubbed "focoism," was popularized in the West by the French philosopher Regis Debray, who, along with Fidel Castro, was largely responsible for propagating the work of Guevara after his death while attempting to foment guerilla warfare in the jungles of Bolivia in 1967.

According to focoism, small groups of highly trained guerillas, "focos," could act as agents for socialist revolution by creating through their actions alone the conditions that would enable a large-scale mass revolution. Tactical wins and losses, though important, were less so than the mass identification with revolutionary possibility that such actions could create by proving to the dispossessed, according to Debray, "that a soldier and a policeman are no more bulletproof than anyone else" (51). The inevitable losses incurred when a small fighting force encountered a trained army did not necessarily have to be a deterrent to fomenting revolution: "For a revolutionary, failure is a springboard. As a source of theory it is richer than victory: it accumulates experience and knowledge" (23). The implication of Guevara's theory of revolution as read through Regis Debray was that, win or lose, focos could become through exemplary action alone a revolutionary vanguard for a soon-to-follow revolution.

"ARMED PROPAGANDA" AND THE VANGUARD OF THE REVOLUTION

Groups like the Black Panther Party were not only excited by the possibility that a small-scale organization could provoke a broader engagement with governmental forces and elicit a mass response, they were empowered by the seemingly audacious claim that if small, armed groups created the conditions of revolutionary struggle, ultimately *they could win.* In the short film *Black Panther,* Huey Newton explained from prison:

> We're not a self-defense group in the limited fashion that you usually think of self-defense groups. I like to use the example of when Fidel Castro started the revolution along with Che Guevara. There were only twelve of them altogether. They realized they wouldn't be able to topple the oppressive regime in Cuba. What they were was essentially an educational body. They engaged with the Army. They fought with the Army in order to show the people that the army was not bullet proof. The police were not bullet proof and that Batista's regime was not a regime that was impossible to topple. So the people started to feel their own strength. The Black Panther Party feels very much the same way. We think that this educational process is necessary and it's the people that will cause the revolution. ... And we plan to teach the people the strategies and necessary tools to liberate themselves.

Newton's belief that military action could have a value beyond basic wins and losses by serving as revolutionary propaganda was drawn primarily from the example of the Cuban revolution. Fidel Castro had affirmed in 1962 at the Second Declaration of Havana: "What Cuba can give to the peoples, and has already given, is its example. And what does the Cuban revolution teach? That revolution is possible, that the people can make it." *The Black Panther* would quote Jose Marti's advice that "the best way of showing is doing," while Huey P. Newton would argue in "The Correct Handling of the Revolution," "When the Vanguard group destroys the machinery of the oppressor by dealing with him in small groups of three and four, and then escapes the might of the oppressor, the masses will be overjoyed and adhere to this correct strategy. When the masses hear that a Gestapo policeman has been executed while sipping coffee, and the revolutionary executioners fled without being traced, the masses will see the validity of this approach to resistance" (*Black Panthers Speak,* 41, 20).

Regis Debray labeled this "armed propaganda" in his highly influential *Revolution in the Revolution? Armed Struggle and Political Struggle in Latin America,* which attempted to continue and elaborate on the work begun in Guevara's *Guerilla Warfare* (47). Debray, who had been arrested in Bolivia during Guevara's Bolivia campaign and served three years in prison as a result, greatly favored, as did Fidel Castro and Che Guevara himself, revolutionary praxis over revolutionary theory. Guevara vigorously denigrated "coffee-shop theories" and "the do-nothing attitude of those pseudo-revolutionaries who procrastinate under the pretext that nothing can be done against a professional army" (*Selected Works,* 204, 375). He urged instead, "Where one really learns is in a revolutionary war; every minute teaches you more than a million volumes of books. You mature in the extraordinary university of experience" (386).

The notion of "armed propaganda" suggested that not only could revolutionary war be a learning experience for revolutionaries, it could also be a teaching experience for the masses of people not yet directly involved in the revolution. In his theoretical reworkings of Guevara's writings, Debray would consistently reinforce Castro's theme from *The Second Declaration of Havana* that "the duty of every revolutionary is to make the revolution," first in an essay-length account of the Cuban revolution entitled "Castroism: The Long March in Latin America," which initially appeared in 1964 in *Les Temps Modernes* and was later reprinted in the *New Left Review,* and then in *Revolution within the Revolution.* Both texts would offer the revolutions in Cuba and throughout Latin America as blueprints for revolutionary action worldwide. Castro's maxim was made so central by proponents of Guevara-style revolution that even Carlos Marighella would paraphrase it as the reason for revolution in his highly influential 1969 *Minimanual of the Urban Guerilla:* "No matter what your philosophy or personal circumstances, you become a revolutionary only by making revolution" (39).

Though Debray, Castro, and Guevara consistently denigrated action that was social, political, or strategic rather than strictly military in nature, Guevara had also continuously cautioned that all military action had to have symbolic value that could be easily read and understood by the masses of people not yet involved in the revolution: "The people must be shown that social wrongs are not going to be redressed by civil means alone" (*Guerilla Warfare,* 111). For his part, Debray cautioned: "The guerilla struggle ... must have the support of the masses or disappear; before enlisting them directly, it must convince them that there are valid reasons for its existence so that the 'rebellion' will truly be—by the manner of its recruitment and the origin of its fighters—a 'war of the people'" (*Revolution within the Revolution?* 47). For groups like the Black Panther Party, whose numbers were initially quite small—the initial Oakland chapter numbered not more than five at its inception— the philosophy of Guevara and its investment in symbolic acts of military violence that could be accomplished in small groups to great results held an obvious appeal. Ultimately, however, it would be the Black Panther Party's interventions into the realm of symbolic, rather than military, culture that would have the most lasting effect in helping to define and position post-1965 African American culture as hypervisible, radically defiant, and the site of a contradictory empowerment and disempowerment.

RICHARD PRYOR AND THE CREATION OF A REVOLUTIONARY CULTURAL POLITICS

As the Panthers attempted to recreate symbolic culture, they began to have widespread influence on the transformation taking place in African American culture and aesthetics. Richard Pryor, whose work came of age through and with the Black Panther Party, declared in his autobiography, "I knew that I could stir up more shit on stage than in a revolution" (*Pryor Convictions,* 121). Pryor embodied the ways in which the cultural politics of groups like the Black Panther Party were influencing a developing African American popular culture. Before the 1970s, Pryor's routines were largely devoid of the explicit political references and references to African American vernacular culture that he would later make famous. After undergoing a series of personal problems, he relocated to the San Francisco Bay Area, where he came into contact with a number of radically politicized African American artists and intellectuals, including Huey P. Newton.[2] In an atmosphere that he would characterize in his autobiography as "a city of spectacles" and "a circus of exciting, extreme, colorful, militant ideas. Drugs. Hippies. Black Panthers. Antiwar protests. Experimentation. Music, theater, poetry" (115), Pryor had a personal and artistic epiphany: "One night I served as the disc jockey on a radio station, playing Miles and rambling on about Nixon, the Vietnam War, the Black Panthers, and shit. I didn't know anything about that shit. But who better to talk about it?" (118). This sort of saturation in radical culture resulted in a moment of personal transformation in which, according to Pryor, "I had a sense of Richard Pryor the person. I understood myself. I knew what I stood for. I knew what I thought. I knew what I wanted to do" (121).

The Panthers' belief that performative action could serve not only as a heuristic tool but also as a provocation to revolution enabled them to understand a variety of activities beyond military action as revolutionary: "The main purpose of a vanguard group should be to raise the consciousness of the masses through educational programs and certain physical activities that the party will participate in. The sleeping masses must be bombarded with the correct approach to struggle through the activities of the vanguard party. Therefore, the masses must know that the party exists.

The party must use all means available to get this information across to the masses" (Foner, 43). Pryor's belief that he "could stir up more shit on stage than in a revolution" echoed the ambiguities that were developing in the relationship between revolutionary action and revolutionary representation as espoused by the Black Panther Party, whose emphasis on the heuristic and the performative would end up creating revolution as a highly visible and visual affair rather than a series of covert actions that involved anything from public demonstrations to concerts by their in-house group of musicians ("The Lumpen") and the politicizing of popular performers such as Pryor. In "The Correct Handling of a Revolution," Newton explains the process by which revolutionary action will mirror back to the masses images of themselves in the idealized form of revolutionaries:

> The masses are constantly looking for a guide, a Messiah to liberate them from the hands of the oppressor. The vanguard party must exemplify the characteristics of worthy leadership. Millions and millions of oppressed people might not know members of the vanguard party personally or directly, but they will gain through an indirect acquaintance the proper strategy for liberation via the mass media and the physical activities of the party. It is of prime importance that the vanguard party develop a political organ, such as a newspaper created by the party, as well as employ strategically revolutionary art and the destruction of the oppressor's machinery. For example, Watts. The economy and property of the oppressor

was destroyed to such an extent that no matter how the oppressor tried to whitewash the activities of the black brothers, the real nature and real cause of the activity was communicated to every black community. (44)

The Panthers' belief that armed propaganda could provoke people to identify with them as the vanguard party caused them to seek to translate every visual encounter with the Panther ideology into a lived experience of the revolutionary utopian possibilities that ideology presented. In *Do It! Scenarios of the Revolution,* the Yippie leader Jerry Rubin would simply declare: "Revolution is theater in the streets. ... The Panther uniform—beret, black leather jacket, gun—helps create the Panther legend. Three Panthers on the street are an army of thousands" (142). The Panthers thus self-consciously presented individuals and images whose revolutionary representation would provoke the possibility of radical social change by creating an identification between the visual representation and the viewer. The Panthers used their iconic uniform and images of Newton as a nexus to trigger identification among people who would never wear such clothing and who would identify experiences such as Newton's incarceration as radically outside the realm of their own lives.

The Black Panther Party's emphasis on lower-class urban vernacular culture as the expression of "authentic" Blackness also validated Richard Pryor's own celebration of the aesthetics of a lower-class, urban African American vernacular. Pryor, who lampooned the very possibility of positive African American images in U.S. popular culture with the creation of the character of Clark Washington, "a mild-mannered custodian for the *Daily Planet*" who is able to transform into "Super Nigger," epitomizes the ambivalent possibilities for critical African American images in the post-segregation United States. On the cover of his self-titled 1968 album *Richard Pryor,* the comedian posed naked, mocking the portrayal of African people in magazines like *National Geographic.* The album, from its cover art to routines like "Super Nigger" and "T.V. Panel Show," provides a thorough critique of the overdetermination of African American representation in U.S. popular culture up to that point.

Pryor brilliantly mimicked the Panthers' popular rhetorical style and the unlikely fame they had found by 1968 through frequent appearances in mainstream American television in "T.V. Panel Show," which takes to absurd extremes the Panthers' ability to interject their ideology into even the most banal of settings:

Black nationalist: I got something to say, man. You dig? You cats been up here rapping and ain't got nothing to say about the real thing. ... You cats up here rapping about the Jews but what about me? What about my people?

T.V. Host: I don't believe anybody's said anything about the Jews.
Black nationalist: You will! You will!

The incongruity of the Panthers' message and the daytime talk-show format, and the obvious limitations of that setting are unmasked, and Pryor continues throughout the routine to foreground the Panthers' attention-getting rhetorical style, such as when the Black nationalist on the panel interrupts the other participant's discussion of religion to interject "God was a junkie, baby! He had to be a junkie to put up with all of this. You don't just walk around feeling nothing behind all of this."

The title of Pryor's popular 1976 album *Bicentennial Nigger* aimed squarely at African Americans' ambivalent position within U.S. symbolic culture and reflects on the status of the African American image in the socially and historically vexed year of the bicentennial celebration of the nation's founding, twelve years after the passage of the Civil Rights Act and ten years after the Black Panther Party's first major public action. By the release of the album, African American images were so soundly incorporated into U.S. popular culture that Pryor's album cover could chain together the litany of representational possibilities open to African Americans at this time, including a naked slave, an emphatic minister, a victorious boxer, a Civil War–era soldier, a Tuskegee airman, a Black revolutionary, a frightened sharecropper, a policeman, a funky hipster, and a Black businessman. The immediate readability that the album pre-supposes for these images testifies to the extent to which Black images had become a commonplace presence in the shifting terrain of dominant representation between the early 1960s and the late 1970s. While Jerry Rubin would declare that "revolution is theater in the streets" (132), the Panthers would attempt to make a revolution of the limitations of African American representation marked by Pryor's work.

After his sojourn in the San Francisco Bay Area, Pryor reappeared on the comedy scene with a radically reworked comedic persona that in-cluded references to the cost of the war in Vietnam, civil discontent, and police violence at home for African Americans, and provided, according to Mel Watkins, "a crucial breakthrough in African American stage humor" (544). Unlike many biographers of Pryor, who tend to attribute the pivotal change in his humor either to the realization of an individual genius or to a personal transformation that finally allowed him to locate himself within an authentic African American subjectivity that he had previously masked, Watkins sees the shift in Pryor's emphasis as reflective of a "shift in the African American mood" that allowed Pryor to build a fan base among "those under thirty-five, who were increasingly rejecting the traditional black middle-class tactic of de-emphasizing cultural differences between the races and embracing Black Power" (545). Attributing these changes to "militant new voices—the Black Panthers and Stokely Carmichael among others," Watkins concludes: "Pryor's switch to an outspoken Black voice occurred at precisely the right time" (545).

Within a shifting cultural climate made ripe for change by both the Civil Rights Movement and the popular urban unrest it had failed to contain, the Black Panther Party would work, like Richard Pryor, with both popular culture and a popular politics of discontent to challenge the dominant motifs of U.S. culture that spectacularized Black suffering and discontent. But while Pryor was largely content to "stir up more shit on stage than in a revolution" with his challenges to the limited parameters of African American representation, the Black Panther Party would seek to reshape those motifs into a radically aestheticized demand for social change. While Pryor would work through the comic absurdity of Black suffering in routines like "Wino and Junkie" and "Niggers vs. the Police,"[3] the Black Panther Party would push a program of "armed propaganda" aimed at demonstrating the necessity for armed struggle and also to argue for a violent visual and discursive moral persuasion that would move African Americans from a position of victimhood to a position of righteous indignation characterized by Carlos Marighella as the "moral superiority" that "sustains the urban guerilla" (47).

Marighella argued in *The Manual of the Urban Guerilla:* "Where the urban guerilla's weapons are inferior, he gains through moral superiority. In moral superiority the urban guerilla has undeniable superiority. ... Moral superiority allows the guerilla to attack and survive, and to succeed in his main objective" (47). The Panthers would turn Pryor's tragic/comic cry for the positive recognition of racial difference into an unapologetic cry for self-defense through a moral suasion that relied on intense identification provoked by its performance of vanguardism. Their model of identification was dependent on recreating African American identity around revolutionary action. In her autobiography, Assata Shakur explores her transformation from someone who shared the African American middle-class aspirations of the 1950s to a Black revolutionary throughout the 1960s and 1970s with the declaration: "I love Black people, I don't care what they are doing, but when Black people are struggling, that's when they are most beautiful to me" (189).

Seize the Time! Watts, Armed Self-Defense, and the Death of the Civil Rights Movement in California

For groups like the Black Panther Party, Ernesto "Che" Guevara's dictums, when taken together with the limited success of the Civil Rights Movement and the conditions of widespread social discontent following its failures, social revolution seemed not only possible but inevitable. Amiri Baraka notes the way in which the fertile political climate of the 1960s and 1970s had been created by earlier movements. In his account of the birth of the Black Arts Theater, Baraka writes about the way in which the vibrant postwar political culture was reflected in the street culture of Harlem:

> The older black nationalists always talked on their ladders across the street from the Hotel Theresa. Larger forums were held in front of Mr. Michaux's bookstore, called, affectionately, the House of Proper Propaganda. Malcolm had spoken in front of the store often and there was a sign in front of the store ringed by pan-African leaders from everywhere in the black world. (208)[4]

Nowhere did possible social revolution seem more plausible than in the symbolically, culturally, and politically loaded terrain of California. Though unrest would break out in cities across the United States throughout the 1960s, "the Watts Riots" in the Watts section of Los Angeles in August of 1965 would become the emblematic moment of racial unrest to which all other subsequent acts of urban discord would be compared. The uprising in Watts held unprecedented symbolic importance because

"Watts clashed with the entire organized white world as a collective organism," as Harold Cruse claimed in 1967 in *The Crisis of the Negro Intellectual* (384). For Black radicals like the Panthers, the violence of Watts seemed to be a powerful counterpoint to the symbolic successes of nonviolence as a political and cultural imperative. According to Cruse, "the sobering lessons of the Watts rebellion" enabled a change from a discourse of "self-defense" to a discourse of "guerilla warfare" among Black nationalist groups. This is symbolized in Cruse's argument by the evolving philosophy of revolution espoused by Robert Williams, whose political philosophies as articulated in *Negroes with Guns* (1962) were a major influence on the genesis and evolution of the Black Panther Party (Cruse, 386). Panther cofounder Bobby Seale even went so far as to characterize the party's first major action as "Niggers with Guns in the State Capitol" in *Seize the Time,* his 1968 history of the Black Panther Party (153).[5]

Williams, a local leader in a small chapter of the NAACP in Monroe, North Carolina, came to national prominence in the late 1950s when he began advocating that the organization reevaluate its stance on nonviolence and suggesting that it consider "meet[ing] violence with violence" (*Negroes with Guns,* 26). Like the Deacons for Defense, a group that had armed and organized for "Black self-defense" but ended up primarily providing armed protection for civil rights organizers, Williams constantly negotiated between a civil rights–style engagement with American culture and society and a desire to separate completely from American society and culture. This eventually resulted in his censure by the national leaders of the NAACP and exile, first in Cuba, where he befriended Castro and Guevara, and then in China as a guest of Mao Tse Tung.[6]

By 1967, according to Cruse's account, as a direct consequence of the Watts rebellion, Robert Williams began to essentially call for a foco-style revolution by advocating "a new concept of revolution [that] defies military science and tactics. The new concept is lightning campaigns conducted in highly sensitive urban communities with the paralysis reaching the small communities and spreading to the farm areas" (386). For African American radical organizers like Williams, Watts had begun to suggest the limitations of "the good society" of mainstream U.S. social reform and the "beloved community" of civil rights rhetoric. According to Cruse, the contradictions inherent in the embrace of guerilla warfare by the leader of an organization that had been created to defend the pro-integrationist aims of the Civil Rights Movement was typical of the ideological confusion experienced by African American intellectuals in the late 1960s. For poets, playwrights, critics, and cultural workers alike, Watts was a watershed moment that brought the civil rights tradition and its attendant mythology to crisis. For Cruse, Williams's embrace of Watts as providing the impetus for "guerilla warfare" foretold a dangerous trend in a African American radical culture, namely, the tendency to adopt the notion of guerilla warfare without fully exploring or creating the necessary conditions for its eventual success.

In California, the site of several defining moments of the student movement, including the Berkeley Free Speech Movement and the long-running student strikes at San Francisco State University, talk of revolution was so much part of the cultural and political discourse by 1968 that further preparation or exploration may have seemed completely unnecessary. Even the student struggles at San Francisco State, which began in late 1967 and required the intercession of then California governor Ronald Reagan and the appointment of two chancellors in as many years, had the symbolic violence of Watts at their core.

Students for a Democratic Society (SDS) organizer Todd Gitlin would claim of the student strikes at San Francisco State that "they began, as insurrection does in America, with the blacks" (298). Protests by the Black Student Union to contest the racist representation in the school's newspaper as well as the suspension of a popular instructor provided the literal but also symbolic impetus for a campuswide shutdown as the Black Student Union formed coalitions with other campus groups, including SDS, the Peace and Freedom Party, and members of the Experimental College. The student strikes grew so large and were so well sustained that Gitlin posited that the "flood might recede, but the countryside will be permanently changed" (298).

LAW AND ORDER AND BLACK POWER IN CONFLICT

By 1968, California also stood on the brink of transforming its prison system into one of the leading structures of what has come to be characterized as "the prison industrial complex."[7] The assassination of

Martin Luther King Jr. and the social unrest that ensued in urban centers throughout the United States brought the confrontation between the dream of a postsegregation culture and its early realities to the forefront of American culture. Nowhere was the conflict between the promises, the actually realizable potential of the Civil Rights Movement, and the intractability of American social and political culture better epitomized than in the clash between radical African American activist culture, which highlighted the police as an "occupying army" and prisons as "modern day slavery," and the culture of "law and order" as pioneered in California by U.S. president Richard Nixon, a former senator from California, and Ronald Reagan, who became governor of California in 1967, just as the Panthers were becoming a powerful force in U.S. public culture.[8] The rhetoric of law and order positioned African Americans firmly within a discourse of lawlessness and disorder that they had traditionally been assigned by the dominant culture. The Black Panther Party would radically reconfigure this discourse, restructuring the relationship between the African American outlaw figure and a romanticized notion of revolution to provoke identificatory possibilities across a broad spectrum of potential supporters. The Black Panther notion of vanguardism successfully created allies out of the formerly uninitiated and apolitical through the wide-ranging appeal of an ideology scripted through an easily decipherable iconic language of images: the raised fist, the black jacket and beret, and the gun.

The industrialization and modernization of California prison technology in conjunction with Nixon's national calls for law and order spawned a cultural climate and economic order that not only endorsed but actually required the incarceration of a large number of its citizenry in order to continue to function.[9] As the postwar booms in industrial production that had attracted large numbers of low-wage southern migrants to California began to fade, African Americans, who had made up the bulk of the southern migrants in what has come to be known as the Great Migration, became fodder for a growing prison system.

In 1978, the U.S. senator Edward Kennedy addressed the NAACP in a speech in which he called "the underclass" both "the great unmentioned problem of America today" and "a group in our midst, perhaps more dangerous, more bereft of hope, more difficult to confront, than any for which our history has known" (Lehman, 282). Kennedy's speech typifies the way in which urban African Americans were beginning to be demonized as an impending threat even by those who considered themselves proponents of the Civil Rights Movement. The growth of radical Black political movements in the 1960s and 1970s in California existed in an immediately confrontational relationship to the growth of a prison industry and a law-and-order culture, which was also radical in its ability to transform the culture of California and eventually the United States. The Black Panther Party's valorization of "the brother on the block" as a potential fighting force played into mainstream ideas about the threat that the urban African American underclass presented. However, the Panthers' desire to present themselves as the vanguard of the revolution, whose job it was to heuristically perform revolutionary behavior for a mass audience also incited an intense identification that ultimately cut across class and racial barriers, redefining the spectacle of urban poverty.

THE BLACK PANTHER PARTY, THE MEDIA, AND MILITARY ACTION

Though the Black Panther Party would become most strongly associated in its early years with its highly publicized actions to patrol the streets of Oakland in order to monitor police brutality, the party mobilized on multiple fronts. Two such examples include its involvement in local electoral politics, and the party's highly touted "survival programs," which featured screening programs for sickle cell anemia, free breakfast programs, and voter registration drives. The cultural war waged through the Black Panther Party's sophisticated understanding of and engagement with mass media and popular culture created a complex interplay between the radical culture and mainstream American popular culture that it both courted and was courted by. This relationship was simplified and parodied by Tom Wolfe as "radical chic" in his best-selling *Radical Chic and Mau-Mauing the Flak Catchers* (1970) and was also harshly critiqued by Maulana Karenga and his US Organization, the Kuumba Collective, and other cultural nationalists.[10] Much of the contemporary misunderstanding of the Black Panther Party's place in American popular culture and its continuing legacy revolves around the thorny questions of representation, appropriation, and commodification raised by its engagement with American popular and political culture and its embrace of vanguardist philosophy as espoused by Che Guevara, Regis Debray, and Fidel Castro.

Though the specific media training of the early members was limited to cofounder Bobby Seale's professional experience as a stand-up comedian, from the very beginning, the Oakland chapter of the Black Panther Party organized around actions meant to have a specific symbolic cachet that could be easily read when transmitted through dominant media. Seale was working in one of the Johnson administration's Poverty Program job-training offices when he and Huey P. Newton conceived of the Black Panther Party and proceeded to draft the Ten-Point Program after hours in the office on 16 October 1966 (Seale, 59).[11] Newton and Seale met while students at Merritt Junior College in Oakland. Both were active in campus organizing initially in the Afro-American Association, a group organized primarily around the study of African American culture, and later in a breakaway group called the Soul Students Advisory Council. The historian Jeffrey O. G. Ogbar notes the influence of the Revolutionary Action Movement (RAM), which was initially organized on college campuses by African American students involved in SDS, on students like Newton and Seale. Ogbar labels the Soul Students Advisory Council "a RAM front organization" (84). "RAM never attracted the media attention of SNCC or the Panthers," Ogbar notes, and Seale writes that he and Newton became disenchanted with what they perceived as the group's inability to translate their radical political vision off campus to the "brothers on the block" (78). From the beginning, the actions of the Oakland Black Panther Party showed a flair for the audacious and dramatic and a connection to everyday culture. On 21 February 1967, the first real year of action for the fledgling Black Panther Party, the group organized a security detail for the highly publicized visit of Betty Shabazz, the widow of Malcolm X, to the San Francisco Bay Area. The group caught the eye of the Bay Area radical community, including the future high-profile Panther party member Eldridge Cleaver, who would remember as formative to his political education the moment when the Panthers' security detail clashed with police over their refusal to disarm, citing their constitutional right to bear arms (*Post-Prison Writings and Speeches*, 23). A couple of months later, on 27 April 1967, the Panthers released the first crude issue of *Black Panther Community News,* which focused on community outrage over the police murder of an unarmed Black teenager named Denzil Dowell during an alleged arrest attempt in nearby Richmond, California.[12]

Less than a month later, on 2 May 1967, party members garnered national attention when they arrived fully armed on the steps of the state capitol in Sacramento, temporarily diverting media attention from a planned meeting on the capitol grounds between Governor Ronald Reagan and youth groups to Bobby Seale, who read "In Defense of Self-Defense: Executive Mandate Number One," a piece written by Newton in support of the right to bear arms (Seale, 153–55). Because of the strategic and sensational staging and the presence of the media for the youth event, this moment began to form the party's national media profile as not only "armed and extremely dangerous" but also a political force to be reckoned with even though the group was still relatively small at this point. By 29 June 1967, it had consolidated its image as an organization deserving of a national platform—so much so that it was able to name Stokely Carmichael as the "Field Marshall of the Black Panther Party" (Charles E. Jones, 53). Carmichael had been chair of the Student Nonviolent Coordinating Committee (SNCC), one of the most high-profile and radical groups of the coalition of groups that constituted the Civil Rights Movement, when in 1966 it decided to expel its white members in a move to redefine itself as a Black Power group. Highly charismatic, Carmichael was so renowned for his propensity to manipulate media attention that he was nicknamed "Stokely Starmichael" in radical circles.

The Black Panther Party's major action of 1967, which was not strictly tied to the creation of images of militancy and potential power for the group but also had a military component, was the creation of the party's Community Police Patrols, in which armed groups of Panthers patrolled the streets of Oakland in order to provide protection for ordinary citizens against the threat of police violence during traffic stops and arrests.[13] But even these patrols were intended more as guerilla theater than guerilla action, because the confrontation between the Panthers and the police was meant to instruct those who witnessed the confrontations that the police were not above reproach. In the film *Black Panther,* Eldridge Cleaver offers an explanation of why confrontations with the police became the Black Panther Party's primary performative moment for the symbolic staging of their ideology:

You don't find a guy just remaining the same after really seeing the Panthers. The guys on the block out there, they have never been too impressed by America, by what's been happening. They're not too impressed by that. But they're going to stand there in fear of the cops. This is one of the reasons the Black Panther Party focused on the cops, because the cops are out there and visible. This is the direct contact that Black people have with the white power structure, when the Man, the Pig comes down and bothers them. Here comes two niggers with some guns who step out and talk to the cops just the way they've been talked to. People notice that.

The film, which was created to showcase the Panther platform, established the party's other key visual signifiers by cutting directly from Cleaver's explanation of why the group chose confrontation with the police as their primary performative moment to images of uniformed Panther men and women marching in formation, fists upraised, groups of Panther women chanting the party's slogans, and party members lining the steps of the Alameda courthouse. This visual imagery would become as widely associated with the party as the police patrols because it so successfully translated the Black Panther critique of the justice system in the United States into an easily accessible, visual, symbolic language that still circulates with relevance today, even to those who no longer have access to the party's original Ten-Point Platform.

Free Huey! Mobilizing the Image for Social Change

The arrest of Huey P. Newton on 28 October 1967 inadvertently provided the pivotal symbolic moment around which Panther critique and organizing would focus for the next three years, for Newton's image would be deployed to consolidate support for the notion that unjust police repression justified the necessity for revolution.[14] Newton and Glenn McKinney were driving home from a party late at night in Oakland when their car was stopped by a police cruiser. A firefight broke out: it left Newton critically injured, one police officer dead, and a second injured. Newton was later arrested and charged with a number of felonies, including attempted murder. For the Panthers, Newton's trial would provide the perfect performative moment to stage their dissent. Elaine Brown would write of 1967: "It was the year 'Free

Huey' erupted as a kind of universal battle cry that J. Edgar Hoover openly pronounced: 'The Black Panther Party is the single greatest threat to the internal security of the United States'. ... Huey Newton had become more than just another leader of a black organization. He was the symbol of change for Americans questioning everything sacred to the American way of life" (237). The "Free Huey" campaign would provide not only the organizing opportunity for the coalescence of an international movement, making the Panthers objects of admiration for radicals around the world, but it would also allow the relationship between theatrical militancy and radical dissent that had been inherent in the Panthers from the beginning to emerge. Through the movement to free him from incarceration, Newton's image would become synonymous with radical dissent and vanguardist leadership.

In December 1967, the Panthers, in a coalition with the Peace and Freedom Party, an antiwar group based in Berkeley, coined the slogan "Free Huey," which would become an international rallying cry for the campaign of the same name. The group chose 17 February, Newton's birthday, to stage a large rally as a precursor to demonstrations at the trial (Seale, 208– 10). Several thousand people gathered to listen to prominent members of the Student Nonviolent Coordinating Committee and the Panthers, including Stokely Carmichael, H. Rap Brown, James Foreman, and Eldridge and Kathleen Cleaver. In keeping with the vanguardist philosophy of the Panthers, they both spoke about the particulars of Newton's case and used Newton as a vector for understanding the situation of African Americans in general. Stokely Carmichael reminded the crowd: "We're here to celebrate brother Huey P. Newton's birthday. We're not here to celebrate it as Huey Newton the individual, but as Huey Newton parcel of black people wherever we are on the world today. ... And so, in talking about brother Huey Newton tonight, we have to talk about the struggle of black people, not only in the United States, but in the *world* today" ("Free Huey Rally Speech"). Standing under large photographs of Newton, Carmichael continued to insist on the heuristic value of Newton's experience of incarceration, which he collapsed into the experience of Black people in general by claiming: "We must develop an undying love as is personified in brother Huey P. Newton. Undying love for our people. If we do not do that then we will be wiped out." For Carmichael, Newton personified Guevara's demand that "the guerilla fighter as a social reformer should not only provide an example in his own life but he ought also constantly to give orientation in ideological problems" (34). As Huey P. Newton's image became the nexus for vanguardist identification, the Black Panther Party quickly became the spectacle through which the experience of revolution could be translated into what the party would label the "brother on the block" or "the lumpen proletariat."[15]

The austere setting of the rally, which resembled a political meeting more than a birthday party, provided a stark contrast to the explosive rhetoric and animated theatrics of the speakers, many of whom were renowned for their ability to stir crowds in the best tradition of African American oratory. H. Rap Brown asked the crowd: "How many white folks you kill today?" reminding them: "You are revolutionaries! Che Guevara says they only two ways to leave the battlefield: victorious or dead. Huey's in jail! That's no victory" ("Free Huey Rally Speech"). Carmichael reiterated the relationship between policing and state control: "They make us fight; they make us steal; they judge us; they put us in prison; they parole us; they send us out; they pick us up again. Where, in God's name, do we exercise any sense of dignity in this country?" ("Free Huey Rally Speech").

The speakers' invocation of the struggle of Huey P. Newton against the police and justice system was in keeping with Che Guevara's dictum in *Guerilla Warfare:* "The people must be shown that social wrongs are not going to be redressed by civil means alone" (111). Brown and Carmichael hoped to use the incarceration of Newton to incite revolution against what they saw as a growing police state. Newton's image would become an iconic shorthand that translated his personal struggles with the police, the court system, and his lengthy incarceration into a treatise on Panther ideology. Organizers of the event hoped to transform the "talk about law and order" into talk about "justice in America," as Carmichael urged, and also to transform discourse about revolution into actual revolution by provoking an increase in Black Panther Party membership as an initial means of securing the "progressive radicalization" that Guevara spoke of as a necessary step toward revolution (81). Earl Anthony, who was only the eighth person to join the party, claims that at the time of the Free Huey Rally, "there were still, actually, only about thirty hardcore members; the Free Huey Campaign would be the ticket to flood the membership rolls" (*Spitting in the Wind,* 43). Between Newton's arrest and trial, membership in the Black Panther Party mushroomed so much that when the actual trial began on 15 July, more than 450 Black Panther Party members were present and over 5,000 spectators ringed the Alameda County Courthouse in what was to become a daily, ritualized display of chants, marches, singing, speeches, and slogans throughout the length of the trial.

CULTURE AS CONDUIT OF REVOLUTIONARY CHANGE

When images of the courthouse reached the world via the televisual news-media, print media, and alternative journalism, the Black Panther Party successfully transformed the courthouse from its representative role as a vehicle for state power into a theater for the display of a spectacular blackness that was potent in its presentation and seemingly potentially revolutionary in its consequences. The moment the Panthers triumphantly transformed the courthouse into a site for contestation of law-and-order ideology in image culture would become emblematic for the successes of the Black Panther Party, whose biggest victories would largely continue in the terrain of the symbolic through a transformation of image culture in relation to notions of race, power, and potential in the United States.

The conflict between the group's stated goal to become a potential vehicle for "self-defense" and military action along the lines of *Guerilla Warfare,* and the more political or social-reform agendas inherent in its decision to organize as a political "party" with political education goals was present from the start. This tension is apparent even in the potentially contradictory name the group almost gave itself: "The Black Panther Party for Self-Defense." The conflict between those who saw the group as a possible vehicle for radical military intervention and those who saw it as a vehicle for political education, and, therefore, a more potentially social reformist platform, would be a constant and growing problem as the years brought ever increasing levels of governmental and police repression.

The Black Panther Party would successfully, spectacularly appropriate U.S. image culture to their own advantage when they managed to literally "Free Huey" from prison when all charges against him were dropped on 5 August 1970. But had they achieved what Che Guevara outlined as "the essence of guerilla warfare," "the miracle by which a small nucleus of men— looking beyond their immediate tactical objective—becomes the vanguard of a mass movement, achieving its ideals, establishing a new society, ending the ways of the old, and winning social justice" (*Guerilla Warfare,* 114)? At the Free Huey Rally, Stokely Carmichael stressed to the audience that revolution would only be possible through "organizing our people and orienting them towards an African ideology which speaks to our blackness," but the exact relationship between armed struggle and the struggle for a liberated African American radical culture was never clearly articulated by Guevara, Debray, Castro, or the Panthers themselves. They would repeatedly decry those whom they labeled "cultural nationalists," mostly notably the US Organization, a Los Angeles–based group led by Maulana Karenga.

The rivalry between the Panthers and US would eventually lead to an armed confrontation over the direction of the Black studies program on the campus of UCLA on 17 January 1967. During this confrontation, John Huggins and Alprentice "Bunchy" Carter, important leaders in the Southern California chapter of the Black Panther Party, were killed.[16] Scholars such as Ward Churchill, Jim Vander Wall, and Kenneth O'Reilly, as well as Panther accounts of the period, have documented how the conflict between the Panthers and the US Organization was targeted and inflamed by the FBI under COINTELPRO, but with or without FBI interference, a lack of clarity over the role that the cultural struggle would play in the armed struggle was all too real for the Panthers.[17] Newton would repeatedly contrast what he labeled "cultural nationalism" or "pork chop nationalism" with "revolutionary nationalists," which included the Black Panther Party. According to him, cultural nationalists "feel the African culture will automatically bring political freedom," which could potentially lead to political leaders who "oppress the people but ... promote the African culture"; in contrast, he continued, the Panthers "believe that culture itself will not liberate us. We're going to need some stronger stuff" ("Correct Handling," 50). For the Black Panther Party, the "stronger stuff" was the promotion of an armed struggle through the creation of a dynamic image culture. Ironically, the Panther image culture proved to be such a powerful complement to the party's vanguardist politics that its images would eventually eclipse the party's actual political presence.

Feelings of ambiguity with regard to gains made in the cultural realm were exacerbated by the Panthers' relative success in that realm versus their relative failure to convert those gains into genuine gains in a popular armed struggle. This became especially problematic as violence around the Panthers intensified after the inception of the "Free Huey" campaign in 1967. According to Russell Shoats, "The Panthers were a potentially strong Black fighting formation that was forced to take to the field before they were ready [because they chose a] high-profile operation, characteristic of the Civil Rights Movement, that relied heavily on television, radio, and print media" (5,7). Consequently, Shoats says, the Panthers floundered "as groups tried to combine the activities of the political and military workers in one cadre" (5).

To view the Panthers' high level of engagement with popular media culture simply as a strategic mistake that preceded immense military and political failures, as Shoats does, not only paints a limited portrait of the Panthers' contribution to U.S. society and culture but also puts unnecessary limitations on what constitutes political and cultural change. The Black Panther Party evinced a more sophisticated understanding of the relationship between African Americans and American popular culture and the centrality of visual culture to African American cultural life than they were or are often given credit for. Examinations of the Black Panther Party legacy continue to be guided by misunderstandings of the central role of cultural work in the Panther struggle, and the Panthers are frequently painted as the victims, unwilling dupes, or scheming manipulators of American media culture. From their first appearance on the front page of the *New York Times* in a photograph showing several Panthers brandishing firearms at the California Statehouse and the inception of the party's official newspaper, the Black Panther Party created an especially sophisticated relationship to broadcast and print media that acknowledged the incipient possibilities for disruption existing in a burgeoning mainstream visual media culture. By doing so, they were able to create a canon of images, slogans, and gestures that codified these symbols into an iconic language of revolution.

The Black migration into northern urban centers paralleled the movement of Black images into mainstream visual culture via television culture; Melvin Patrick Ely has characterized African American presence in postwar television culture as "the Great Black Migration into America's living room" (64). The Panthers were successful in seizing television culture, one of the most important arbiters of public opinion during the Civil Rights Movement and early postsegregation era, and were unquestionably more successful than Karenga and the US Organization or any other organization of the era in manipulating the cultural order against Nixon's notion of law and order.

The Civil Rights Movement's ideology of nonviolence held an obvious appeal for most Americans, but from the onset of the "Free Huey" campaign, the Black Panther Party successfully conveyed the notion that armed struggle was not only justifiable for African Americans but, in fact, mandated by the treatment of African Americans in the United States. In a certain sense, they were successful precisely because they utilized both the romance and the threat of violence endemic to constructions of Blackness in the United States to win support for their cultural war against the notion of law-and-order culture, even though they could never really fulfill either the role of romantic revolutionary or violent impending threat. Their tremendous success in seeming to convince popular culture of the necessity of a mandate against law-and-order culture would be mocked by those who insisted on downplaying gains made by the party in the cultural realm: thus, party members were dubbed "media star revolutionaries," and much focus was placed on the party's inability or unwillingness to be seen as simply fulfilling the role of revolutionary hero or being a dangerous threat.

The Panther Look A Visual Language for Social Change

In "Afro Images: Politics, Fashion, Nostalgia," Angela Davis herself writes of the manner in which the current circulation of images associated with her political work from the 1960s and 1970s often occurs without reference to its origins in Black radical politics. After an encounter with a young man who directly identifies her with the Afro hairstyle that she wore throughout the 1960s, Davis ruminates, "It is both humiliating and humbling to discover that a single generation after the events that constructed me as a public personality, I am remembered as a hairdo. It is humiliating because it reduces a politics of liberation to a politics of fashion; it is humbling because such encounters with a younger generation demonstrate the fragility and mutability of historical images, especially those associated with African American history" (29). Davis is most deeply disturbed when reconstructed images from her time as a fugitive appear along with images of Che Guevara in a fashion spread of a popular music magazine, "emptied of all content so that it can serve as a commodified backdrop for advertising." For Davis, the mutability of such images is a particular problem because it allows for the specific details of African American radical historicity to be unfixed in such a way that lays it open for a troubling nostalgia. This nostalgia offers a romantic vision of the past that is in the end highly commodifiable.

For Davis's account, the commodification of social movements is a contemporary phenomenon associated with a commodified nostalgia that exists in the place of what might be a more genuine historical memory. According to Davis, the recirculation of the images from the 1960s and 1970s radical culture testifies to the strength of those images to continue to speak in myriad ways to audiences removed from the direct political reality that they portray, but she insists on maintaining a strict boundary between commodification and politicization that risks perpetuating a nostalgia of its own for a political era free of the trivialization and commodification of the raw material of historicity by market forces. This nostalgia for an era "back in the day when everyone was Black and conscious / Freedom was at hand and you could just taste it," as a contemporary song puts it,[18] ignores the ways in which contemporary nostalgia was in fact created and enabled by the visual politics of vanguardism that dominated the radical culture of the time.

Black radical culture of the 1960s and 1970s would continually seek out and define the symbolic language and visual tools that could convey the potential for social and political revolution to African Americans who had grown used enough to oppression to incorporate it into even the everyday language of humor as Richard Pryor had done. The transformation of the symbolic artifacts of everyday culture into potent political symbols was perhaps achieved most consistently by the Black Panther Party, but Angela Davis's Afro spoke as powerfully as their leather jackets and raised fists of the climate of repression and disappointment during the early postsegregation period. Taken together, these symbols created an iconography whose power lay much more in its translatability to commodity culture than in its distance from it.

A vision of the 1960s and 1970s radical culture as one of pure politics free from commodification fails to recognize the complicated role the Black Panther Party played in perpetuating their own mystique throughout commodity culture. Angela Davis's Afro, with which she is now so deeply identified and to which she so greatly regrets being reduced, was cultivated as much for its dramatic performative ability to speak a reductive symbolic political language in a vanguardist manner as "the Panther look." Far from being simple media opportunists, many of the Panthers saw the wide dissemination of their example across U.S. culture as the radical mandate of a vanguard party to model revolutionary behavior. Huey Newton, who seemed to understand the Black Panther Party's primary role as that of educating through symbolic action rather than leading an actual armed insurrection, made it clear in his writings that he believed symbolic action could provide instruction that far outlasted both the action and the teacher.

In "The Correct Handling of the Revolution," Newton emphasized the importance of creating moments of dynamic performative action that would then create the visual symbols that would become shorthand instructions for other revolutionary actions: "The brothers in East Oakland learned from Watts a means of resistance. ... The first man who threw a Molotov cocktail is not personally known by the masses, but yet the action was respected and followed by the people. If the activities of the Party are respected by the people, the people will follow the example. This is the primary job of the Party" (41). At no time, however, did Newton or the Black Panther Party in general limit their notion of "action" to military action in the streets. While Newton and the party's minister of culture Emory Douglas, a skilled illustrator, placed particular emphasis on the creation and circulation of nontextual visual representations of the Black Panther Party, there were other equally significant nonvisual articulations of it. These ranged from Panther songs and slogans from Elaine Brown's album dedicated to the party, to the chants and slogans created for demonstrations such as "Black is Beautiful / Free Huey!" and "No more brothers in jail / The Pigs are gonna catch hell," which successfully imprinted the party ideology onto American popular culture.

One of the most consistently circulated articulations of the Black Panther Party ideology, however, was the party's official newspaper, the *Black Panther.* In his memoir *This Side of Glory,* David Hilliard records how the paper's prominence quickly grew after Emory Douglas, a skilled graphic artist and illustrator, joined the party: "In a short time, the paper becomes the most visible, most constant symbol of the Party, its front page a familiar sight at every demonstration and in every storefront-window organizing project throughout the country" (149).[19] The paper's circulation eventually grew so large, Hilliard records, that it would at times become the primary source of income for the Oakland chapter of the party (154).

Serving both to provide information and to promote the party, the *Black Panther* combined graphic images of police brutality and urban black misery with uplifting illustrations and textual analysis of events in American popular and political culture. In the 19 June 1971 issue are found an article on the lack of scientific research on sickle cell anemia; a lengthy analysis of the film *Sweet Sweetback's Baadasssss Song!* that includes movie stills alongside illustrations by Douglas; a press statement on the Richmond Five; and an article on and picture of Jo Etha Collier, a young Black woman killed while celebrating her graduation from the white high school in Drew, Mississippi, that she had integrated. The careful mélange of popular and political culture in the *Black Panther* suggests how the party would successfully operate within popular culture to create an enduring critique of U.S. culture in general. At the same time, this mix also suggests how the Black Panther Party's investment in popular culture would leave it open to co-option and appropriation by the same commodity forces driving the popular culture that it critiqued.

Material from the early days of the Oakland chapter of the Black Panther Party, now archived in the Dr. Huey P. Newton Foundation Collection held in Palo Alto by Stanford University, suggests the seemingly limitless extent of the creative nature of its engagement with American popular culture. Whereas Panther efforts to imprint the notion of Black Power and an end to police brutality through the newspaper and rallies is widely known, the extent and sophistication of their engagement with popular culture is not.

In *This Side of Glory,* Hilliard makes brief mention of "large contributions" and "remunerative book deals" as important sources of income for the Black Panther Party (154). The extent of its financial dealings and the sophistication of its interaction with popular culture, however, is not generally acknowledged or explored in the numerous Panther autobiographies and writings about the party. The control of the lucrative book contracts of the prison activist George Jackson, who was seen as a movement martyr; the creation of films to document the Panther struggle and prominent members of the party; and plans for the creation of an Eldridge Cleaver watch dispel myths that members of the Black Panther Party were unaware, unwitting pawns in their interaction with the American culture industry. The name of the entity created to oversee the economic interests of the party demonstrates that the Panthers fully understood the ambiguous nature of such ventures. Elaine Brown notes that Huey P. Newton created "Stronghold Incorporated" as "a one-word idea that captured what the Party intended to erect inside the walls of the citadel of capitalism" (244).

In his final will and testament, George Jackson directed that "anything that I may in capitalist terms seem to possess should be passed on as directed below to further my political ideals." At the time of his death at the hands of California corrections officers in an alleged escape attempt in 1971, he had risen from the ranks of California's ever-growing anonymous prison population to become one of the most widely recognized prison rights activists, and the group best situated to further those ideas was the Black Panther Party. Jackson directed all the proceeds from his latest book, *Blood in My Eye*, to "the Black Panther Survival Programs through the Berkeley Branch of the Black Panther Party." Jackson had already authored one of the most widely circulated antiprison manifestos in contemporary American history, *Soledad Brother*, and publishers were anticipating equal success for *Blood in My Eye*. Contractual records show that in 1971 Random House agreed to pay $100,000 in advance royalties for the book to the party, which also controlled the rights to Jackson's other work and was actively negotiating for the Spanish and Norwegian rights to *Soledad Brother*.[20]

Members of the Black Panther Party have long been portrayed as "media star revolutionaries," but facts like these that attest to the extent to which the party actively, successfully sought and controlled media attention as a means to spread its message are often ignored. During the most active years of the Black Panther Party, Huey P. Newton and Bobby Seale authored texts that would be as widely circulated as *Blood in My Eye*. The party was also involved in several attempts to document the ideology on film, in *Black Panther* and *May Day Panther*, which were created by the Third World Newsreel Collective. The party was also involved with American Documentary Films in the creation and distribution of the films *Stagolee: A Conversation with Bobby Seale in Prison* and *Huey!* and it participated in the creation of a documentary on the 17 February 1968 "Free Huey" Rally by Agnes Varda, an important director of the French New Wave film movement. In this same period, the critically renowned San Francisco Mime Troupe produced a piece with the cooperation of the party that centered on the court trials of Newton and Seale.[21] Collaborative book and film deals were just one means by which the party increased visibility, controlled and circulated its image, and generated income to further and continue its efforts.

Brian Ward records the significant inability of civil rights organizations to successfully utilize recording culture to either translate their message musically or to profitably produce and distribute recordings of various movement events, such as the 1963 March on Washington (268–75).[22] The Black Panther Party, with far fewer connections to established cultural venues, was able to do this and much more, authorizing recordings of various party members and events and producing (among others) *Huey! / Listen Whitey!* an album that placed a recitation of the Ten-Point Platform next to reactions to the murder of Martin Luther King Jr. recorded during a live radio call-in show. The party also successfully promoted benefit concerts at which their own band, the Lumpen, or other progressive, more established groups, such as the Grateful Dead, might perform.[23] Members of the Black Panther Party had a notorious run-in with Ike and Tina Turner at one such event, which culminated in a series of threats and lawsuits.

Reflecting their deep investment in and understanding of American popular culture, the party created a series of greeting cards featuring the images of the more prominent members of the party; they also at one time planned to market an official "Seize the Time" Panther watch featuring a picture of Eldridge Cleaver with arms outstretched, pointing time with a raised gun as one watch hand and an upraised finger as the other.[24] Like the slogan "Black is Beautiful," these items reflect a complex understanding of the deep influence of lived, everyday culture on people's political, social, and cultural perceptions and represent the party's attempts to insinuate itself successfully into popular consumer culture.

Such participation in the commodified arena of American popular culture, as Angela Davis has pointed out, would facilitate the Panthers' work against the state but also its absorption by it. Recent attempts by former Panthers to market everything from a cookbook to hot sauce seem to mock the party's countercultural stance and legacy, but complicated issues around an item such as the "Seize the Time" watch existed from the earliest days of the party as it attempted to negotiate both contesting and flourishing in U.S. aesthetic and political culture.[25] Does it matter that Bell Time, the company that proposed to make the watch, offered similar watches with the face of Moshe Dayan, Israel's minister of defense, while the Black Panther Party staunchly supported the efforts of the Palestine Liberation Organization? Or that the company also offered a P.I.G. watch featuring the image of a pig in a police uniform that the party had popularized along with the slogan *P* for Pride, *I* for Integrity, and *G* for Guts, which was advertised as being "endorsed and worn by law enforcement agencies throughout the USA"?[26] Did the commodification of such images as an armed and belligerent Cleaver cheapen the complexity of his writings even as those images simplified and promoted certain party stances? Whether such a strategy of commodification of its ideology best served the interests of the Panthers or the forces that brought down the party is disputable. What is not in question, however, is the fact that through carefully crafting and circulating its image, the Black Panther Party enabled its critique of the criminal justice system to live and grow long after the demise of the party itself, ultimately allowing it to continue to serve the teaching function that Newton had originally intended as its primary role.

NOTES

1. In *Revolutionary Suicide,* party cofounder Huey P. Newton listed Che Guevara's *Guerilla Warfare,* along with Frantz Fanon's *The Wretched of the Earth* and the collected works of Mao Tse-Tung, as the books he and Bobby Seale "pored over" when initially conceiving the idea for the Black Panther Party (111), and cofounder Bobby Seale cited the same list of sources for the party's ideology in *Seize the Time* (82).

2. In *On The Real Side,* his landmark study of African American comedy, Mel Watkins lists Cecil Brown, Ishmael Reed, Al Young, Claude Brown, and David Henderson as the Bay Area writers and intellectuals who influenced Pryor in these years (541). Richard Pryor cites these literary figures as well but also significantly includes "characters worse than me," including "really scary people like Huey Newton," though he insists, "Newton didn't bother me" (*Pryor Convictions,* 119–20).

3. "God Is a Junkie" is on the album *Super Nigger* (Loose Cannon Records, 1982); "Super Nigger" is on *Richard Pryor* (Dove/Reprise Records, 1968); and "Wino and Junkie" and "Niggers vs. the Police" are on *That Nigger's Crazy* (Partee/Stax, 1974).

4. Amiri Baraka documents the social, cultural, and political atmosphere that contributed to the rise of Black Power in *The Autobiography of Leroi Jones.*

5. Huey P. Newton also cites *Negroes with Guns* as "a great influence on the kind of party we developed" in *Revolutionary Suicide,* his account of the creation of the Black Panther Party (112).

6. Timothy Tyson chronicles Robert Williams's history from the formation of the Monroe, North Carolina, chapter of the NAACP to his exile in Cuba in *Radio Free Dixie.*

7. The term "prison industrial complex" has its origins in the New Left critique of the military industrial complex—the creation of an industry around the proliferation of armed conflicts and interventions involving the United States (see A. Davis, "What Is the Prison Industrial Complex?").

8. Huey P. Newton outlined the relationship between the California state government, police brutality, and the Black community in "In Defense of Self-Defense: Executive Mandate Number One" (40). The relationship between policing and government oppression is also articulated by Seale and Newton in the "Ten Point Program," three points of which directly address the criminal justice system and focus particularly on issues of policing and courtroom justice.

9. California has the highest incarceration rate in the United States, and the United States has had the highest rates of incarceration in the world since the late 1980s (see Schlosser, "Prison Industrial Complex").

10. The Kuumba Collective, a Chicago-based art and cultural collective, issued an official response to an edition of the Black Panther newspaper that was largely devoted to celebrating the film *Sweet Sweetback's Baadasssss Song!* as a "black community event" (Newton, *To Die for the People,* 146). The collective remarks, "We don't know what film Huey Newton watched (or any other perverted, confused, or badly misguided folks who agree with him). … In terms of black aesthetics, 'Sweetback' fails an essential principle—that black art must be functional." The Kuumba Collective specifically criticized the film's graphic violent and sexual content and its glorification of street life. The collective characterized several of the scenes as "more fit for stag films—to be shown to white people— than as part of any film for black people" (Kumba Collective, unpublished position paper, Dr. Huey P. Newton Foundation Collection, Stanford University Special Collections, Palo Alto, CA).

11. Seale's *Seize the Time* provides a detailed account of the early history of the Black Panther Party.

12. The official history of the paper is given in "The Black Panther: Mirror of the People" (see Foner, *Black Panthers Speak,* 8–14). David Hilliard also speaks at length about the creation and daily importance of the paper in his autobiography, *This Side of Glory,* and Mumia Abu-Jamal mentions the paper's importance in helping to educate and coalesce Panther ideology for Panther recruits in *We Want Freedom* (111–14).

13. Huey P. Newton details the community patrols in his autobiography, *Revolutionary Suicide* (120–27). Bobby Seale discusses the formation and implementation of the patrols at length in *Seize the Time* (85–99), and David Hilliard writes about the patrols in relation to the formation of the party and their effect on the community in *This Side of Glory* (117–19).

14. The details of Newton's arrest and his trial are provided by Edward M. Keating, a member of Newton's legal defense team, in *Free Huey!*

15. Newton devotes an entire chapter of *Revolutionary Suicide* to "the brother on the block" as an integral force in the Black Panther Party (73–78). Chris Booker considers the "lumpenization" of the party its "critical error," claiming, "The criminal element within the lumpen developed a modus operandi that created a sociocultural milieu inimical to a stable political organization" ("Lumpenization," 38).

16. Elaine Brown gives a detailed account of the incident in her autobiography, *Taste of Power.* Huey P. Newton contends that the shooting was carried out by two FBI informants, who were subsequently convicted and sentenced to prison but, according to Newton, were allowed to escape and were never apprehended (*Revolutionary Suicide*, 78–81). Ward Churchill and Jim Vander Wall discuss the murder of Huggins and Carter in relation to the effective propaganda campaign created by the FBI's Counter Intelligence Program (COINTELPRO) to foment dissent between radical Black activist groups in Los Angeles (*Agents of Repression*, 42–43).

17. COINTELPRO was the code name for actions taken by the Federal Bureau of Investigations Counter Intelligence Program to disrupt a wide array of political groups between 1940 and 1971 through the now infamous use of often illegal tactics ranging from organized harassment and wiretaps to outright assassination (Churchill and Vander Wall, *Agents of Repression*, 37–39).

18. Me'Shell NdegéOcello, "I'm Diggin' You (Like an Old Soul Record)," *Plantation Lullabies* (Warner Brothers, 1993).

19. *This Side of Glory* provides an important firsthand account of the paper's significance to the party.

20. The Random House contract with the Black Panther Party and Mary Clemmy's 24 January 1972 letter to Huey Newton can be found in the Dr. Huey P. Newton Foundation Collection, Stanford University Special Collections, Palo Alto, CA.

21. John Holden, Agreement between San Francisco Mime Troupe and the Black Panther Party, 2 October 1970, Dr. Huey P. Newton Foundation Collection, Stanford University Special Collections, Palo Alto, CA.

22. From 1964 to 1970, SNCC members published a newsletter called the *Movement,* SNCC's closest equivalent to the *Black Panther.* Even a brief comparison of the two demonstrates the relative sophistication of the Black Panther Party's use of this type of mass media in comparison with that of established civil rights organizations. The *Black Panther* is professionally typeset, with professionally rendered illustrations and photographs; most of the work was done in-house by party members themselves, and the paper was able to maintain a fairly consistently large national distribution. The *Movement,* in comparison, never had more than a limited circulation and more closely resembled a high school newspaper than a national newsweekly. C. T. Vivian writes that "publicity was of the highest strategic importance" in winning the hearts and minds of the general public to the cause of civil rights, but the focus of movement strategists tended to be on using mainstream media to reveal the horrors of segregation. The Black Panther Party borrowed that technique from the Civil Rights Movement but also went further in attempting to use other avenues available in popular culture. For example, Brian Ward highlights "the difficulties faced by enthusiastic but inexperienced SNCC members when they attempted to take their beg-steal-and-borrow fundraising philosophy into the cutthroat world of commercial entertainment and record production" (qtd. in Clayborne, 270). The Black Panther Party was also inexperienced, but it managed to create a far more professional product in almost every instance than comparable civil rights organizations.

23. Panther ideology was also successfully disseminated through the posters that advertised various party events, many examples of which are available in the Dr. Huey P. Newton Foundation Collection at Stanford University, including the Assassinated Malcolm X Poster of 21 February 1971 and the Revolutionary Intercommunal Day of Solidarity [with] Bobby Seale, Erika

Huggins, Angela Davis, Ruchell Magee and Post-Birthday Celebration for Huey P. Newton, 5 March 1971.

24. Both the greeting cards and the Eldridge Cleaver watch are in the Dr. Huey P. Newton Foundation Collection, Stanford University Special Collections, Palo Alto, CA.

25. The watch was to be produced by the Bell Time Company, a wing of the Dirty Time Company, the novelty watch company that also produced the high-selling "Spiro Agnew Watch" (see Donald A. Marton's letter to the Black Panther Ministry of Information, 12 July 1971, Dr. Huey P. Newton Foundation Collection, Stanford University Special Collections, Palo Alto, CA). For a discussion of how the Huey Newton Foundation trademarked the slogan "Burn, Baby Burn" in order to use it to market hot sauce, see Rick DelVecchio, "Black Panthers Hot Again," *San Francisco Chronicle,* 20 July 2005, A2. Also, David Hilliard stressed the importance of being "creative with our radical marketing" and "using our history as a marketing resource" in "Using the Black Panther Name to Market New Products" on National Public Radio's *All Things Considered* on 16 August 2005.

26. A copy of the Bell Time Company advertisement is housed in the Dr. Huey P. Newton Foundation Collection, Stanford University Special Collections, Palo Alto, CA.

"We Waitin' on You"

Black Power, Black Intellectuals, and the
Search to Define a Black Aesthetic

Amy Abugo Ongiri

DUTCHMAN, THE BLACK ARTS REPERTORY THEATER, AND THE BIRTH OF THE BLACK ARTS MOVEMENT

On 24 March 1964, LeRoi Jones's *Dutchman* opened at the Cherry Lane Theater, an off-Broadway stage. The play, which was both ground-breaking and controversial, would go on to win an Obie Award. Langston Hughes would characterize 1964 as "The Jones Year," noting that Jones's plays were so controversial that of the five staged in New York in 1964, two were shut down by order of the police (*Black Magic,* 251). Less than a year later, Jones would join up with a group of artists and activists to form the Black Arts Repertory Theater School in Harlem, which would stage a number of his plays, including *Dutchman.* In his 1968 manifesto "The Black Arts Movement," Larry Neal claims that the Black Arts Repertory Theater "represented the most advanced tendencies in the movement" and presented work of "excellent artistic quality" (261). *Dutchman* was typical of the Black Arts Repertory Theater's performances in its polemi-cal narrative and its experimental, highly stylized content. Centered on the seductive interplay between a black male and a white female subway rider, an interplay that culminates in the murder of the man by the woman, the play performs what Phillip Brian Harper terms the "anxious identities and divisional logic" that would come to mark the Black Arts polemical "call" for the unification of the race against the white oppressor.[1]

Amy Abugo Ongiri, "'We Waitin' on You': Black Power, Black Intellectuals, and the Search to Define a Black Aesthetic," *Spectacular Blackness: The Cultural Politics of the Black Power Movement and the Search for a Black Aesthetic*, pp. 88-123, 201-202. Copyright © 2009 by University of Virginia Press. Reprinted with permission.

In Larry Neal's account of the Black Arts Repertory Theater, which lies at the heart of his call for the formation of a Black Arts Movement, the theater opened, like *Dutchman,* to almost immediate controversy and widespread acclaim. The theater's organizers and participants included some of the most important artists, activists, and cultural workers of the day, from Sonia Sanchez, Harold Cruse, John Coltrane, and Sun Ra to LeRoi Jones himself. The confluence of cultural, political, and intellectual events that led to the Black Arts Repertory Theater's production of *Dutchman* would be replicated across the country as debates concerning the relationship between aesthetics, politics, and representation resulted in a vibrant burst of cultural production. By the summer of its opening year, however, the Black Arts Repertory Theater had ceased operations, having survived for less than three months. During its short life, the Black Arts Repertory Theater was rife with the ideological, aesthetic, and monetary crises and critical questions that would create, shape, and ultimately lead to the demise of the Black Arts Movement as a whole.

In its attempt to produce "art that speaks directly to Black people," the Black Arts Repertory Theater created a vibrant alternative to dominant Western culture that continues to be the primary way through which African American culture and identity are created and understood (Neal, "Black Arts Movement" 258). The notion of African American cultural production as "race memory ... art consciously committed, art addressed primarily to Black and Third World people," as Larry Neal declared in "Reflections on the Black Aesthetic," as well as the notion that African American identity is born out of a struggle with racism, urbanity, and the consequences of slavery, are both a direct legacy of the Black Arts Movement's struggle to redefine African American cultural production (14).

In this chapter, I examine the failures and successes of the Black Arts Movement through its theorization of a "Black aesthetic" and its continuing legacy in order to challenge the commonly held assertion that this movement—with its spectacular successes and failures—offered little more than racial essentialism, a hyperbolically divisive ideology, and a formalistic and essentially flawed aesthetic theorization. I look beyond dismissive evaluations of the Black Arts Movement to argue that the historical moment of both the Black Power and the Black Arts Movements was *the* formative moment, not only for contemporary understanding of African American identity, but also for ideas of blackness in African

American cultural production, characterized by artists and intellectuals of the era as "the new thing" but naturalized into contemporary African American culture as "authentic" Blackness. Don L. Lee noted in 1971: "The decade of the sixties, especially that of the mid-sixties, brought us a new consciousness, a perception that has come to be known as a *black consciousness*. ... Along with the new awareness, we get a form that on the surface speaks of newness" (226). I explore the shape and implications of that "new awareness" and the new forms it enabled, as well as the continued importance of the death of civil rights–era symbolism for the form, discourse, and ideology created and shaped in the Black Arts/Black Power moment.

By 1968 the Black Arts Movement and the Black Power Movement had successfully seized the cultural arena as the primary site of political action. The African American freedom struggle in the United States would begin to be represented and debated in virtually *every* artistic and cultural format in the terms defined by the Black Arts Movement: from the politically progressive experiments of free jazz musicians such as Ornette Coleman, Albert Ayler, and Pharoah Sanders to Black popular music, in which James Brown sang "Say It Loud, I'm Black and Proud" as the Impressions urged African Americans to "Keep on Pushing"; from the Black Arts drama of Ben Caldwell, LeRoi Jones, and Ed Bullins to the poetry of Sonia Sanchez, Don L. Lee, Larry Neal, and Jayne Cortez; and in the unprecedented boom in film productions chronicling the African American experience.

In 1971 Larry Neal issued the cry for "an art that speaks directly to the needs and aspirations of Black America" from the pages of *The Black Aesthetic,* a collection of essays on theory, music, poetry, drama, and fiction edited by Addison Gayle (257). In this chapter, I explore the Black Arts Movement's theorization of a Black aesthetic through a discussion of one of its seminal texts, *Black Fire! An Anthology of Afro-American Writing,* coedited in 1968 by LeRoi Jones and Larry Neal. *Black Fire!* collected work by some of the most significant artists, musicians, and theoreticians of the Black Arts Movement, including Sun Ra, Victor Hernandez Cruz, Henry Dumas, John Henrik Clark, Stanley Crouch, Calvin Hernton, Stokely Carmichael, A. B. Spellman, David Henderson, and Sonia Sanchez. In the process of defining a diverse artistic practice, *Black Fire!* participants also created definitions of community, identity, and authenticity that continue to be central to African American cultural production.

"Ethnic Propaganda" The Black Arts Movement and Its Detractors

In its own time the movement was criticized by everyone from Ralph Ellison (who claimed LeRoi Jones's *Blues People,* when "taken as a theory of Negro American culture," could "only contribute more confusion than clarity"), to J. Saunders Redding (who, as Houston Baker has noted, labeled the movement "an intellectually unsound discourse of 'hate,' a naive racism in reverse").[2] Like the Black Power Movement itself, which was criticized as reactionary, racist, and theoretically unsound by the civil rights orthodoxy it was attempting to displace, the Black Arts Movement's detractors viewed it as dangerous and critically untenable, in particular its demand that "the cultural values inherent in Western history must be radicalized or destroyed," as well as the observation that "the only way out of this dilemma is through revolution."[3] Many critics of the movement refused to engage with the Black Arts Movement's call for racial unity even as a self-conscious political strategy or as a rhetorical stance that reacted to the perceived failures of the Civil Rights Movement. This fostered a climate in which Black Arts creations were more likely to be dismissed as "ethnic propaganda," as Stanley Crouch says in "The Incomplete Turn of Larry Neal" (5), than seriously critically and examined. Crouch's reductive description of Neal's contributions during the Black Arts period is typical in this regard:

> One encounters the philosophical attacks on the systems of the Western world, romantic celebrations of African purity, denunciations of the purported Uncle Toms who didn't embrace separatist and violent "solutions" to the American race problem, and the demand that all serious young black artists commit themselves to a particular vision of political change. Such writing is now more important in terms of the thought processes that underlay the work of a generation that produced nothing close to a masterpiece, that failed, as all propaganda—however well intentioned—inevitably fails. (4)

Crouch's subsequent declaration that the Black Arts Movement "exists more as evidence of a peculiar aspect of social history than any kind of aesthetic achievement" represents the general disregard in which the work of the period is held in many scholarly accounts. This disregard stands in stark contrast to the actual continuing importance of the Black Arts legacy to African American cultural production.

In fact, the Black Arts Movement continues to be one of the most influential and yet least studied moments of African American literary and cultural production. In a 1991 review of the period for *American Literary History,* David Lionel Smith writes of "the paucity of scholarly literature on this body of work":

> A review of the *MLA Bibliography* for the past 10 years gives the clearest picture of this dearth ... one seldom finds more than three or four listings in any given year ... in most years there are only a couple of articles under these headings that one can easily obtain through normal channels. Furthermore, many of the movement's basic documents ... are now out of print. (93)

Smith's statement is borne out by a 1985 special issue of *Callaloo* devoted to honoring Larry Neal, which represents one of the most extensive scholarly treatments to date of Neal and the movement he helped engineer. The guest editor Kimberly W. Benston begins his introduction by noting, "We do not yet have a coherent history of the great Afro-American cultural movement that began in the mid-1960s" (5).[4] Smith attributes the lack of scholarship on the Black Arts Movement to the fact that "the extremes of this writing are so egregious that we may come to equate all the work of the movement with its worst tendencies" (93). Lorenzo Thomas's 1978 exploration of the influence of the Umbra Writers' Workshop on the Black Arts Movement, "The Shadow World," concludes simply: "It is much too soon to say what ultimate results this movement might produce, just as it is not yet time to evaluate all the works of its principal participants" (70).

The sense that African American critical theory has necessarily "moved on" from the politically charged moment of the 1960s and 1970s that birthed the Black Arts Movement predominates, perpetuating an understanding of the movement as simply a politically didactic but critically unimportant moment in African American intellectual and cultural history. However, the effects of Black Arts Movement, especially the critical assumptions that underpin the notion of the Black aesthetic, continue to lurk in often unacknowledged ways in the shadows of accepted African American critical thinking and artistic production.

"Real" and "Out Loud" The Influence of the Black Arts Movement on Contemporary African American Cultural Identity

Though the movement was already beginning to dissipate soon after the publication of *The Black Aesthetic* in 1971, its discourse, along with other of the Black Power–era discourses—on Blackness, the arts, politics, and culture—continue to be formative influences on contemporary under-standing of race in America. For everything from hip-hop culture to contemporary urban fiction and contemporary cultural assertions about what constitutes African American identity, the Black Arts Movement's notion of authentic Blackness continues to be the predominant mode for understanding African American identity and culture. Its investment in urban vernacular culture resulted not only in the cultivation of "street" poetry and poetics but also in a positioning of urban vernacular at the center of African American aesthetics.

The impact of the Black Arts Movement on urban American vernacu-lar poetry can simply not be overstated. In an almost verbatim echoing of Larry Neal's statements on the Black Arts Movement and the Black aesthetic, Miguel Algarin writes in *Aloud: Voices from the Nuyorican Poets Cafe*, "The poet of the nineties is involved in the politics of the movement. There need be no separation between politics and poetry. The aesthetic that informs the poet is of necessity involved in the so-cial conditions the people of the world are in" (11). Though Algarin is speaking of the vibrant, multiethnic Slam poetry movement and the poetry of the Nuyorican Poets Cafe, with its ties to the hip-hop culture and its roots in Puerto Rican and African American oral traditions, his constitutive aesthetic values are the same as those first defined by Neal and the Black Arts Movement. Written in 1971 for *The Black Aesthetic*, the categorical analysis of "the black poets of the sixties" produced by Don L. Lee (Haki Madhubuti) could easily be read as a description of the elements of contemporary spoken word poetry:

1. polyrhythmic, uneven, short explosive lines

2. intensity; depth, yet simplicity; spirituality, yet flexibility

3. irony; humor; signifying

4. sarcasm—a new comedy

5. direction; positive movement; teaching, nation-building

6. subject matter—concrete; reflects a collective and personal lifestyle

7. music: the unique use of vowels and consonants with the developed rap demands that the poetry be real, and read out loud. (226)

Black Arts' influence is evidenced by the Slam poetry aesthetic, particularly in Lee's demand that poetry "be real, and read out loud." It is not surprising that *Aloud: Voices from the Nuyorican Poets Cafe* opens with a quote from the *Black Fire!* contributor Sun Ra, or that poems by the contributors Victor Hernandez Cruz and David Henderson appear in its "founding poems" and "poems of the 1990s" sections, respectively. The influence of the Black Arts Movement runs consistently not only through the Slam poetry and the spoken word movements, which prides themselves on orality, vibrancy, and populism, but also within a hip-hop culture that positions urban vernacular traditions at the core of its aesthetic.

The influence of the Black Arts Movement extends far beyond the formal elements of African American poetry to the ways in which African American culture is defined and produced. In the introduction to *The LeRoi Jones/Amiri Baraka Reader,* William J. Harris summarizes the importance of the Black Arts Movement for a variety of emergent literary traditions:

> The Black Arts Era, both in terms of creative and theoretical writing, is the most important one in black literature since the Harlem Renaissance. No post-Black Arts artist thinks of himself or herself as simply a human being who happens to be black; blackness is central to his or her experience and art. Furthermore, Black Arts had its impact on other ethnic groups primarily through the person of Baraka ... He opened tightly guarded doors for not only Blacks but poor whites as well and, of course, Native Americans, Latinos, and Asian-Americans. We'd all still be waiting for an invitation from *The New Yorker* without him. He taught us all how to claim it and take it. (xxvi)

Harris highlights the importance of the Black Arts Movement challenge as a critical practice as well as an aesthetic demand. Jones, Neal, and other Black Arts practitioners and critics positioned social change and identity struggle at the center of an aesthetic agenda for an entire emergent African American literary tradition and intellectual class. Their demand to clarify the aesthetic dimensions of "Black Art" in relation to the political demand for the creation of discrete spaces in which to articulate that aesthetic shaped the way in which an entire generation of critics and practitioners would define their role within culture and society.

Though Black Arts Movement practitioners were most deeply invested in creating an alternative to mainstream culture, contemporary popular culture remains the domain in which the Black Arts Movement's influence continues to be most openly celebrated. The African American presence in U.S. popular culture continues consistently to pay homage to the Black Arts Movement's cultural politics through actual allusion and in the way an African American cultural aesthetic is articulated and authenticated. While political groups like the Black Panther Party successfully incited a lexical revolution through the popularization of slogans such as "Black is Beautiful!" that were meant to transform the American Negro into a powerful Black revolutionary, it was within the arena of popular, rather than political, culture that notions of authentic blackness as soulful, urban street life, and ghetto-fabulous masculinity were popularized and defined and continue to have an acknowledged resilience today.

Like the Black Arts and Black Power movements themselves, popular culture's tributes to these movements continue to locate the essence of African American culture in the street-savvy urban dweller rather than within the African American folklife of the South celebrated by earlier African American literary and cultural movements. From Snoop Doggy Dogg's warning that he can "clock a grip like my name was Dolemite" and Tupac Shakur's tributory Black Panther Party tattoos, to the name of Notorious B.I.G./Biggie Smalls, which is drawn from Hiawatha "Biggie" Smalls, the ill-fated gangster from the 1975 Blaxploitation film *Let's Do It Again* (1975), the urban poor, yet occasionally ghetto-fabulous, "brother on the block" constructed during the Black Arts Movement as a representational standard continues to provide the most pervasive assumption of essential Blackness in contemporary understandings of race and racial politics. "The Corner," from Common's 2005 album *Be*, is typical in that it proclaims the contemporary urban ghetto landscape to be marked by, as well as to mark, the spiritual and psychic dimensions of African American identity, in addition to configuring the spatial parameters and configurations of racialized urban poverty. The video for "The Corner" trades on the Black Arts Movement's focus on art as a concrete documentation of African American life and its belief that African American identity is profoundly urban by proclaiming itself to be shot on location in the artist's hometown of Chicago. The video not only explicitly references Black Power culture through raised fists and self-conscious markers of ghetto identity, it also includes an appearance by the Black Power–era spoken-word artists The Last Poets, who proclaim the corner to be "our Rock of Gibraltar, our Stonehenge, our Taj Mahal." In keeping with the Black Arts Movement's belief that the free articulation of African American expressive culture would create spontaneous articulations of both political and cultural value, The Last Poets declare: "The corner was our magic, our music, our politics / Power to the people, black power, black is beautiful."

Some of the other more self-conscious tributes to the Black Arts/ Black Power Movements in hip-hop include the 1995 compilation album *Pump Ya Fist: Hip Hop Inspired by the Black Panther Party,* which includes contributions from some of the most respected artists in hip-hop, including KRS-ONE, Grand Puba, Jeru the Damaja, Yo-Yo, The Fugees, and Tupac Shakur; Talib Kweli's 2004 album *The Beautiful Struggle,* on which he asserts that he is "from a place where real is real;" and Ras Kass's 1998 album *Soul on Ice,* which references the title of Eldridge Cleaver's 1968 book. Direct and indirect tributes to the Black Power/ Black Arts era represent far more than a nostalgic yearning for the panache of 1960s and 1970s street culture; they reveal the unheralded and pervasive ascendancy of the very aesthetic championed by the Black Arts Movement.

Hip-hop culture has continued to draw extensively on African American culture of the 1960s and 1970s and to reenvision the era's cultural politics as its most extensive legacy. In *Soul Babies: Black Popular Culture and the Post-Soul Aesthetic,* Mark Anthony Neal notes the way in which a pivotal line from the popular 1970s sitcom *Good Times* becomes the important refrain for a song by Outkast on their cutting-edge 1998 hip-hop album *Aque-mini.* According to Neal, the repetition of the phrase "damn, damn, damn, James" is a lament both for the loss of the traditional African American family structure and for the lost opportunity and broken promises that accompanied African American migration from the South to northern cities (62–64). Thus, *Aquemini* not only directly recycles the culture of the 1960s and the 1970s, it continues its debates on community, family, and "home."

In "Stakes Is High: Conscious Rap and the Hip Hop Generation," Jeff Chang argues that though "political rap" was more prevalent in the 1980s, "conscious rap" artists, such as Talib Kweli and Dead Prez, as well as "gangsta rap" acts, such as Scarface, Trick Daddy, and DMX, continue to negotiate the cultural politics of the 1960s and 1970s. And in 2004, Dead Prez attempted to explicitly mix the "gangsta rap" genre with "political rap" on the album *RGB: Revolutionary but Gangster*. Its track "I Have a Dream, Too" articulates a desire to "turn drive-bys revolutionary" and ends with the invocation of the names of such Black Power–era activists as Assata Shakur, Geronimo Pratt, Bunchy Carter, George Jackson, and Ruchell McGee. Rather than offer a critique of capitalist structures that create criminality, as the Panthers sought to do, the album's single "Hell Yeah (Pimp the System)" describes a number of criminal scenarios and ends by commanding its audience to "Get that paper till we get our freedom / We got to get over." The album's powerful call to action and its seeming inability to resolve the relationship between revolutionary action, capitalism, and cultural production comes as a direct result of debates in the 1960s and 1970s on aesthetics, community, and culture.

THE BLACK AESTHETIC, THE DEATH OF THE CIVIL RIGHTS MOVEMENT, AND THE BLACK ARTS MOVEMENT'S SEARCH TO DEFINE A BLACK COMMUNITY

The search for a Black aesthetic began and was inextricably tied, according to Larry Neal, Addison Gayle, Hoyt W. Fuller, and Don L. Lee in *The Black Aesthetic,* to the advent of the Black Power Movement. The Black Arts Movement considered itself the academic and cultural branch of what was intended to be an armed revolutionary political struggle. As such, the Black Arts Movement's search to define and codify a Black aesthetic became a search for the trace elements of community as a necessary means to lay representational claims to that community. If Stokely

Carmichael and members of the Student Nonviolent Coordinating Committee, the Congress of Racial Equality, the Black Panther Party, and other participants in the Black Power Movement were busy creating and defending the Black community, the task of defining it fell to the artists and intellectuals of the movement. Had the movement failed to provide an answer to the question K. William Kgositsile emphatically posed in the *Black Fire!* anthology—"Who are we? Who are we?" (228)— or to provide evidence to "let Black people understand / that they are the lovers and sons / of lovers and warriors and sons / of warriors," as Amiri Baraka declared in "The Black Arts Movement," the political claims of the Black Power Movement to represent the community would have been without validity.

The Black Arts Movement asserted its definition of "Black community" as an open contestation to the Civil Rights Movement's utopian vision of community based on racial inclusion, integration, and cultural harmony. A poem by Clarence Franklin from *Black Fire!* offers "Two Dreams (for m.l.k.'s one)" (364). As the poem imagines "the cosmic pistol" held by "a million black hands / linked like chain, surrounding the world," a discourse connecting African American identity with violent African American resistance emerges in contrast to Martin Luther King's famous vision of a nonviolent utopia as articulated in his "I Have a Dream" speech. Franklin's vision lacks the symbolic force of grand oratory, a historic location, or a mass audience, but—characteristically for the Black Arts Movement— what it lacks in symbolic capital, it makes up for in boldness, irreverence, and attention to the plain-speaking bravado of the streets, in which "the cosmic pistol was cocked and the / finger was squeezing ... squeezing ... and suddenly." Franklin's rhetorical celebration of violent action mirrored the hyperbolic language of groups like the Black Panther Party, who defended their use of such rhetoric in speeches as the rhetoric of the Black ghettoes. The Panther David Hilliard was arrested by federal agents for making terroristic threats against Nixon two weeks after he said, in an antiwar rally in San Francisco, "Fuck that motherfucking man! ... We will kill Richard Nixon" (265). Hilliard and the Panthers seemed genuinely surprised by the arrest. Hilliard writes in his autobiography: "The whole thing is absurd. Any number of tapes will prove I spoke the words. But it's equally clear I'm not about to kill the President. What do they imagine— I'm going to order some ICBMs to bomb the White House?" (65). Hilliard and the Panthers defended the use of hyperbolic language as typical of the urban street aesthetic that they wished to embody (272).

Franklin's suggestive terseness complements the hyperbolic action in a manner disallowed by the lyrical traditions of African American oratory to which King subscribed. Franklin's poem continues: "and a million liquid bullets were shot into the heart of / the city and everything was wet and running, / like open wounds." It is hard to imagine Franklin's vision of destruction emanating from King, not only because of its confrontational and aggressive narrative point of view, but also because its equally confrontational and aggressive vernacular "street" poetic style clashes with the tradition of African American oratory that King's performance of Blackness embodied and was so much in evidence at the March on Washington. In developing the African American urban vernacular as an aesthetic, the Black Arts Movement attempted to reclaim the artistic merit of the poetics of a people for whom, as Don L. Lee put it, "poetry on the written page ... was almost as strange as money" (223).

The twin guiding precepts of the Civil Rights Movement, nonviolence and a vision of an integrated "beloved community," were the ones most contested by the Black Arts and Black Power movements. This contestation is epitomized by the Student Nonviolent Coordinating Committee's (SNCC) shift away from its early orientation as the student wing of the Civil Rights Movement to its later attempts to re-create itself as a radical advocate of Black Power. In his *In Struggle: SNCC and the Black Awakening of the 1960s,* Clayborne Carson documents the process by which the group's shift resulted in the controversial expulsion of all of its white members and the eventual dissolution of the organization. Martin Luther King Jr. would remark on the challenges to civil rights ideology from "various black nationalist groups" as early as 1963 in "A Letter from the Birmingham Jail": "I am further convinced that if our white brothers dismiss as 'rabble-rousers' and 'outside agitators' those of us who are working through the channels of nonviolent direct action and refuse to support our nonviolent action, millions of Negroes will ... seek solace and security in black nationalist ideology."

King devoted the entire opening chapter of his final book, *Where Do We Go from Here: Chaos or Community,* to contesting Black Power ideology. For King, Black Power represented a distinct move away from the ideals of community he wished to enshrine as the core values of the Civil Rights Movement, and toward disorder, violence, and chaos. King begins the chapter with an anecdote about the announcement of the shooting of James Meredith to a group of young civil rights workers who subsequently refused to sing the song "We Shall Overcome," which had become the movement's anthem. Instead, they suggested "We Shall Overrun" as an appropriate substitute (King, *Where Do We Go from Here* 26).

The year in which the *Black Fire!* anthology was initially published, 1968, marked several key moments in the destruction of symbolic markers of the civil rights era, especially in the transition away from a mass-movement politics and nonviolent struggle and to a post–civil rights era of vanguardism and violent repression. On 3 April 1968, members of J. Edgar Hoover's counterintelligence program who were based in San Francisco first expressed grave concern in a report to Hoover about Oakland's Black Panther Party; this would eventually lead Hoover to declare the party "a major threat to U.S. internal security of the country" and to initiate a campaign of state-sanctioned violence against it and other organizations like it (Haskins, 122). Exactly one day after the report was filed, on 4 April 1968, Martin Luther King was assassinated on the balcony of a Memphis hotel in circumstances so suspicious that decades later, historians, activists, and conspiracy theorists alike continue to speculate about the exact nature of and political motivation for the killing.[5] However, of even greater significance than the ambiguity surrounding the circumstances of King's violent death is what his assassination would come to represent in terms of a definitive, symbolic end to the popularity of nonviolence as a cultural phenomenon in African American social protest, thus marking the beginning of the end of the civil rights era.

Two days after the assassination, Eldridge Cleaver composed a scathing condemnation of King's legacy of nonviolence titled "The Death of Martin Luther King: Requiem for Nonviolence," in which he declared: "The assassin's bullet not only killed Dr. King, it killed a period of history. It killed a hope, and it killed a dream" (*Post-Prison Writings,* 74). In Cleaver's account of King's assassination, King's philosophy and rhetoric of nonviolence are what render him "dead"—as much from the symbolism as from the social forces at work in his actual assassination. Cleaver connected the literal violence of the King assassination to a symbolic violence in a time when "words are no longer relevant" (78):

> In the last few months, while Dr. King was trying to build support for his projected poor people's march on Washington, he already

resembled something of a dead man. Of a dead symbol, one might say more correctly. Hated on both sides, denounced on both sides—yet he persisted. And now his blood has been spilled. The death of Dr. King signals the end of an era and the beginning of a terrible and bloody chapter that may remain unwritten, because there may be no scribe left to capture on paper the holocaust to come. (74)

Cleaver ends the essay by declaring 1968 "the Year of the Black Panther," a year in which "action is all that counts," and presumably an era in which "action" would replace "dead symbols" (78).

The King assassination did indeed trigger violent unrest across the country, with major outbreaks of rioting in 131 U.S. cities as African Americans struggled both physically and intellectually with the civil rights legacy of nonviolent protest (Allen, 106). By the early summer of 1968, the brief, tenuous alliance between SNCC—the organization that had made a radical break with the Civil Rights Movement when its members coined the phrase "Black Power"—and the Black Panther Party had fallen apart. The schism that had grown between SNCC and the Panthers was symptomatic of the altered political and cultural terrain of the post–civil rights era as African Americans searched for meaning, direction, and leadership in the wake of the King assassination and the unrest that followed. Intellectuals, artists, and activists alike struggled to come to grips with the fallout from the Civil Rights Movement and the new "Black Power" in articulating a cultural agenda appropriate to the events that preceded and followed 1968.

The End of Beloved Community Larry Neal and the Beginning of a "Black World"

The stirrings of a post–civil rights cultural revolution as represented by the Black Arts Movement were brought to fruition with the 1968 publication of *Black Fire! An Anthology of Afro-American Writing,* edited by Larry Neal and LeRoi Jones, the two most prominent proponents and spokespersons for the Black Arts Movement. They attempted, in anthologizing African American literature at this point, to perform an intervention that was as much political as it was cultural. In "The Black Arts Movement" Neal claimed, "Poetry is a concrete function, an action. No more abstractions. Poems are physical entities: fists, daggers, airplane poems, and poems that shoot guns" (260). Appearing first in a 1968 issue of *Drama Review,* Neal's essay was to become the movement's manifesto, and it remains the definitive statement of its goals and ideas, especially when taken together with Jones's famous exhortation in "Black Art," "We want 'poems that kill'/Assassin poems, Poems that shoot ... /We want a black poem. And a/Black World." The claim that poetry is "an action" speaks to the Black Arts Movement's profound belief in the positive transformative effects of cultural change.

According to James Smethurst in "Poetry and Sympathy," as a staff writer and later the arts editor for New York's important Black radical arts and news venue the *Liberator,* Larry Neal helped shift African American discourse away from leftist politics toward nationalism (270). In "Reply to Ba-yard Rustin," Neal criticized civil rights leaders, labeling critics of the Black Power Movement " 'civil rites' intellectuals" and further criticizing "Black intellectuals of previous generations for failing to ask" questions such as "whose vision of the world is finally more meaningful, ours or [that of] the white oppressors? ... whose truth shall we express, that of the oppressed or of the oppressors?" ("Reply to Bayard Rustin," 7). From the pages of the *Liberator,* Neal used every opportunity to declare the necessity of African American artistic self-determination and celebrated the earliest impulses of those participating in the Black Arts Movement.[6] In a 1965 discussion of the controversial rejection by the Pulitzer Prize Advisory Board of a music jury citation for Duke Ellington, Neal wrote: "I am proposing that what we understand is the necessity of establishing *our own* norms, our own values; and if there must be standards, let them be our own. Recognition of Duke Ellington's genius lies not with white society that has exploited him and his fellow musicians. It lies *with us,* the Black public, Black musicians and artists. Essentially, recognition of that sort, from a society that hates us and has no real way of evaluating our artistic accomplishments, is the meanest kind of intrusion upon the territory of Black people" ("Genius and the Prize," 11).

The major dilemma of the post–civil rights era was how to face the twofold problem that integration and desegregation presented: What would be the consequences for African American intellectuals and the African American middle class of their entry into the majority institutions and arenas of the United States? And would programs for desegregation and integration result in the destruction of the very African American community and traditions that had birthed the African American freedom struggle in the first place? In 1995, Manning Marable described the crisis facing the African American community in the 1990s as being rooted in the racial, cultural, and social politics of the 1960s. Noting that sharp disjunctions in African American class advancement since the 1960s, when coupled with the significant changes in the social composition of the African American community, make it almost impossible to speak today of shared "black experience," Marable states:

> One cannot really speak about a "common racial experience" which parallels the universal opposition blacks felt when confronted by legal racial segregation. Moreover, contemporary black experience can no longer be defined by a single set of socioeconomic, political and/or cultural characteristics. For roughly the upper third of the African American population the post-1960s era has represented real advancement in the quality of education, income, political representation and social status. Social scientists estimate that the size of the black middle class, for example, has increased more than 400 per cent in the past three decades. The recent experience of the middle third of the African-American population, in terms of income, has been a gradual deterioration in its material, educational and social conditions. For example, between 1974 and 1990, the median income of black Americans compared to that of white Americans declined 63 per cent to 57 percent. However, it is the bottom one-third of the black community which in this past quarter of a century has experienced the most devastating social consequences: the lack of health care, widespread unemployment, inadequate housing, and an absence of opportunity ... The resultant divisions within the black community ... contributed to a profound social and economic crisis within black households and neighborhoods. (128–29)

By focusing on African American cultural expression as creating a sort of unifying continuity, the "Black Aesthetic" as articulated by Neal implicitly asserted that the "devastating social consequences" that make up "the Black experience" for the bottom one-third of the African American community would have symbolic, spiritual, and real material consequences for the upper third of the African American community who were situated to reap the benefits of desegregation.[7]

It is no accident that Marable's discussion of a post–civil rights African American community in crisis in the late 1990s comes at the end of the contemporary debate about African American studies and multicultural-ism in the university, a primary and ongoing site of struggle in the battle for desegregation. Marable locates a shift in the political and social condi-tions of what he terms "the post-1960s era" specifically in the failed project of integration and the attendant "ghettoization" within African American studies departments of a social-change agenda in U.S. universities. While he does not directly relate the early post–civil rights era intellectual struggles to the questions he lays out for contemporary African American studies, his emphasis on post–civil rights shifts in notions of "black experi-ence" and the possibility for "black community" reflect the fact that con-temporary debates on African American identity have their foundational moments in the early post–civil rights intellectual struggles and questions of community and culture as exemplified by the Black Arts Movement.

The Black Arts Movement began its negotiations around class, inclu-sion, and cultural production precisely when changes created by the Civil Rights Movement and the end of legalized segregation fostered opportunities for economic advancement and inclusion. The Black Arts Movement would try to negotiate the economic opportunities and the class rifts such changes would create by posing the question of how the artist and intellectual would be accountable to the masses of African American people and, conversely, how the masses of African American people were to be included in dominant culture. The creation of African American studies departments during the Black Arts Movement was one means by which the problem of inclusion within U.S. institutions was addressed. The Black Arts Movement attempted ultimately to provide a model for African American advancement that would avoid the pitfalls of mainstream institutional inclusion, includ-ing the disintegration of African American culture and community that was believed to have been produced by the Civil Rights Movement.

"Black Theater Go Home!" Conceptualizing the Black Aesthetic and the Black Experience

The search by Larry Neal, Addison Gayle, and LeRoi Jones to define a Black aesthetic was related to attempts to determine what constituted "Black community" and "the Black experience." *The Black Aesthetic,* edited by Gayle in 1971, is divided into five major sections: theory, music, poetry, drama, and fiction. Most of the text is given over to music, poetry, and drama, forms that are not only primarily communal but also have their foundations in the African American oral folk cultures. In "The Black Arts Movement," an essay in *The Black Aesthetic,* Larry Neal explained the relationship between Black Arts drama and African American people as rooted in the give-and-take between creator and audience that is made possible by the performative nature of the genre: "Theatre is potentially the most social of all of the arts. It is an integral part of the socializing process. It exists in direct relationship to the audience it claims to serve" (263).

For Neal, it was the theater's imagined populist ability to communicate aurally and orally directly for and to African American people that was at the heart of the Black Arts Movement's embrace of it as an efficacious form. Neal and the other writers on theater in *The Black Aesthetic* conceptualize it as freely available in a variety of ways to the masses of African American people still by definition anchored in the extreme specificity of an African American identity born of the struggle against racism. Ronald Milner writes in "Black Theater—Go Home!":

> If a new black theater is to be born, sustain itself, and justify
> its own being, it must go home. Go home psychically, mentally,
> aesthetically, and, I think, physically. First off, what do I, myself,
> mean by a new *black* theater? I mean the ritualized reflection and
> projection of a new and particular way of being, born of the unique
> and particular conditioning of black people leasing time on this
> planet controlled by white men. A theater emerging from artists
> who realize that grinding sense of being what we once called the
> blues but now just term: *blackness.* (288)

In "The Black Arts Movement," Neal writes succinctly of what he presumes to be the natural and inextricable relationship between African American people and African American poetry: "The poem comes to stand in for the collective conscious and unconscious of Black America— the real impulse in the back of the Black Power movement" (261).

Neal and Milner both articulated a desire to create a cultural and artistic tradition that would feed rather than feed off of African American people and the traditions they had created in their struggle to survive America's repressive social and economic order. For this reason, Richard

Wright's "Blueprint for Negro Writing," with its demands that "Negro writers ... stand shoulder to shoulder with Negro workers in mood and outlook," is one of the only works by the previous generation of African American writers or artists to be included in *The Black Aesthetic*. The Black Arts Movement dreamed of creating an artistic tradition that not only celebrated the cultural impulses of the African American community but also became a natural part of constructing and maintaining that community.

In *The Autobiography of LeRoi Jones,* Baraka recounts how the concept of a Black Arts Movement arose from the Black Arts Theater after a discussion between Baraka, Neal, and the Revolutionary Action Movement organizer Max Stanford in which Baraka "felt particularly whipped and beaten" by his inability to define the relationship between his role as an artist and his role within the African American community (197). Baraka had previously wondered in discussions with Neal "what was going on in the world, who were we in it, what was the role of the black artist" (197). Baraka notes that not only had Stanford "had communications with exiled Rob Williams," he "was actually distributing his newsletter, *The Crusader*" (197). Stanford's ability to marry radical political action, community organizing, and cultural work created an imperative that Baraka felt he could not ignore. Baraka wrote: "To me, the young tireless revolutionary I saw in Max was what I felt I could never be" (197). For Baraka, the conversation with Stanford became the catalyst for reimagining a relationship between artist and community with radical political activism at its center. It also became the genesis for the creation of the Black Arts Theater. Baraka writes: "One evening when a large group of us were together in my study talking earnestly about black revolution and what should be done, I got the idea that we should form an organization" (197).

The search to define a black aesthetic that arose directly out of a shared community-building racial episteme termed "the Black experience," and the attempt to convert the vernacular rhythms and behavior of everyday African American life into a viable poetics and powerful praxis formed the central cultural and aesthetic agenda of the Black Arts Movement. The Black Arts agenda manifested itself in the desire to directly convert the rhetoric and poetics of the movement into the creation of active, independent African American–owned venues for African American artistic and cultural production, not as an extension of the movement, but as the foundation for further cultural development. For the Black Arts Movement the conditions of African American artistic production were obviously and inextricably linked to the aesthetic concerns of its product. Ekkehard Jost writes of the impact of social conditions on the creation of "free jazz":

> Free jazz shows precisely how tight the links between social *and* musical factors are, and how one cannot be completely grasped without the other. Several of the initiators of free jazz, for instance, had to contend for a long time with systemic obstruction on the part of the record industry and the owners of jazz clubs (who continue to control the economic base of jazz). This circumstance is by no means void of significance for the music of the men concerned. Being without steady work means not only personal and financial difficulties; it also means that groups may not stay together long enough to grow into real ensembles, that is, to evolve and stabilize a concept of group improvisation— an absolute necessity in a kind of music which is independent of pre-set patterns. (9)

According to Jost, free jazz, like other forms born out of the social conditions of the era, was foundationally shaped, both aesthetically and socially, by its attempts to combat systematic exclusion while maintaining a productive cultural and aesthetic integrity. The presumption that free jazz was forged out of the linkages between repression, cultural production, and resistance, as Jost claimed, helped to enshrine it in the lexicon of the Black Arts Movement as a barometer of "all the hurt, pain, and good times which black people share through their daily experience," as Peter Labrie declared in "The New Breed" (64).

When Robert Williams began broadcasting from exile in Cuba a radio program directed at the United States, jazz, particularly the jazz experiments of Max Roach and Ornette Coleman, formed a significant part of the musical selection. Williams claimed free jazz enabled his efforts to create "a new psychological concept of propaganda" by providing "the type of music people could feel, that would motivate them" (Tyson, 288). The free jazz aesthetic celebrated by Robert Williams and the Black Arts Movement was, according to them, a direct consequence of the process by which an independent African American musical style was created and articulated under the duress of exclusion and partial inclusion. The Black Arts Movement struggled to create the venues that would allow for the free articulation of a Black aesthetic fully supported by the people whose ideas it articulated.

As was the case with the Black Arts Repertory Theater, many of the attempts to establish institutions that reflected the Black Arts agenda were short-lived. But as with the free jazz movement, the attempts and attendant critical shifts and ruptures that they caused often resulted in major shifts in the cultural and aesthetic agendas of the various media in which they participated. It is as impossible to imagine contemporary jazz without the influence of Ornette Coleman, for example, as it is to imagine the creation of contemporary African American poetry without the presence of Amiri Baraka, whose every challenge ultimately aided African American poetry's institution in mainstream anthologies and classrooms.

Black Fire! Anthology Production, Historical Trauma, and Cultural Production

Black Fire! An Anthology of Afro-American Writing, edited by Larry Neal and LeRoi Jones and published in 1968, raised important questions about the shape a viable African American poetics might take in a postsegregation African American context. It also highlighted questions about the function of artistic and intellectual work in the formation of notions of "the Black community" in the postdesegregation period. Reexamining *Black Fire!* provides the opportunity to challenge or to acquiesce in Larry Neal's final statement in the anthology that "the artist and the political activist are one" within African American cultural production (656). The Black Arts Movement revolutionized African American literary and intellectual life with its insistence that artists and intellectuals be directly accountable to the masses of Black people and vice versa. It also revolutionized African American life by politicizing the aesthetics of popular music and film, as well as the culture of everyday African American life as reflected in clothing, food, speech, and expressive or "soul" styles. Manning Marable claims: "The politics of soul in the 1960s was the personal and collective decision to fight for freedom" (*Beyond Black and White,* 95). The Black Arts Movement successfully rescripted the challenges of African American inclusion and exclusion in American culture as a cultural imperative in a historical moment in which not only were the political goals of the Civil Rights Movement increasingly at risk, but the very project of Black emancipation seemed to come under fire.

By late 1968, the Civil Rights Movement was mourning the highly publicized deaths of the four little girls killed in a Birmingham church bombing, and also those of Medgar Evers, Malcolm X, James Earl Chaney, Jimmy Lee Jackson, Sammy Young Jr., and countless others who had given their lives to the struggle for civil rights. It was not only vulnerable African American bodies, however, but also newly formed African American institutions that came under siege. The early post–civil rights period is most frequently characterized not by the destruction of nascent cultural ventures, such as the Black Arts Repertory Theater, but rather through the much more brutal and high-profile disruption of African American radical political organizing as epitomized by the destruction of the Black Panther Party and the Revolutionary Action Movement by law enforcement and the federal government, and by the deaths of civil rights leaders. However, the destruction of political organizations was also a direct attack on the civil rights symbolism of "beloved community," which served as the key organizing principle for much of the civil rights and early post–civil rights culture. Thus, the civil rights period can be characterized as a period of intense, systemic repression and historical trauma as well as one of intensely positive social change and transformation. This resulted in a tremendous anxiety regarding the future not only of African American institutions but of African American culture itself.

Larry Neal had been in the auditorium of the Audubon Ballroom selling *Black America,* the newspaper for the Revolutionary Action Movement, on the day that Malcolm X was assassinated. The moment of Malcolm X's assassination, according to Neal, "was an awesome psychological setback to the nationalist and civil rights radicals" ("On Malcolm X," 128). He characterized the moment as one that traumatized individuals as well as a movement, writing, "Malcolm's death—the manner of it—emotionally fractured young Black radicals," and he went on to speculate about how the fracturing of young African American radicals extended to a breakdown in collective organizing:

> Some of us did not survive the assassination. Strain set in. Radical black organizations came under more and more official scrutiny, as

the saying goes. The situation made everyone paranoid, and there were often good reasons for being so. People were being set up, framed on all kinds of conspiracy charges. There was a great deal of self-criticism, attempts to lock arms against the beast we knew lurked outside. Some people dropped out, rejecting organizational struggle altogether. Some ended up in the hippie cults of the East Village. Some started shooting smack again. Some joined the poverty programs; some did serious work there, while others, disillusioned, and for now, weak, became corrupt poverticians. Malcolm's organization, the Organization of Afro-American Unity (OAAU), after being taken over briefly by Sister Ella Collins, Malcolm's sister, soon faded. But the ideas promulgated by Malcolm did not. ("On Malcolm X," 129)

According to Neal, Malcolm X's death led to a fragmentation and then a flowering of African American radical culture based on Malcolm X's ideas that led directly to the founding of the Black Arts Repertory Theater School of Harlem.

Neal claimed in "On Malcolm X" that "what was happening in Harlem was being repeated all over the United States" (129). But just as Malcolm X's death was both traumatic and productive for an African American radical culture, the Black Arts Repertory Theater School of Harlem would prove a consistently contested and productive site for cultural production. Neal pointed to the systematic defunding of the Black Arts Repertory Theater School of Harlem by government arts agencies as a symbolic starting point in the destruction of African American radical culture by the government. LeRoi Jones would flee the Black Arts Repertory Theater collective in Harlem to organize in Newark, New Jersey, when infighting turned ugly, and Neal himself would be shot when leaving the theater one night.[8] The destruction of the Black Arts Theater, like the death of Malcolm X, would not result in the defeat of the movement but would rather signal the need for the rebirth of such ventures in African American communities throughout the country, or, as Neal claimed: "The Black Arts group proved that the community could be served by a valid and dynamic art. It also proved that there was a definite need for a cultural revolution in the black community" (257).

Since anthology production is almost inherently a collective venture, anthologies such as *Black Fire!* and the collections that followed it provided one way of preserving and transmitting the notion of cultural collectivity that had developed out of the Civil Rights Movement and was very much under siege by 1968. The publication of *Black Fire!* set off a virtual explosion of African American anthology production: more than thirty new African American literary anthologies were published in the years between 1967 and 1973 alone. Structured around categories of genre or identity, these anthologies were as varied in shape and tone as their titles indicate: Toni Cade's *The Black Woman,* Dudley Randall's influential *The Black Poets,* Etheridge Knight's *Voices from Prison,* and Arthur P. Davis and Saunders

Redding's popular classroom text *Cavalcade: Negro American Writing from 1760 to the Present.* Many of the anthologies consciously identified with the Black Arts Movement or were edited by the key figures of the movement themselves, from Sonia Sanchez's *We Be Word Sorcerers: 25 Stories by Black Americans,* to Dudley Randall's *Black Poetry: A Supplement to Anthologies which Exclude Black Poets,* Ed Bullins's *New Plays from the Black Theatre,* Ahmed Alhamisi and Harun Kofi Wangara's *Black Arts: An Anthology of Black Creations,* Gwendolyn Brooks's *A Broadside Treasury,* and Addison Gayle's *The Black Aesthetic.*[9]

Black Fire! created the climate for the later anthologies, not only in its multigeneric format and its powerful drive to document African American art and culture, but also in its strident political and aesthetic challenges to the preexisting codes and canons of American literature. Bullins, San-chez, and Alhamisi—who would all later edit anthologies that challenged the parameters of established generic codes in theater, the short story, and "the arts"—published their own work initially in *Black Fire!* The opening essay of *Black Fire,* "The Development of the Black Revolutionary Artist," by James T. Stewart, reiterates the need for a separate aesthetic: "The black artist must construct models to correspond to his own reality" (3). The essay section also contains work by some of the key intellectual and political figures of the Black Power era, including Stokely Carmichael, Harold Cruse, John Henrik Clarke, and Nathan Hare. In placing Stewart's essay at the beginning of the anthology, Neal and Jones obviously hope to posit a model for artistic construction that is "Black" and "revolutionary," but one that is, above all, *communal:* the anthology represents a radical call to create a community of revolutionary artists and cultural workers in the face of a fractured African American community and an increasingly fractured Black liberation movement.

Several of the writers in *Black Fire,* including Lorenzo Thomas, Henry Dumas, A. B. Spellman, Lance Jeffers, Calvin Hernton, David

Henderson, Joe Goncalves, and Ronald Snellings, had been involved with the influential artistic collectives that were clustered around small magazines such as *Umbra* and *Dasein* and around radical journals such as the *Liberator*.[10] In general, journals and magazines of this type had relatively limited circulation and often enjoyed only short life spans. Nonetheless, the collectives that formed around these projects provided a forum for intellectual exchange and collectivity around African American poetics that was unmatched and helped create a climate in which anthology publication would later flourish.

The beginning of the Black Arts Movement was rooted in the spirit of collectivity as evidenced by the establishment of the Black Arts Repertory Theater, which was founded the day after the assassination of Malcolm X through the efforts of an artists' collective that included LeRoi Jones, Charles Patterson, William Patterson, Clarence Reed, and Johnny Moore and was instituted by a fund-raising concert that featured John Coltrane, Betty Carter, Albert Ayler, McCoy Tyner, and Archie Shepp, among others (Neal, "Black Arts Movement" 261). Once established, the Black Arts Repertory Theater School became a meeting place for such black artists and intellectuals as Harold Cruse, Sonia Sanchez, and Stokely Carmichael to meet and to teach others. Efforts like the repertory theater school meant not only to showcase the Black Arts creations of the influential collective that had participated in its birth but also to provide an arts and cultural education to black youth in the area, who would then go on to form its repertory company (Riley, 21). While the Black Arts Repertory Theater was unable to survive the pressures created by government interference and repression and group infighting, the anthologies provided a permanent place of exchange and challenge to consolidate the ideas of a movement that was increasingly under fire.

The Beautiful Day Transforming a Western Cultural Aesthetic

The Black Arts project was not only about transforming the notion of the black community as the spirit of a new politicized collectivity, it was also about preserving old notions of community as they came under siege in the late 1960s. James T. Stewart's essay in *Black Fire,* "The Development of the Black Revolutionary Artist," declares, "Revolution is fluidity" (4). The collection of writers anthologized in *Black Fire!* became a revolutionary African American community through their determination to articulate African American culture and community as a cohesive experience, and through their insistence on discarding old models, old markers, old forms, and old conventions in their search to declare a new Black aesthetic. For these writers, the dismantling of corrupt social and political structures would necessarily go hand in hand with the destruction of the culture that underpinned that structure. This revolution went far beyond the simple social-protest formula made famous by Black writers like Richard Wright. As Larry Neal would write in *Black Fire:* "The West is dying and offers little promise of rebirth ... The West is dying, as it must, as it should. However, the approach of this death merely makes the power mad Magogs of the West more vicious, more dangerous like McNamara with his computing machines, scientifically figuring out how to kill more people. We must address ourselves to this reality in the sharpest terms possible. Primarily, it is an address to black people. And that is not protest, as such" (64). The critical re-evaluation of Western culture and African American people's place in it would not be accomplished through the simple, formulaic "mau-mauing" to which later evaluations of the period would reduce it.[11] Rather than simply protesting Western norms, the Black Arts Movement sought to provide new paradigms for understanding experience that shed light on the destructive nature of existing paradigms.

In "The Beautiful Day #9," a poem dedicated to the U.S. Secretary of Defense Robert McNamara, A. B. Spellman reenacts the bitter ambivalence that characterized the post–civil rights era's attitude toward social change, a mindset that by the poem's publication in 1965 had become an awesome apocalyptic possibility:

> stateside shades
> watching the beast in his jungle
> biting blackness from the sides of
> ibo, shinto, navajo, say
> no mo, charlie

by biting i mean standing before
all that is human
ripping the shadow from a man's back
throwing it in his face
& calling it him.

but what if the shadow was the beast
gray as the grave and hanging on?
what if his mirror was blackness
the knife was the shadow
the thaw of the times?

With his chant of "ibo, shinto, navajo, say / no mo, charlie," Spellman invokes the genocidal politics of the U.S. government in relation to the indigenous peoples of Africa and the Americas and the historical resistance to those practices as epitomized by the Viet Cong saying "no mo, charlie." However, the line also invokes the complicated complicity of nonwhite people in the U.S. war machine through its invocation of the Navajo "code talkers" of World War II. When Spellman rejects the possibility of "ripping the shadow from a man's back / throwing it in his face / & calling it him," he is exploring the Black Arts ambivalence toward contemporary human experience that would seem to lock injustice and human suffering into everyday practices as a quiet inevitability.

Though now largely forgotten, Spellman was a major figure in New York City's Black Arts scene and a close associate of LeRoi Jones; he was also involved with the Umbra group.[12] While a student at Howard University, Spellman had studied with Sterling Brown, and his poems, according to Aldon Nielsen, "mark a site of convergence for all the tendencies linking the various black practitioners of the newer poetics who formed the generation that first began publishing after World War II and established the formal structures that would subsequently be taken up as a vocabulary of aesthetics during the Black Arts Movement" (98). The Black Arts Movement represented both a continuation of and a notable break with the poetics of a Sterling Brown or a Langston Hughes, whose jazz poetics, as Nielsen notes, continued to exert considerable influence over the jazz-inspired poetry of Spellman and other Black Arts practitioners.

"The Beautiful Day #9" continues Brown's investment in African American vernacular English and Hughes's interest in descriptive, rhythmic wordplay, but it is equally shaped by its stern confrontation with the vicious, cold mechanization of state repression and the difficulty of tearing that repression from the fabric of everyday experience. Spellman asks of his metaphoric "beast, sexless & fragile, frail / as machine, his energy made, whiter / than air, strength leaking from every / hole, & richer than god, what do you do with him?" The contradictions of the "fragile, frail / as machine" beast who nonetheless has "strength leaking from every / hole, & richer than god" and the stanza's ambivalent spacing, which leaves every descriptor in the stanza hanging half-declared, create a feeling of tepid, unresolvable instability for the reader. This is only reinforced by the stanza's last question: "what do you do with him?"

It is no accident that Spellman's series of "Beautiful [Vietnam era] Days" poems are as numerically categorized and itemized as Hills 881s, 861, 861a, 558, 950, and 1015, the names given to the hills that surrounded the decisive battle at Khe Sanh. In 1964, in his infamous "An End to History" speech delivered at the University of California, Berkeley, Mario Savio, one of the leaders of the Berkeley Free Speech Movement, pronounced, "The most crucial problems facing the United States today are the problem of automation and the problem of racial injustice" (194). While the grouping of "automation" with "racial injustice" may seem arbitrary in a contemporary context, Savio's hyperbolic fear of technological culture would seem to be borne out by the mechanized horror of the Vietnam War. Spellman's "sexless & fragile, frail / as machine" beast is realized in the impotent war machine that prepared to defend Khe Sanh during the Tet Offensive of 1968:

> Circling the skies above Khe Sanh for thirty miles in every direction, aircraft took high-resolution photographs, scanned the ground with radar for evidence of enemy movement, and recorded the findings of an array of complex, highly classified gadgets designed to locate enemy positions and movements: acoustic sensors that picked up voices; seismic sensors that registered vibrations from marching soldiers, trucks, and armored vehicles; infrared heat sensors that could identify cooking fires; and electrochemical analyzers that could detect high concentrations of human urine. Technicians in an airborne electronic laboratory read, collated, and interpreted the data. (Dougan and Weiss, 42)

For Spellman and for other *Black Fire!* poets, most notably David Henderson, Joe Goncalves, and LeRoi Jones, the wanton destruction that characterized the post–civil rights era produced texts in which the destruction and re-creation of language and language forms were an inherent part of the composition. Nielsen concludes, "Spellman was willing to advance into the shadowy text of the world's future, but he could not know what he would find there" (*Black Chants*, 105).

Black Fire! pieces like Jones's "Three Movements and a Coda," Henderson's "Neon Diaspora," and the technopaegniac experiments of Joe Goncalves preserve a wordplay tradition rooted in African American oral and musical traditions at the same time that they suggest that the new forms and formulas of expression are necessitated by the social instability of the times. The challenging street language of urban rebellion is matched in Jones's "Three Movements and a Coda" by a challenge to create poetry as "the music" that matches the destruction and reconstruction of meaning inherent in such events. *Burn, Baby, Burn: The Los Angeles Race Riot, August 1965,* Jerry Cohen and William S. Murphy's sensationalist account of the Watts rebellion, offers an intriguing account of the way a popular radio deejay's trademark tagline ("burn, baby, burn") was transformed into a powerful rebellion invective with a life of its own: "Not once during the rioting did Montague mention the violence on his three-hour program, and he immediately ceased using the expression. His station's news reports covered developments closely as a public service, and one of its mobile units was stoned. But unintentionally Magnificent Montague had given rioters a rallying cry. The first night a few teenagers shouted it in jest, then defiantly, and finally, with fire in their eyes and rocks in their fists. Young adults seized on it later. Then so did their elders. As mobs shrieked 'Burn, baby, burn,' large parts of Los Angeles would do just that" (76–77).

Black Arts poets wished to harness the transformative power of language as epitomized by the call "burn, baby, burn" to new forms worthy of the radical new possibilities that revolutionary change would bring. Joe Goncalves's experiments in concrete poetry "Now the Time Is Ripe to Be" and "Sister Brother" swirl hopeful statements about the spiritual possibilities for Black people around the single exclamatory statement "OH!"[13] Because they appear on the page in the form of a circle, the poems force the reader to perform a repetitive cyclical motion to read them. This motion literally suggests the cycles of change and transformation that the poems' simple declarative statements of hope, such as "Our kingdom was not of this world but it has come now," and "your hand is here and I know we are on our way," wish to enact. These statements are also enclosed within illustrations of a pyramid and a star of David, symbols that evoke mystical connections between the Black struggle in the United States and the history of ancient Israel and Egypt.

Converting the political "action" of urban unrest and the rhetoric of Black Power into a workable cultural aesthetic became the focus of the Black Arts Movement, which demanded that "the black artist must link his work to the struggle for his liberation and the liberation of his brothers and sisters," as Larry Neal declared in "Shine Swam On," the afterword to the *Black Fire!* anthology (655). Politically and socially, the book was meant to function as more than just a simple showcase for African American literary production. Despite Eldridge Cleaver's pronouncements that 1968 was a year in which "words are no longer relevant" and "action is all that counts," the contributors to *Black Fire!* believed in the power of their intellectual efforts to, as Neal put it, "make literature move people to a deeper understanding of what this thing is all about, [to] be a kind of priest, a black magician" (655). Sun Ra, already present as an influential innovator of free jazz, contributed several pieces of poetry to the anthology. His "To the Peoples of the Earth" is a succinct testament to the perceived possibilities of language for the Black Arts Movement:

> Proper evaluation of words and letters
> In their phonetic and associated sense
> Can bring the peoples of earth
> Into the clear light of pure Cosmic Wisdom. (217)

As LeRoi Jones, writing under the name Amiri Baraka, states in the foreword to the collection, "Black Fire" represents "the black artist. The black man. The holy holy black man. The man you seek. The climber the striver. The maker of peace ... We are they whom you seek. Look in. Find yr self ... We are presenting. Your various selves" (xvii). Like Sun Ra, Jones believed in the power of words to create—not simply describe—social change and community itself.

The Black Arts Movement used language to invoke a cultural and social unity that was increasingly difficult to claim in the face of post–civil rights social changes. The participants in the *Black Fire!* anthology most often grappled with the class dynamics of an emergent intellectual class that had no desire to be anyone's "Talented Tenth" by positioning themselves in the manner that Jones's foreword and as the meaning of Jones's new name—"enlightened prince/spiritual leader/blessed one"—would suggest. The contributors to *Black Fire!* contradictorily imagined themselves as both the leaders ("the climber the striver" and "the holy holy black man") and the incarnations of the "various selves" of the masses of African American people. The vanguardist, yet insistently populist, demand of the Black Arts Movement created a dynamic in which Black Arts poets stood not for what the average African American man or woman *could* strive to be, as in the earlier Du Boisian "Talented Tenth" model, or what they *should* want to be, as in even earlier "uplift" paradigms, but rather what African American people *would* naturally and essentially be if it weren't for their lack of spiritual enlightenment and political consciousness. The poet Edward S. Spriggs's contribution to the volume, "We Waiting on You," begins and ends with the invocation of the title (337), and this could be a summation of the anthology's sometimes contradictory stance on intragroup politics, class or otherwise.

"Anxious Identities and Divisional Logic"
Fracturing Communities, Class Divisions, and the Black Arts Movement

Instead of expressing the cultural unity that they sought, the Black Arts Movement's desire to articulate concepts such as Black aesthetic, Black experience, and the Black community created what Phillip Brian Harper has labeled in a discussion of Black Arts poetry "anxious identities and divisional logic" (49). Ironically, the Black Arts Movement's most glaring class-based omission was its failure to acknowledge or critique the increasingly important role African Americans were playing in American popular culture.

For Larry Neal as for most of the Black Arts practitioners and critics, the notion of African American community was so closely linked to the popular and vernacular traditions of African American folk and folklore that he found it difficult to factor in all the elements of urban commodification necessary to form a complex understanding of postmigration

African American artistic practice. In *Hoodoo Hollerin' Bebop Ghosts,* Neal lamented the move from the rural South as an authentic and primary site for the articulation of African American culture, while in "Shine Swam On," he struggled to articulate a relationship between the ascendancy of African American popular music culture and the potential for creating a literary aesthetics with a connection to African American mass culture: "The key to where Black people have to go is in the music. Our music has always been the most dominant manifestation of what we are and what we feel, literature was just an afterthought, the step taken by the Negro bourgeoisie who desired acceptance on the white man's terms. And that is precisely why the literature has failed" (654).

Much of the tension in the Black Arts Movement's reception of popular culture resulted from the fact that the Black Arts Movement expressed a desire for separate spheres of articulation at the precise moment when African American culture saw increasing inclusion in the mainstream. It was difficult enough for Neal to imagine an African American community constituted as a market; it would ultimately be impossible for him to understand the market value of African American culture within mainstream American popular culture. The Black Arts Movement's failure to provide complete intellectual guidance for the radical political movements of the time was ultimately linked to an inability to define or find significance in the relationship of African American culture to American popular culture in general and the wider dissemination of African American culture throughout American popular culture. In *The Crisis of the Negro Intellectual,* Harold Cruse asserts: "The Black Arts was not a failure in achievement, so much as a failure in its inability to deal with what has been achieved" (539). Though Cruse does not address the specific developments in postwar culture that Jones and the Black Arts Movement were unable to relate, he correctly identifies ambivalences in their role as intellectuals in a developing cultural movement that negotiated changing class, cultural, and political positionings for African Americans.

Phillip Brian Harper locates what he labels the "divisional logic" of the Black Arts Movement in the need to be "*heard* by whites and *over*heard by blacks" (*Are We Not Men,* 53, emphasis in original). He discusses how this "divisional logic" invokes a fantasy of African American unity in order to both create and negotiate intragroup hierarchies: "For according to this fantasy, not only would to be *heard* be to annihilate one's oppressors, but to be *over*heard would be to indicate to one's peers just how righteous, how nationalistic, how potently Black one is, in contradistinction to those very peers, who are figured as the direct addressee of the Black Arts works" (53).

The "insistent use of the second-person pronoun," which Harper characterizes as the address convention of Black Arts poetry, is very much in evidence in *Black Fire,* from Sonia Sanchez's "to all sisters" and Reginald Lockett's "Die Black Pervert," to Bobb Hamilton's "Poem to a Nigger Cop" and "Brother Harlem Bedford Watts Tells Mr. Charlie Where It's At" (47). Harper indicates that the "anxious identities and divisional logic" of Black Arts poetry are rooted in phallocentric, homophobic gender politics, which the Black Arts Movement is often also reduced to in contemporary rememberings of the period:[14]

> The Black Aestheticians' development of such potent gender-political rhetoric through which to condemn perceived failures of Black consciousness is significant … for at least two reasons: First, it can clearly be seen as establishing a circular dynamic whereby Black Arts writers' own need not to be deemed racially effeminate fueled the ever-spiraling intensity of their repudiative formulations, including the divisional *I-you* constructions … second, it indicates the Black Aestheticians' preexistent anxiety regarding their own possible estrangement from the very demands of everyday black life that were repeatedly invoked as founding their practice. If the routine figuration of such estrangement as a voluntary and shameful effeminization was a powerful signal practice in Black Arts poetics, this may well be because the estrangement itself was experienced as the unavoidable effect of inexorable social processes—specifically, the attenuation of the Black Aestheticians' organic connection to the life of the folk (to invoke the Gramscian concept) by virtue of their increasing engagement with the *traditional* (Euro-American) categories of intellectual endeavor, through which they largely and inevitably developed their public profiles in the first place. (*Are We Not Men,* 51)

As Harper indicates, what is most central to the Black Arts project and its strongest point of tension and contention is the question of inclusion: How exactly were the masses of African American people and the rich traditions of the African American culture to be included and maintained within the decentralizing project of integration? How would the intragroup politics of the African American community be negotiated as it increasingly fractured?

Although heteronormative hypermasculinity is widely on display throughout *Black Fire,* as is "anti-white" performativity, it is definitely tension over intragroup class divisions and the possibilities for class ascendancy that most consistently permeates the anthology and much of Black Arts writing. It is also that which gets the least critical attention in scholarly studies of the period. In one of the opening essays in *Black Fire,* "The Screens," C. E. Wilson writes, "The changing world often makes some terms obsolete and requires new names and concepts in order that men can communicate with one another" (133). Wilson hopes to elucidate a term that describes those for whom " 'Uncle Tom' is no longer apt." He claims that " 'Uncle Toms,' 'Handkerchief Heads' or 'Aunt Jemimas' " are a thing of the past, since increasingly, "whites have had to recruit willing, middle-class Negroes to do their dirty work for them" (133). His subsequent labeling of this group as "the screens" is dependent on a class politics that would have the readers of *Black Fire!* define themselves against a group he variously labels "the have-resume-will-travel professionals" and "the poverticians" (136). Similarly, David Llorens in "The Fellah, The Chosen One, The Guardian," borrows terms from the political struggle for independence in Northern Africa to castigate those whom it labels traitors to the "Fellah" class of African Americans.

Marvin E. Jackmon's (Marvin X's) one-act play *Flowers for the Trashman* is exemplary of Black Arts attempts to negotiate the role of the intellectual among characters who represent standards within the Black Arts vision of Black community. In the play, Joe, an African American college student, spends an unexpected night in jail with his hip, "hoodlum friend" contemplating his relationship to his family, especially his brother, who is in prison, and his father, who owns and operates the community's flower shop and whom he views as having impotent "establishment" values. Joe's anxiety over his inability to communicate with or to understand either his jailed brother or his broken father ends when he connects action for social change with the potential end of his alienation, declaring, "That's why I gotta start doin' somethin'—I wanna talk to ma sons" (*Black Fire,* 558). *Flowers for the Trashman* suggests that action for social change as a sort of community-building project will alter the dynamic that has caused Joe, the representative intellectual, to be estranged from those to whom in an ideal world he would logically be close, his incarcerated brother and streetwise friend, who are both representatives of the African American lower classes. The "race as family" model that is the premise of the play allows elision of trickier questions concerning the unifying social action to be taken, but it also wishes away the myriad conflicts that created the African American establishment father, the hip outlaw, and "the brother on the block" as representational figures for Black Arts literature in the first place.[15]

In "le roi jones talking," a 1964 essay that appeared in *Home,* a collection of his essays published in 1966, Jones writes about the agonies of writing: "I write now, full of trepidation because I know the death society intends for me. I see Jimmy Baldwin almost unable to write about himself anymore. I've seen Du Bois, Wright, Himes driven away—Ellison silenced and fidgeting in some college" (179). It is noteworthy that even as early as 1964, Jones conflated Baldwin's silence and Du Bois's, Wright's, and Himes's exile with Ellison's employment at "some college" as potential forms of death facing the African American writer. For Jones, the college campus, the site of so many contentious and ultimately at least partly victorious civil rights battles, is clearly not a desirable location for the racially conscious African American to inhabit according to the Black Arts Movement, which wanted to "keep it all in the community." A large portion of the Black Arts impulse, as evidenced by Jones's title, *Home,* comes from an anxiety to claim an appropriate "home" site for an emergent intellectual class. Larry Neal's "Ghost Poem #1," which appeared after the publication of *Black Fire,* invokes similar conflicts about "home"; it is a moving meditation on rural to urban migration and what Cornel West labeled "black nihilism" (*Black Popular Culture,* 271):

> You would never shoot smack
> or lay in one of these Harlem
> doorways pissing on yourself
> that is not your way not the
> way of Alabama boys groomed slick
> for these wicked cities momma
> warned us of
>
> You were always swifter than that:
> the fast money was the Murphy game
> or the main supply before the cutting—
> so now you lean with the shadows

(at the dark end of Turk's bar)
aware that the hitman is on your ass

You know that something is inevitable
about it
You know that he will come as sure as shit
snorting blow for courage
and he will burn you at the peak of your peacocking
glory
And when momma gets the news
she will shudder over the evening meal
and moan: "Is that my Junie Boy runnin
with that fast crowd?" (7–8)

Here Neal attempts more than simply to document, discover, or revive what is valuable about African American folk and mass culture in two of its most mythic locations, Harlem and Alabama. The tension of the poem, as indicated by its irregular line breaks and spacing and its fluid, understated narrative, is the sum total of a culture that is in the midst of an intense transition. Like the liminal figure of the ghost who is caught between the worlds of the living and the dead, Neal's "Ghost Poem #1" is an attempt to maintain a cohesive culture in the midst of intense social, economic, and political transformation while marking the inevitability of its eventual change. The character who "lean[s] with the shadows / (at the dark end of Turk's bar)" is saturated with the fatalism and precariousness of the social forces that are about to do him in, and the poem anticipates the problems of the urban underclass as clearly as it signifies Neal's inevitable estrangement from that class.

The Black Arts Movement's critics and practitioners responded to the question of "Black Art" and the postsegregation problematic of African American artists and intellectuals by calling for an art that would, as Larry Neal writes, "speak directly to the needs and aspirations of Black America" ("Black Arts Movement," 257). The desire to articulate a collective identity as the basis for the form and function that is designated the Black aesthetic necessitated that the Black Arts Movement be, as Neal writes, "radically opposed to any concept of the artist that separates him from his community" (257). The notion of community that the Black Arts Movement constructs is constituted around oppositional struggle, and the function of "art" within that struggle is the primary criterion for judging it through the Black aesthetic. As Ron Karenga writes in "Black Cultural Nationalism," which appears in *The Black Aesthetic,* "all African art has at least three characteristics: that is, it is functional, collective, and committing or committed," and, "Black art, like everything else, must respond positively to the reality of revolution" (32, 31). This, according to Karenga, is in marked contrast to the African American cultural and critical practices of other eras. Neal, Karenga, Jones, and other Black Arts practitioners desired to create an aesthetic that was, in the words of Etheridge Knight, "accountable ... only to the Black people" (*The Black Aesthetic,* 259).

While Karenga, Jones, and Neal would agree for the need for a revolutionary Black aesthetic, the question of exactly how that aesthetic would be constituted was very much up for debate. Whereas Neal and Jones struggled to define a revolutionary cultural practice within existing African American practices, Karenga's US Organization and its philosophy of "kawaida" called for the complete overthrow of existing cultural norms and practices and the instilling of new practices based in a direct reclamation of African culture. The US Organization based its entire doctrine of nationalist change deeply within the transformation of culture. According to Karenga, "Kawaidists are essentially the new nationalists, spiritual and theoretical heirs of Garvey and Malcolm and the immediate products of the fire, feelings, and formations engendered by a decade of Black revolts," and while their imperative for change was political, their mechanism would largely come through a reorganizing of culture ("Kawaida and Its Critics," 126). While Larry Neal saw radical possibilities especially in existing musical forms such as gospel and the blues, Karenga as US's spokesman declared such folkloric practices as the blues "invalid" (*Black Aesthetic,* 36). Baraka was deeply involved in the philosophy of kawaida before he left the US Organization to embrace a more aggressive form of Marxism, but from his earliest writings as LeRoi Jones to his later writings as Imamu Amiri Baraka, he struggled more positively with the place of existing African American practices in the development of a racial aesthetic in a way that kawaida's strict articulation of cultural change would not allow. Though Karenga would dismiss Baraka in 1977 as "essentially a man of arts and letters ... neither a theorist nor an accomplished organizer," ultimately, the Black Arts Movement's debates about the relationship between cultural and political practice and the everyday lives of African American people would prove to be the major nexus around which Black radical politics would come to be defined (136).

Today, the attempt to realize and define an intellectual endeavor "accountable ... only to Black people," or accountable *even* to black people, remains as unrealizable as attempts to resolve the dilemmas highlighted by the Black Arts project. As African American intellectuals rapidly enter a post–affirmative action, postsegregation era, the questions raised by the Black Arts Movement take on an even greater urgency, demanding scrutiny more than ever.

NOTES

1. In Harper's words, the Black Arts project calls for the liberation of " 'all Black people' but not, evidently for 'you' " (*Are We Not Men?* 53).
2. Ellison, *Shadow and Act,* 253; Baker, *Afro-American Poetics,* 161.
3. L. Neal, *Visions of a Liberated Future,* 63, 76.
4. This has been somewhat rectified by the recent publication of several literary and cultural histories of the movement, including work by Cheryl Clarke, Harry J. Elam, James Smethurst, and Komozi Woodard.
5. David J. Garrow's *The FBI and Martin Luther King, Jr.* provides documentation of government excesses under COINTELPRO and the FBI's systematic campaign of harassment against King. Philip Melanson's *Who Killed Martin Luther King?* examines some of the most glaring inconsistencies in the investigation into the murder of King by the House Select Committee on Assassinations. Both books extensively document the U.S. government's attempts to derail the Civil Rights Movement, and both implicate government agencies in King's assassination.
6. Larry Neal, LeRoi Jones, Houston Baker, Ossie Davis, and Clayton Riley, among others, all contributed to the *Liberator* either as writers or by serving on its editorial board.
7. In *Beyond Black and White,* Marable goes on to cite the following factors as evidence of this crisis: "The infant mortality rate for black infants is twice that for whites. Blacks, who represent only 13 per cent of the total United States population, now account for approximately 80 per cent of all premature deaths of individuals aged fifteen to forty-four—those who die from preventable disease and/or violence. There are currently more than 650,000 African-American men and women who are incarcerated,

and at least half of these prisoners are under the age of twenty-nine. In many cities the dropout rate for nonwhite high-school students exceeds 40 per cent." (129).

8. Komozi Woodard gives the most complete account of the conflicts and infighting that surrounded the cultural projects of the Black Arts/Black Power era, including the Black Arts Repertory Theater School, in *A Nation within a Nation*, 63–68.

9. A partial list of significant anthologies produced during the period of the Black Arts Movement includes R. Baird Schuman's *Nine Black Poets*, J. Saunders Redding and Arthur P. Davis's, *Cavalcade: Negro American Writing from 1760 to the Present*, Dudley Randall's *Black Poetry: A Supplement to Anthologies which Exclude Black Poets*, Ed Bullins's *New Plays from the Black Theatre*, Gwendolyn Brooks's *A Broadside Treasury*, Toni Cade Bambara's *Tales and Stories for Black Folks*, Ahmed Alhamisi and Harun Kofi Wangara's, *Black Arts: An Anthology of Black Creations*, Etheridge Knight's *Black Voices from Prison*, and Orde Coombs's *We Speak as Liberators: Young Black Poets*.

10. Lorenzo Thomas explores the formation and impact of literary collectives such as Umbra in "The Shadow World." James Smethurst explores the impact of the Black Leftist tradition on emerging Black nationalism in literary journals such as *Liberator, Journal of Black Poetry,* and *Black Dialogue* in "Poetry and Sympathy." Smethurst gives the most complete history to date of the Black Arts Movement's literary collectives and Black Arts publications in *The Black Arts Movement*.

11. In "The Black Arts Movement and Its Critics," David Lionel Smith cites Henry Louis Gates's dismissal of the Black Arts Movement and his desire "to take the 'mau-mauing' out of the black literary criticism that defined the 'Black Aesthetic Movement' of the 60s and transform it into a valid field of intellectual inquiry" as formative for the way in which the Black Arts Movement continues to be received.

12. Nielsen, *Black Chant*, 101, 98; Thomas, "The Shadow World," 54.

13. Joe Goncalves served as the editor of *Journal of Black Poetry* and the poetry editor of *Black Dialogue*. "Now the Time Is Ripe to Be" and "Sister Brother" appear in *Black Fire!* (265–66).

14. For example, in "Controversies of the Black Arts Movement," a section in his longer discussion of the Black Arts Movement that appears in the 1997 *Norton Anthology of African American Literature*, Houston A. Baker Jr.

uses such troublesome subcategories as "anti-Semitism" and "misogyny, homophobia" in discussing the movement (1804–6).

15. It is not surprising, given the post–civil rights era context in which *Black Fire!* appeared, that the figure of the Black preacher is the most frequently castigated representational figure in the anthology. Ben Caldwell's "Prayer Meeting, or the First Militant Preacher" goes so far as to suggest a conversion scenario for a civil rights–era Black member of the clergy based on his encounter with a Black criminal.

DISCUSSION QUESTIONS

1. What is *focoism*? Explain its connection to Guevara's theory of revolution.

2. How did the Cuban Revolution, as well as revolutions throughout Latin America, inspire the Black Panther Party? Why was Guevara's concept of revolution both different and scary?

3. What is the purpose of a vanguard group? How did the Black Panthers act as a vanguard to political/social revolution?

4. How did comedian Richard Pryor's public transformation reflect a "shift in the African American mood," as well as to provide an affront to the limited representations of blacks within the media?

5. How did the Watts Riots reshape the expression of civil rights?

6. How had the Black Panthers accomplished Che Guevara's ideals through the use of popular culture and social media?

7. In what ways did the Black Arts Movement provide a contemporary understanding of African American identity?

CPSIA information can be obtained
at www.ICGtesting.com
Printed in the USA
LVHW100324180119
604306LV00006B/17/P